Here to Stay

HERE TO STAY

American Families in the Twentieth Century

———

MARY JO BANE

———

Basic Books, Inc., Publishers

NEW YORK

To my mother

and the memory

of my father

Library of Congress Cataloging in Publication Data

Bane, Mary Jo.
  Here to stay.

  Bibliography: p. 176
  Includes index.
    1. Family—United States. I. Title.
HQ536.B3   301.42'0973   76–44877
ISBN: 0–465–02927–2 (cloth)
ISBN: 0–465–09726–x (paper)

Contents

CONCLUSIONS
Persistent Commitments; Persistent Dilemmas 139

Acknowledgments

THIS BOOK grew out of a project on "alternative approaches to child rearing" supported by a grant from the Carnegie Corporation of New York to the Center for the Study of Public Policy (CSPP), Cambridge, Massachusetts.

A number of other documents, which complement this one, were produced by the CSPP project. A series of descriptive articles on playgroups, communal arrangements, congenial work settings, day care centers and so on, written primarily by William Ronco, Gail Howrigan, and Andrew Kopkind, illustrate how families cope with the demands of work and child care. Much of the analysis of social policy in the second half of this book grew out of reflection on these examples of families successfully solving their own problems without professional or governmental interference.

Two reviews of the psychological literature by Gail Howrigan provide a more detailed discussion than is contained in this book of what is known about the effects on children of separation and divorce and of working mothers. Two papers, by Gregory Jackson and by Heather Weiss, look in detail at the reasons why mothers go to work. Two memos by Mary Corcoran, on work incentives and economic determinants of family behavior, examine economic correlates of other family decisions. Finally, a paper by William Ronco on changing attitudes toward women provides background data for the discussions of women's status that occur throughout the book. All these papers are available from the Center for the Study of Public Policy.

An anthropological study of two-worker families begun as part of the original Carnegie-CSPP project has now taken on a life of its own. This continuing study, directed by Laura Lein, is described in reports to the National Institute of Education and the National Institute of Mental Health. The findings of Lein's study have informed this book in many ways.

As indicated, the child-rearing project was supported by the Carnegie Corporation of New York, and my biggest debt of gratitude is to them. Part of the writing of the book was aided by a summer stipend from the National Endowment for the Humanities.

A number of people were of enormous help to me in actually writing the book. Gail Howrigan provided research assistance, and Nancy Lyons gave editorial help. Christopher Jencks and Kenneth I. Winston read several drafts of the entire manuscript and made both substantive and editorial comments that were extremely helpful. Others whose comments helped improve the manuscript include Barbara Brenzel, Mary Corcoran, Robin Dimieri, Carolyn Elliott, Rosabeth Kanter, David Kirp, Mary Shanley, and William Ronco. Janet Lennon was responsible for the typing of the manuscript. Jim Bane was a conscientious and patient proofreader.

Any book on the family is inevitably colored by the family experience of the author. I have tried to stick very closely to data in this book and to draw conclusions only from evidence. I am aware, however, that my conclusions also reflect a basic optimism about family life and a deep conviction that family relationships can be fulfilling and liberating. This bias must be at least partially blamed on my two families: on my mother, late father, and brother; and on my husband. It may have flawed the objectivity of the book, but I nonetheless thank them for it, very profoundly.

Introduction

The family in the Western world has become a mere shadow of what it was. The causes which brought about the decay of the family were partly economic and partly cultural. In its fullest development, it was never very suitable either to urban populations or to seafaring people. . . .

BERTRAND RUSSELL, 1929 [1]

The American family is falling apart.

ITHACA JOURNAL, 1975 [2]

OBSERVATIONS that the family is declining are not new. But in our time there is more widespread belief than ever before that the family will finally succumb to the assaults upon it. One alleged villain is the ever-accelerating tempo of modern life, marked by transiency, rapid obsolescence, and impermanence. The lives of Americans are characterized by movement from place to place and by goods designed to be used quickly, thrown away, and replaced. The lack of permanence in material life seems to be carried over into emotional and social life. Several recent commentators have described friendships and marriages as becoming more and more like automobiles, short-lived and replaceable.[3] How can the family, which Westerners have long seen and still see as requiring unconditional, permanent bonds between people, survive such assaults?

Even if it can, attacks upon the family may also be coming from another quarter—from the slow but inevitable movement toward sexual equality. Many conservatives and some radical feminists see equality between men and women as incompatible with family life.[4] Perhaps equal work opportunities for women will destroy any incentives men have to live in and care for families. Perhaps women will reject bearing and raising children in favor of independence and economic success. Perhaps competition for dominance and conflict over task division within marriage will destroy the fabric of affection and concern that makes family life worthwhile. Is the contemporary family in the process of being replaced by people living basically alone, coming together only for business or for transient sociability?

The arguments predicting the imminent decline of the family seem to be supported by a good deal of statistical evidence: rising divorce rates, declining fertility rates, rising numbers of women leaving the home for paid work, diminution of the family's productive economic functions, the disappearance of the extended family. Are these statistics not sufficient proof that the family as an institution is reaching the end of its days? Should we not be developing public institutions to replace the family with other forms of living arrangements and other methods of child care? When I began investigating the situation of families and their children in contemporary America, I believed that the answer to both questions was yes.

Yet, as I delved further into the data that describe what Americans do and how they live, I became less sure that the family was in trouble. Surprising stabilities showed up, and surprising evidence of the persistence of commitments to family life. The title of this book changed many times as the work went on. As the final title suggests, I became convinced that the time has not yet come to write obituaries for the American family or to divide up its estate.

I also became convinced that answering my questions about the family—separating myth from reality—was important as well as interesting. Public decisions affecting the family are being made regularly, and public debate about abortion and divorce reform, sexual equality, welfare, taxation, and public services for children and families is both persistent and heated. Questions about specific bills or court decisions cannot be answered by historical and demographic study of American families. However, facts can be used to explore the basic assumptions and values behind particular policies and to describe the effects that policies may have. Assuming that the family is dead or dying may lead to policies that, in their desperate attempt to keep the patient alive, infringe unnecessarily on other cherished values and prove once again that the cure can be worse than the disease. On the other hand, too hasty concern for replacing the "dying" family may in fact bring about its untimely death. Both of these harmful responses can perhaps be avoided by more accurate diagnosis of the family's current condition.

The first part of this book looks at contemporary American families in the perspective of changes during this century. The second part explores some of the policy areas that I believe can be illuminated by the findings of Part I. In describing American families, I look at data on family formation, family dissolution, and living arrangements derived chiefly from census surveys and polls. There are other kinds of data, of course, that could be looked at as indicators of the state of family life: diaries, child rearing manuals, newspaper reports, portrayals of families in TV situation comedies and commercials. I rely on demographic indicators principally because they give a more accurate picture of what people actually do than reports of what outside observers think they do. For example, historians have noted innumerable discrepancies between personal observations of family size and numerical data on actual households.[5] One contemporary example illustrates the point: A person relying only on television portrayals of American families would probably conclude that almost no women have paying jobs, while the statistics give a quite different picture.

Quantitative data allow for little psychological interpretation of the sort that has recently become fashionable, but they have the advantage of being reasonably straightforward and trustworthy. Behavioral data provide a good basis for describing what is happening and likely to happen. Readers will, however, have to provide their own explanations for why things are happening the way they are.

Readers should also be aware that neither Part I nor Part II attends to the special needs of special groups—the retarded and physically handicapped, for example—which certainly call for public attention and remedy. Nor does the book deal explicitly with the families of black, Spanish-speaking, and Native Americans. I believe that the general picture of families that emerges from the data applies to most minorities as well as the white majority: lower fertility and higher divorce rates are characteristic of all groups, for example. But ethnic groups do seem to differ in the structure and strength of ties between the nuclear and the expanded family and also in the characteristic roles of men and women. Readers should keep this in mind and realize that the general picture of family life presented here does not necessarily portray accurately all families or all ethnic groups.

Another word of caution: It should not be assumed that families in Western countries have always exhibited the characteristics of North American families. From the colonial period on, North American families seem to have been nuclear in structure, private, and relatively child-centered. In continental Europe, however, the private, child-centered family developed only since the seventeenth century. Before that time, European families were more public and had more permeable boundaries; adults and children lived more fully in the community and less intensely in the home. That earlier family belonged, however, to a quite different time, a time of high death rates, especially high infant mortality rates, and brutal poverty for the mass of men and women. It was not the jolly extended family of American myth and, unless one looks only at aristocrats, warrants little nostalgia.[6] At any rate, it is not part of the American past and thus not part of the story of this book.

PART
I

The Persistence of
Commitment

Chapter One

PARENTS AND CHILDREN

WORRY ABOUT THE FAMILY is mostly worry about the next generation. Falling birthrates, rising divorce rates, increasing numbers of working mothers, and other indicators of the alleged decline of the family would probably seem much less alarming if adults alone were affected by the making and dissolving of families. People are distressed by these trends not because they signal a decline in the quality and richness of adult lives but because they seem to threaten the next generation. If the trends continue, will there be a next generation? Will it turn out all right? Will it be able to maintain and perhaps even improve the world?

These feelings about the importance of generational continuity lie, I suspect, behind the implicit and explicit comparisons that one generation makes with the generations before it. Modern families and modern methods of child rearing are almost always measured against the families of earlier times. The comparison is usually unfavorable to modern families. In contrast, when modern technology and economic institutions are evaluated against earlier times the judgment is far more often made that things are better. In technology, progress is the standard. In social institutions, continuity is the standard, and when change occurs, it is seen as decline rather than advance.

Decline and *advance* are not easily defined terms, of course. What some people see as good child rearing, others may see as stifling repression and yet others as rampant permissiveness. But some agreement probably exists on the basic principles of how a society ought to treat its children: Children should receive secure and continuous care; they should be neither abused nor abandoned. Children should be initiated into adult society with neither undue haste nor unduly long enforced dependency—in other words, allowed to be children and permitted to become adults. Probably most important, Americans believe that children should be wanted both by their parents and by society.

Arguments that modern families are failing their children usually cite rising divorce rates and the rising proportion of mothers working as evidence that children are less well cared for by their parents now than in the past, that their environments are less secure and less affectionate. In addition, statistics on falling birthrates are sometimes used as evidence that modern Americans want and value children less than earlier generations. But data on parental care, family size, and the ties between generations can be used to make a different argument: that discontinuities in parental care are no greater than they were in the past; and that changes in fertility rates may lead to an environment that, according to generally agreed on criteria, is more beneficial for children.

Demographic Facts and the Age Structure of Society

Intergenerational relationships are profoundly influenced by the age structure of society, since that structure determines how many generations are alive at any one time and what proportion of the population has living ancestors or descendants. The age structure can also influence whether a society "feels" mature and stable or young and vibrant. Certain activities or patterns may seem characteristic of a society because they are characteristic of the largest age group in the population.

A combination of birth and death rates creates the age structure of a society. These two rates also determine the rate of growth of the population, which can in turn affect the density and structure of living arrangements. Birth- and death rates thus define the demographic context within which the relationships between generations must be worked out. As technology provides the basic facts of economic life, demography defines the basic facts of social life.

Today's great-grandparents were born during a period when the population of America was growing at a rapid rate. The European populations from which the American colonists had come had been relatively stable in size, with death rates balancing birthrates over long-term cycles of prosperity followed by epidemics and famines. In the seventeenth-century, death rates began to fall dramatically and steadily, probably because of general improvements in nutrition and the physical environment.[1] Death rates fell at all ages; not only did mature people live longer, but more infants survived to childhood and more children to maturity. And more women lived to have more children. The result was a rapid population growth that has characterized the United States at least since the U.S. Census began in 1790, and probably much earlier.[2]

Falling death rates, however, have been partially balanced by falling birthrates.[3] In the United States, birthrates have been gradually falling for as long as data have been collected. They probably began to fall about 1800 or possibly earlier, and in the last few years they have fallen below replacement level. If they remain at replacement level, the United States will reach a stable population level about the year 2000.[4] In the United States, therefore, the rate of natural population growth was probably highest in the early and mid-nineteenth century. Around 1800 the population grew at a rate of almost 3 percent per year. By 1880 it was growing at around 2 percent per year and by 1974, at six-tenths of one percent.[5]

A rapidly growing population is different from a stable population in several ways. One is age structure. Demographers find that the average age of populations that are not growing can range from about twenty-seven years when mortality rates are very high (probably characteristic of pre-industrial Europe) to about thirty-eight years when mortality rates are very low (the United States of the future).[6] In contrast, a rapidly growing population is young. The median age of the population of the United States shown in Table 1–1 illustrates the point.

As population growth has slowed down, the American population has become gradually older. This aging is perhaps the most important difference between the world of our great-grandparents and our own world, and

TABLE 1–1
Median Age of the U.S. Population,
1820–1970

Census Year	Median Age of Population
1820	16.7 years
1850	18.9 years
1880	20.9 years
1910	24.1 years
1940	29.0 years
1970	28.0 years

SOURCE: U.S. Bureau of the Census, *Statistical Abstract*, Table 25.

contributes to many of the changes that have taken place in family and intergenerational relationships.

It may seem strange that a population becomes younger as death rates fall. As people live longer should the population not become older? The reason it does not is that in all the societies that demographers have studied, death rates are highest both late in life and early in life.[7] Declines in death rates are usually most dramatic among infants. More infants survive, contributing more children to the population. More women survive to reproductive age and contribute even more children to the population. Thus lower mortality rates result in a younger average age of the population even though average life expectancy at birth rises.

Imagine, for example, a population in which half the babies died at birth and half lived to be 50. The average life expectancy would be 25 years, and the average age of the population would also be 25 years. Now imagine that infant mortality rates fell, so that everyone lived to be 50. The average life expectancy would then be 50. The average age of the population would still be 25, if the population remained stable in size. But if birthrates remained the same as they were when death rates were high, the population would be bound to grow, since more women would live to reproductive age and there would be more babies and children than older people. Thus lower mortality rates would have produced a younger rather than an older population.

Another interesting characteristic of a rapidly growing population, related to its age structure, is that working-age adults comprise a relatively small proportion of the population. Working-age adults (age 15–64) made up 58 percent of the rapidly growing population of the United States in 1880. In contrast, 68 percent of the population of the United States in 1940 was made up of working-age adults.[8] The nonworkers in a rapidly growing population are almost all children, since the proportion of old people is extremely low. On the other hand, when death rates are low and the population is stable in size, almost half of the nonworkers are over 65.

A third feature of a rapidly growing population is that it must every year induct a relatively large number of young people into adulthood and into the work force. More must start work than retire. This can put a strain on adult society in general and on the economy in particular. If the economy is not growing as rapidly as the population, the problem of what to do with young people can become acute.

Changes in the rate of population growth produce changes in the age structure of a society that are in turn reflected in the problems the society must cope with, the mechanisms it uses to do so, and the general feel of the society. In a rapidly growing population, children and adolescents must be more visible. A young, childlike society may be a more congenial place for children to live.[9] But it may not. Children may be more precious when they are relatively rare. A more mature society may have more physical and emotional resources to give to the care of children. It may display a greater ease in inducting children—since there are fewer of them—into the adult society.

Teenagers may cause major social problems when they make up a disproportionately large segment of the population. When they are fewer, especially when the number entering the labor force equals the number retiring, they can be integrated much more easily. This interpretation might partially explain cycles of concern over youth. It might also partially explain societal attitudes toward children. Dr. Spock, after all, advocated permissive child-rearing in the first edition of his book in 1947, when children were relatively rare. He changed his mind in 1968, for a variety of reasons no doubt. But whether Spock realized it or not, he may simply have been reacting to what must have seemed a veritable surfeit of children. In the coming decades, children and adolescents will make up a small proportion of the population. Through this simple demographic change, they may become less of a problem and more of a precious resource.[10]

Childlessness and Family Size

Declining birthrates not only change the position of children in society as a whole, but they can also affect the status of children in individual families. Low birthrates that occur because fewer women are having children should probably be interpreted differently from rates that are low because many women are having a smaller number of children. High rates of voluntary childlessness in the society might reflect a cleavage in the society. If people who did not have children were different from those who did—if, for example, they were better educated or concentrated in the professional occupations—the potential for social conflict would be great. Public support for children would certainly be hard to master if only low-status (or only high-status) parents had children. At the same time, the family environments of children would not necessarily change much. If fewer women had children but still had large numbers, most children would continue to be brought up in large families.

If, on the other hand, low birthrates occurred because most people continued to have children but had fewer of them, political divisions between the childless and others would be less likely. But an important change would take place in the family environments of children. More children would be brought up in small families. The consequences would more likely be beneficial to both the children and the society.

Decreasing family size rather than increasing childlessness accounts for most of the declining fertility in the United States. The U.S. Census first gathered data on the total number of children women had had over their reproductive years in 1910. The census data is probably accurate for women born as early as 1846 [11] and as late as 1935, since most women now complete their childbearing before age 35. The fertility of women born after 1935 can be predicted from two sources: from Census Bureau questions that ask women how many children they expect to have, and from projections of fertility rates based on the number of children they have had so far. These combined sources provide fairly accurate descriptions of the fertility history of women born since the middle of the nineteenth century.

Between 90 and 95 percent of women marry at one time or another. The proportion has fluctuated over the years, with a slight increase in recent decades in the proportion of women marrying. The proportion of married women who have no children has also fluctuated over the years— first up, then down. The childless proportion rose from about 8.2 percent of married women born 1846–55 to a high of over 20 percent of the married women born between 1901 and 1910. Childlessness then fell to 7.3 percent among married women born 1931–35.[12]

It is hard to say why childlessness rose during the nineteenth century, but it may have to do with the unhealthful conditions facing women in the factories or the economic difficulties experienced especially by the immigrants.[13] One explanation for the high rates of childlessness among married women born around the turn of the century is the economic depression of the 1930s. When unemployment rates are high, birthrates almost always fall. In the 1930s unemployment reached a new high and birthrates a new low.

The decline in childlessness since the 1930s is equally hard to explain. It may have to do with improvements in general health and with new medical treatments for sterility and infertility. Involuntary childlessness may have virtually disappeared. Predictions about the future are thus predictions about voluntary childlessness, which is now possible through the relative ease of birth control and abortion.

Predictions might be based on the characteristics of women who remained childless in the past. Among women born before 1920 who were surveyed by the 1970 census, those who were childless were more likely to be black,[14] to have been born in the Northeast,[15] to have married at older ages, to have gone to college, to have lived in urban areas,[16] and to have been married to professional or white-collar workers rather than farmers or laborers.[17] In general, the childless were better educated and better off. High rates of childlessness among blacks are the exception and may be explained by health conditions.

These correlates suggest that childlessness should have increased over time as more women became better educated and better off. But that is the opposite of what actually happened. The cross-sectional data also suggest that childlessness should decrease during hard times since fewer people are well-off. But this too is precisely the opposite of the historical fact. The economic and demographic correlates of childlessness are, therefore, not very useful bases for making predictions about what will happen.

Some predictions can be made, however, on the basis of what women say about the number of children they expect to have. In 1975 less than 5 percent of wives who were interviewed about family plans expected to remain childless. This proportion was relatively constant throughout the age groups.[18] The proportion of women who expect to remain childless went up slightly from 1967–1974, but then went down again in 1975.[19] Better-educated women and white women are more likely to expect to remain childless, but the difference is not great.[20]

The most interesting thing about these figures on expected childlessness is that they are so low. If as few women remain childless as say they expect to, the childless proportion among women born between 1940 and 1955 will be the lowest ever recorded. Even if the rate of childlessness for all women were equal to the expected rate for college women, childlessness would still be at its lowest recorded level.[21] Under either condition, however, the country is due for some upswing in births, as those who have put off having children begin to have them.[22] One problem with the data is that the Census Bureau interviews only married women about their family plans, not unmarried women who may or may not marry and may or may not expect children in the future. Another is that women who now see themselves as putting off children may later be unable to have them, or decide not to. This problem can be partially corrected by making projections from birthrates by age. One demographic study uses these rates to estimate that 10 percent of women born around 1945 will actually remain childless, rather than the 5 percent who expect to.[23] The Census Bureau made a series of projections from similar data, with similar results.[24] These studies project a slightly higher rate of childlessness than that found among women born during the 1930s, but still lower than that among women born 1901–10. It seems safe to say that the vast majority of American women will continue to have at least one child.

Although there has been no systematic increase over the century in the proportion of women who have no children, there has been a systematic and dramatic decrease in the number of children each mother has. The average married woman in colonial Massachusetts may have had as many as eight children. The average mother born 1846–55 had 5.7 children. The average number of children decreased steadily for sixty years, reaching 2.9 children among women born 1911–15. It then rose for a short period during the postwar baby boom; women born 1931–35 have had an average of 3.4 children per woman with children. It is now once again falling.[25] Yet the proportion of women having no children or having only one child has not increased over the century. The big change has thus been in the proportion of women having very large families, a change which has occurred for all races and education levels.[26] Many fewer women have five or more children; many more women have two or three.[27]

Looking at these numbers from the viewpoint of the children illustrates the change that has taken place over four generations. Statistics about average family size do not accurately reflect the size of the family into which the average child is born. The family of the average child is larger than the average family because more children are born into larger families.

If this sounds like a riddle, imagine ten families distributed as follows:

> 1-child—4 families
> 2-child—3 families
> 3-child—2 families
> 4-child—1 family

The average family size is $4(1) + 3(2) + 2(3) + 1(4) \div 10 = 2$. But the twenty children are distributed as follows:

> 1-child families—4 children
> 2-child families—6 children
> 3-child families—6 children
> 4-child families—4 children

The average child is born into a family of $4(1) + 6(2) + 6(3) + 4(4) =$ $50 \div 20 = 2.5$ children, and has an average of 1.5 brothers and sisters. When large families are included in the calculations the differences between average family size and the average number of brothers and sisters can be very dramatic.

From the point of view of the child, a better indication of family size than average family size is the average number of brothers and sisters that children of different generations have. The great-grandparents of today's children had on the average six brothers and sisters. Their grand-parents had five brothers and sisters. Their parents—depression babies— had on the average three brothers and sisters. Today's children may have as few as two.[28] The low birthrates of the depression occurred partly be-cause of high rates of childlessness and only children. There were, how-ever, many large families. In contrast, the low fertility rates of the early 1970s are the product of low rates of childlessness and only children, accompanied by extremely small numbers of large families. Most children in the 1970s are born into two- or three-child families. If these patterns continue, the average child born in the next decade will have only two brothers and sisters.

Small families mean a quite different life for children. Some of the differences are probably detrimental to children, but, on the whole, small families seem to be beneficial. A number of studies suggest that children from small families do better in school and score better on standardized tests than children from large families. Part of the explanation is that smaller families are usually better off financially. But even when these families are equally well-off, children from large families do not get as much education, as good jobs, or as high earnings as children from small families.[29]

One of the most interesting studies on family size and achievement investigated the reasons for the superior performance of children from small families.[30] The study first looked at the amount of time that parents and other adults spent with children.[31] Middle children in large families received considerably less adult care and attention than children in smaller families or than first and last children in larger families. Parental attention must be shared by more people when the family has more children living at home, a condition that affects middle children in large families more than others.

The study then looked at the effect of family size on achievement. It found that a variable representing the child's share of family time and financial resources had a more important effect on achievement, both edu-cational and occupational, than most other background characteristics.[32]

Children from large families seem to be somewhat slower in physical development than children from small families. Emotional and social differences have not been so clearly documented, although there is some evidence that children from small families are more likely to think well of themselves. On the other hand, cross-cultural studies have shown that children who care for younger children are more nurturing and responsible and less dependent and dominant than others.[33] Because children are more likely to have taken care of younger siblings when they come from larger families, smaller families may produce fewer independent and helpful children. In general, though, the trend toward smaller families among all segments of the population has probably done more to increase and equalize cognitive development and schooling than any other demographic trend.

The data on childlessness and family size, in short, do not suggest a societal abandonment of children. A large increase in childlessness now that involuntary childlessness is almost nonexistent would indicate that a substantial portion of the population wanted no children, but this has not occurred. The vast majority of adults have at least one child. Average family size has decreased, but the decline has taken place mostly in larger families. Family size is converging for the entire population on the two- or three-child ideal. These smaller families seem to be advantageous for children rather than a sign of societal indifference.

Living Arrangements of Children

Another indicator of the place of children in the society is whether parents and children live together. Children who live with their parents are certainly better off than children raised in orphanages. They may or may not be better off than children raised by relatives or foster parents. At any rate, whether or not children live with their parents provides some indication of the strength of ties between parents and children.

Many people assume that the rising divorce rates of the last few decades mean that fewer children now live with their parents. This assumption is not completely accurate. The data suggest that the proportion of children who live with at least one of their parents rather than with relatives, with foster parents, or in institutions has been steadily rising.

The U.S. Census has published information about the living arrangements of people only since 1940. Since then the proportion of children living with at least one of their parents in a separate household has gone steadily up, from about 90 percent in 1940 to almost 95 percent in 1970.[34] The increase seems to have occurred for two reasons. The first reason is that the proportion of children who lost a parent through death and divorce combined fell gradually during the first half of the century and probably fell before that as well. Among children born between 1911 and 1920, about 22 percent lost a parent through death and 5 percent had parents divorce sometime before their eighteenth birthday. Gradually declining death rates meant that fewer children lost parents as the century went on. Smaller families had the same effect, since more children were born to younger parents. The result was that about 20 percent of the children born during the 1940s lost parents through death or divorce. Only for children born around 1960 did rising divorce rates begin to counteract the effects of falling death rates. The proportion of children who experienced a parental disruption fell until then; only recently has disruption increased.[35]

The second reason for the rise in the proportion of children living with at least one parent between 1940 and 1970 is a dramatic increase in the proportion of widowed and divorced women who continued living with their children after their marriage ended. In 1940 only about 44 percent of women with children but without husbands headed their own families. The rest must have sent their children to live with their grandparents or other relatives or to orphanages. By 1970 almost 80 percent of divorced, separated, and widowed women with children headed their own families.[36] Some women, especially the young and unmarried, continue to leave their children with their grandparents. Most, however, now keep the family together. The children may not live with both their parents, but they do live with at least one. In 1975, despite rising divorce rates, only 2.7 percent of children under 14 lived with neither of their parents. The aggregate figures do conceal a racial difference: In the same year, 1975, 7.5 percent of non-white children were living with neither parent, compared with 1.7 percent of white children. But for non-whites as well as whites, the percent living with neither parent has been going down, from 9.8 percent for non-whites in 1968 to the present figure.[37]

Although the proportion of children living with at least one parent has risen, rising divorce rates since 1960 have caused a decrease in the proportion of children under 14 living with both parents. In 1960, 88.5 percent of all children under 14 lived with two natural or adoptive parents; by 1974 the number had fallen to 82.1 percent. This trend is likely to continue. Estimates from death and divorce rates indicate that nearly 40 percent of the children born around 1970 will experience a parental death, divorce, or separation and consequently live in a one-parent family at some point during their first eighteen years.[38] The proportion living with neither parent, however, is likely to remain small.

The effects on children of these changes in living arrangements are not well understood. Hardly anyone argues that the divorce or death of parents is good for children, but the extent of the harm done has not been documented. There is some evidence that children from broken homes do not do as well in school as children from unbroken homes. Much of the disadvantage seems to come, however, from the fact that many one-parent homes are also poor. Moreover, children whose parents divorce are no worse off than children whose homes are unbroken but also unhappy. Although the evidence is scanty, it suggests that most children adjust relatively quickly and well to the disruption and that in the case of divorce the disruption may be better than the alternative of living in a tension-filled home.[39]

No studies have looked at the effects on children of various living arrangements after divorce. This is surprising, given the significant change that has taken place over the last thirty years in what normally happens to children. Probably children who stay with their mothers are better off than children who are sent to institutions. They may also be better off than children with foster parents or relatives, although individual circumstances can vary widely.[40] Staying with the mother may make the event less disruptive and less distressing; only one parent is lost rather than both. The increased tendency of widowed and divorced mothers to keep their children may, therefore, be good for the children.

The effect of the growing tendency of women with children but without husbands to set up separate households rather than live with relatives or friends is less clear. Since single-parent families seem to live on their own whenever they can afford to,[41] they must see advantages to the arrangement. On the other hand, single parents have the almost impossible responsibility of supporting and caring for a family alone. The absence of other adults to relieve the pressure must increase the tension and irritability of single parents (unless, of course, the presence of other adults would increase tension and irritability even more). Children in separate households gain the undivided attention of their mothers and often establish extremely close supportive relationships.[42] But they lose the company of other adults and the exposure to a variety of adult personalities and role models that larger households might provide. Separate households are clearly what most single parents want, but it would be interesting to know exactly what they give up in having them.

Child Care Arrangements

Like data on living arrangements, data on child care arrangements are often cited as evidence of the state of parent-child relationships. People often talk as if children are best off when they are taken care of exclusively by their mothers. The rise in the proportion of mothers who hold paid jobs is, therefore, cited periodically as an indicator of the decline of the family. Most concern, of course, is focused on young children; Americans have long believed that older children should go to school and play on their own, not be continually supervised by mother. But even care arrangements for young children involve more than simply care by the mother. Care arrangements have changed over the century, but it is not clear that families and mothers have become less important. Nor is it clear whether the changes are good or bad.

The most important activity of contemporary children up to the age of 14 is watching television. The average preschooler seems to watch television about thirty-three hours per week, one-third of his waking hours. The average sixth-grade child watches about thirty-one hours.[43] Since television sets only became common during the 1950s, the importance of television has clearly been a development of the last quarter century. It represents a tremendous change in how children of all ages are cared for. Television is by far the most important new child care arrangement of this century.

The next most important activity of children's waking hours is going to school. Children now spend an average of about nineteen hours a week in school.[44] A larger proportion of children of all ages go to school now than ever before. They start school earlier and stay in school longer. The most dramatic change of the last ten years has been in the proportion of very young children enrolled in nursery school and kindergarten. In 1965 about 27 percent of all 3- to 5-year-olds were enrolled in school; by 1973, 41 percent of this age group were in school.[45]

Other important changes have occurred in the length of the school year and in average daily attendance. In 1880 the average pupil attended school about eighty days per year. By the 1960s the typical school year was

180 days and the average pupil attended about 164 days.[46] Both these changes mean that children enrolled in school spend more time there. School, therefore, has steadily gained in importance as a child care arrangement.

Compared with these two dramatic changes in child care arrangements—the growth of television and school—changes caused by mothers working outside the home appear almost trivial. It is true that the proportion of mothers with paid jobs has risen sharply over the last twenty-five years, particularly among mothers of preschool children. In 1950, 12 percent of married women with children under six were in the labor force; by 1974 the proportion had grown to nearly 40 percent.[47] Many of these working mothers arranged their schedules so that they worked only when their children were in school or when fathers were at home to take care of the children. About 70 percent, however, made other child care arrangements. The most common was to have a relative or sitter come to the home and care for the children. Only about 10 percent of the preschool children of working mothers went to day care centers.[48]

How much of a difference these arrangements make in the lives of children depends on what actually happens to them and who actually spends time with them. There is no evidence as to how much time mothers a century ago spent with their children. Undoubtedly, it was less than contemporary nonworking mothers, since mothers of a century ago had more children and probably also had more time-consuming household tasks.

Contemporary nonworking mothers do not spend a great deal of time exclusively with their children. A national study done in 1965 found that the average nonworking mother spent 1.4 hours per day on child care.[49] A study of 1,300 Syracuse families in 1967–68 showed that the average nonworking mother spent sixty-six minutes a day in physical care of *all* family members and forty-eight minutes in other sorts of care on a typical weekday during the school year.[50] The amount of time varied with the age and number of children.[51]

A small 1973 Boston study, by White and Watts, found that of the time they were observed mothers spent about a third interacting with their children (but one expects that mothers being observed by Harvard psychologists might depart somewhat from their normal routines). The children in the study, age 1 to 3, spent most of their time in solitary playing or simply watching what went on around them.[52]

Working mothers spend less time on child care than nonworking mothers, but the differences in the amount of time mothers spend exclusively with their children are surprisingly small. In the Syracuse study, the correlations between the amount of time women spent on physical care of family members and whether or not they were employed were very small, once family size and children's ages were taken into account. When all family members, not just wives, were looked at, the correlations were even smaller.[53] There is some evidence that working mothers especially in the middle class try to make up for their working by setting aside time for exclusive attention to their children. They probably read more to their children and spend more time in planned activities with them than do nonworking mothers.[54]

There is no evidence that having a working mother per se has harmful effects on children. When a mother works because the father is incapacitated, unemployed, or paid poorly, the family may be poor and disorganized and the children may suffer. In these cases, however, the mother's working is a symptom and not a cause of more general family difficulties. In other cases where mothers work, children are inadequately supervised and may get into trouble. Again, though, the problem is general family difficulty. The Gluecks' study of lower-class boys, often cited as evidence that working mothers raise delinquent children, shows no direct link between the mothers' employment and delinquency. It did find that in lower-class homes children of working mothers were less likely to be adequately supervised, and that there was a tie between lack of supervision and delinquency whether the mothers worked or not.[55] In families where the mother's employment is not a symptom of deeper family trouble, children seem not to turn out any differently from other children.[56]

Parents and Teenagers

For the last century or so, Americans have become attuned to the existence and peculiarities of that stage in life between childhood and adulthood that we call adolescence. Adolescence is apparently a creation of relatively recent times; at least its problems have only recently attracted widespread attention. Certainly, as Margaret Mead showed so well, adolescent difficulties do not occur universally.[57] Whatever the distinctive characteristics of the adolescent personality, however, there have been some noticeable changes over the last century in the living and working arrangements of adolescents. The general trend is to tie adolescent boys to parents for an increasing length of time and to begin to liberate adolescent girls.

In mid-nineteenth-century America, it was common practice for young men, and to a lesser extent young women, to leave their parents' house and live for a few years as a lodger or servant in some other older person's house before marrying and setting up independent households.[58] The best information on family structure in the mid-nineteenth century comes from Michael Katz's study of Hamilton, Ontario. Boarders and lodgers were then an important feature of life. In 1851 more than half of the young men aged around 20 were living as boarders in the household of a family other than their own.[59] But industrialization was accompanied by business cycles and increased schooling, which in turn brought striking changes in the lives of young people. By 1861 only a third of Hamilton's young men were living as boarders. More lived at home and went to school. Nearly a third were neither employed nor in school. The nineteenth-century specter of gangs of young men roaming the city streets must have arisen because gangs of young men were indeed roaming the streets.

In the United States also, many young men of the middle and late nineteenth century lived for a time as boarders. Boarding was a different phenomenon, however, in rural and urban areas. In cities young men typically lived with families but worked elsewhere. Rural youth were more often live-in farm help.[60] By 1970, boarding out had virtually disappeared; less than 2 percent of 15- to 19-year-olds were living as boarders or servants.[61] Instead they were living at home and going to school. The rise in school attendance was dramatic. In 1910, about 30 percent of 16- to 19-year-old boys were in school compared to about 73 percent in 1970. The employment situation for teenagers is still, as it was in mid-nineteenth-century Hamilton, dreadful. The young men have not been put to work, but they have been induced to stay in school.

Young women, so often forgotten in historical discussions, are working more and going to school more. Typically, young women lived at home performing domestic tasks until they married. In mid-nineteenth-century Hamilton, for example, about 36 percent of the 18- and 19-year-old women were employed and about 5 percent went to school. Another 5 percent were married. The rest must have been living at home, doing domestic chores or doing nothing. During the growth of schooling in the nineteenth century, girls' attendance rates rose even faster than boys'.[62] In 1970 in the United States, young women were still living at home, but they were going to school rather than helping mother. The vast majority

(88.6 percent) of the 16- and 17-year-olds and 41.6 percent of the 18- and 19-year-olds were enrolled in school. Most of the rest were working at paid jobs, and some were raising children.

Among both men and women, there seems to have been a slight increase in the last decade in the proportion who live away from their parents during their late teenage years. Even in 1974, however, this group was a minority. Among 18- and 19-year-old men, about 7 percent were married and living with a wife and only about 6 percent were living on their own. Among 18- and 19-year-old women, 21 percent were married and 9 percent were living on their own.[63] Virtually all 14- to 17-year-olds lived with their parents. The living arrangements of 20- to 24-year-olds will be examined in Chapter Three.

In short, there has been no significant emancipation of teenagers from their families. In comparison with nineteenth-century teenagers in urban areas, in fact, contemporary teenage boys are much more dependent on their parents for shelter and support. What they do at home is another matter, but they do live there.

Children in the Family and Society

In summary, demographic materials suggest that the decline of the family's role in caring for children is more myth than fact. None of the statistical data suggests that parental watchfulness over children has decreased over the span of three generations; much suggests that it has increased. The most important difference between today's children and children of their great-grandparents' and grandparents' time is that there are proportionately fewer of them. They make up a smaller proportion of society, and there are fewer of them per family. Like children born during the 1930s, but unlike children born during the 1950s, children of the 1970s face a predominantly adult world. If the rate of population growth continues to stabilize, the society of the next decades will be older and the families smaller than any previously found in America.

Parent-child bonds also persist despite changes in patterns of disruption and living arrangements after disruption. The proportion of children who lose a parent by death has gone steadily down over the generations. The proportion who live with a parent after a death or divorce has gone steadily up. Even in recent years when family disruptions have begun to rise again to high levels, almost no children have gone to relatives, foster homes or institutions.

The trend toward more mothers in the paid labor force has probably not materially affected parent-child bonds. Even though more mothers work outside the home and more children go to school earlier and longer, the quantity and quality of actual mother-child interaction has probably not changed much. In short, the major demographic changes affecting parents and children in the course of the century have not much altered the basic picture of children living with and being cared for by their parents. The patterns of structural change so often cited as evidence of family decline do not seem to be weakening the bonds between parents and children.

Chapter Two

HUSBANDS AND WIVES

THE MOST FREQUENTLY CITED EVIDENCE of the decline of the American family is the divorce rate. In 1929 the Committee on Recent Social Trends, reporting to President Hoover on the state of American society, pointed to the rising divorce rate as an indicator of strain in the family.[1] The committee's report explained that the family had lost many of its economic functions and was thus held together by more tenuous bonds. The rising divorce rate showed that these social and emotional bonds were not sufficiently strong to ensure marital stability. Almost half a century later social commentators echo the same arguments about the loss of functions by the family. The same evidence, a divorce rate now rising with unprecedented rapidity, is still cited as proof that the new family is not stable.

Family life is inexorably connected in the minds of most Americans with monogamous, life-long marriage. Most Americans, even young Americans, think that marriage should be a permanent commitment between two adults that involves maintaining a household and usually raising children.[2] Thus, marriage is seen as quite different from the transient changing relationships that characterize "dating" and many friendships. It is the transformation of marriage into a short-lived, fair-weather friendship that people see as a threat to family life and that they feel rising divorce rates may be pointing toward.

But Americans have always permitted exceptions to the rule that marriage must last "until death do us part." Insanity, felony conviction, adultery, physical cruelty, impotence, and desertion have long been seen as legitimate grounds for dissolving a marriage. These exceptions recognize that if marriage is to be a vital institution in the society it must provide at least some degree of mutual satisfaction to husbands and wives; marriage is not slavery or penal servitude. The question is whether marriage has become so transient as to destroy its ability to provide a foundation for family life and for strong unconditional bonds among people.

The divorce rate is one indicator of where American society is in this regard, but it is only one. Other indicators include proportions marrying and proportions remarrying after divorce or widowhood; the satisfactions that people say they do or do not derive from their marriages; and whether the reasons that people give for divorce reflect a commitment to the institution or a change to quite different sorts of relationships. Much of this other data suggests that marriage is far from withering away in contemporary America and is, in fact, enjoying unprecedented popularity. Its character, to be sure, is changing substantially, because of declining birthrates and because women hold a different position in contemporary marriages. The change, though, seems to be taking place within a context of strong and persistent commitment to marriage relationships.

Proportions Marrying

Almost everyone in America gets married at some time or other. In early eighteenth-century Andover, Massachusetts, less than 10 percent of women never married. Among Quaker women born before 1786, about 16 percentage remained unmarried until the age of 50. Among women born during the nineteenth and twentieth century, between 90 and 95 percent married at least once. The proportion marrying is somewhat higher among women born in the twentieth century than in the nineteenth.[3]

Whether this will continue is open to question. The Census Bureau does not ask people if they expect to get married the way it asks whether they expect to have children, and so that source of prediction (which would probably, in truth, not be particularly useful) is lacking. The census does collect statistics on proportions married and single at various ages. Between 1960 and 1974 the percentage single increased for both men and women at all ages below 30, and decreased for ages over 30.[4] This means that for those over 30, born before 1944, the proportion marrying at some time or other is continuing to rise. For those under 30, the trend is not so clear, since they may be either postponing marriage or deciding to remain single for life.

Even if the proportion of people who marry does decline somewhat, it is still very high. It is hard to imagine that it will fall even as low as the 90 percent recorded earlier in the century.

Age at Marriage

The age of first marriage for contemporary Americans seems to be considerably lower than it was in colonial times or even in the nineteenth century.

In seventeenth-century Plymouth Colony, men married between the ages of 25 and 27, on the average, and women married at age 21 or 22. Men and women in seventeenth-century Andover, Dedham, and Hingham married at about the same ages as in Plymouth, as did eighteenth-century Quakers.[5] Two hundred years later, in 1890, American men married at an average age of 26 and women at 22. The average age of marriage then dropped steadily until the mid-1950s, to 22 for men and 20 for women.

In the last few years, the average age at first marriage has been rising slightly; in 1974 it stood at 23 for men and 21 for women. A rise of one year in the average age of marriage in the course of two decades is not particularly noteworthy. In 1974, after all, 42 percent of all 20-year-old women were married.[6] But the increasing proportions of single people under 30 may indicate that young Americans are putting off marriage. If they are indeed postponing rather than rejecting marriage, the trend may indicate that young Americans are becoming more cautious about making long-term commitments or that they are doing other things first. Since teenage marriages tend to be less stable than older marriages, this trend may lead to greater marital stability in the future.[7]

The Marital Life Cycle

What has changed most about American marriage during the twentieth century is neither the proportion marrying nor the age at marriage, nor even, I suspect, the proportion divorcing. Instead, the most dramatic change is in the pattern of the marital life cycle—in what husbands and

wives do and in the number of years they spend together with and without children. The change has resulted partly from increased life expectancy, but mainly from changed fertility patterns. Because women spend
a smaller proportion of their time raising children, they spend a larger
proportion doing other things. Changed fertility patterns also mean that
husbands and wives have many more years alone together, without children. Increased life expectancy means more years together after retirement
from paid work. How husbands and wives eventually accommodate to the
changing patterns may well be the key to the future of marriage in this
country.

Arthur Norton used Census Bureau data to put together a description
of the marital life cycles for women born between 1900 and 1939.[8] He
found that the average married couple—a couple who do not divorce—born
in the 1930s will spend about forty-eight years married. During thirty-one
of those years, they may have children living at home with them.[9] They
will have slightly more than a year alone together when they are young,
and fifteen or sixteen years when they are older. The time during which
they will have young children is relatively short. Their last child will start
school, age 6, when the mother is about thirty-seven, having spent sixteen
years with young children at home. Two-thirds of the couples' married
life, therefore, is free of the time- and energy-consuming responsibilities
of young children, and one-third is free of children living at home.

Norton found that the life-cycle patterns of women born between
1900 and 1909 were not very different from those of women born between
1930 and 1939. But because of the peculiar fertility patterns of both these
cohorts, they are not particularly good indicators of what came before or
will come after. The 1900–09 cohort had depression babies and had many
fewer children than earlier cohorts. The 1930–39 cohort had baby-boom
babies and had more children than women born later are likely to have. To
make a more interesting historical comparison, both earlier and later birth
cohorts must be looked at.

Table 2–1 shows hypothetical life cycles for women born in the mid-
nineteenth and the mid-twentieth centuries.

Constructing these life histories involves considerable speculation for
both groups, since detailed fertility histories for the older women do not
exist and the fertility history of the younger women has not yet happened.
The table therefore makes a number of assumptions, principally that
child-spacing patterns do not change over time.[10]

The figures in Table 2–1, if they are anywhere near correct, indicate
that a combination of lower fertility and longer life expectancy will make

TABLE 2–1

Hypothetical Life Cycles: Mean Ages at Major Events of
Women in Mid-nineteenth and Mid-twentieth Centuries.

	Born	
	1846–55 (Six Children)	1946–55 (Two Children)
First marriage	22.0	20.8
Birth of first child	23.5	22.3
Birth of last child	36.0	24.8
First marriage of last child	58.9	47.7
Death of spouse	56.4	67.7
Own death	60.7	77.1

SOURCES: CPR, P-20, No. 263, "Fertility Histories, 1971"; Preston, Keyfitz, and Schoen, 1972.

the marriages of the next few decades follow a quite different pattern from those of a century ago. The marriages that last will last longer; forty-seven years instead of thirty-four.[11] Couples will spend only 18 percent of their married lives raising young children, compared with 54 percent a century ago. Married couples a century ago had only about a year and a half alone together before the birth of children. In contrast, couples marrying now are likely to spend nearly twenty-two years, almost half their married life, alone together with no children in the house—mostly after the children are grown. During a substantial part of this time, neither partner will be in the full-time labor force. The normal age of retirement, now 65, seems to be dropping, while life expectancy for older people continues to increase slightly. People, married or not, will spend over a decade in what might be called "young old age," between retirement from the labor force and the onset of physical disability. For women, who can now expect to live twenty years after they reach age 60, "young old age" will last longer than childbearing, longer indeed than youth.

How this change in the average marital life cycle will affect the stability and happiness of marriages remains to be seen. What women do instead of raising children and what people do instead of working for money varies considerably. How much satisfaction they derive from their lives also varies from one person to another.

Mothers whose lives are centered on their children might be expected to have considerable difficulty adjusting to married life without children. They may feel that their lives have no real purpose after they have raised their children. They may suffer from what sociologists have called the empty nest syndrome and have difficulties finding things to do that are worthwhile and satisfying. Similarly, married couples may feel that they have little in common with each other once the bond created by children is gone.

Marriage without children might be expected, therefore, to be less satisfying; the new marital life cycle might lead to decreased satisfaction and increased divorce. But that does not seem to be what happens. Divorce rates decrease with age; in 1969, the highest divorce rates occurred among 20- to 24-year-olds. Divorce rates seem to be going up faster among the young, with no notable divorce "bump" for the "empty nest" ages.[12]

Reported marital satisfaction also seems to be greatest during those periods before the children come and after they leave home. Respondents to national surveys in 1971 and 1974 were most likely to say that their marriages were very happy either when they were expecting children but had none yet or when all their children were grown. They were least likely to say their marriages were very happy when they were living in relatively large families with school-age children.[13] In another study, Spanier, Lewis, and Cole looked at three local samples and used a more sophisticated measure of marital adjustment. They found that men and women in the middle stages of the family life cycle—with preschoolers out of infancy, school-age children, and adolescents—had somewhat lower scores on the marital adjustment scale than people in either earlier or later stages.[14]

A third study looked at data on general satisfaction with life from national polls during the 1960s and 1970s.[15] This study compared reported satisfaction for men and women age 40–59 who still had children at home and men and women in the "postparental" stage. Both men and women were somewhat more likely to report greater satisfaction if they had no children living at home than if they did. For example, in a 1971 Roper survey, 79.7 percent of the 172 women respondents aged 35–64 who had children living at home said they "mostly enjoyed life," compared with 84.4 percent of the 147 women of the same age who had no children living at home.

None of the studies of general satisfaction and marital adjustment found very large differences between stages in the family life cycle. They are consistent, however, in what they do not find. They do not find that raising young children provides the greatest satisfactions of married life. They do not find that married life without children is a terrible letdown. Instead, they suggest that married couples can work out a quite satisfactory life together after the children are grown—although not all do. The shift in the marital life cycle from a larger proportion of time spent raising young children to a larger proportion of time alone together as a couple ought not pose any special dangers for marriage.

Married Women's Work

Changing fertility patterns have accompanied and probably partly caused another important change in married life, a dramatic shift in wives' work, from work in the home to work outside. From colonial times up until the mid-twentieth century, women's work was mostly done in the home. In colonial America wives made important contributions to the domestic economy, producing a wide variety of goods for family use and for trade. They may sometimes have joined men in work in the fields, but generally they worked in and around the home, caring for their large brood of children at the same time that they gardened, spun, raised chickens, made medicines and candles, and brewed beer.

As production was transferred to factories in the nineteenth century, women's work changed, especially in the cities. Textile production was still done by women, but the early factory workers were unmarried rather than married women. Married women could no longer care for children while they worked, so they had to stop working. Instead of producing food and goods, women began to spend their time on housework. The occupation of wife and mother became the ideal for married women. Women remained in the home. Unlike colonial women, however, women in the nineteenth century did not play an important role in economic life.[16]

In 1940 only 14.7 percent of married women living with their husbands were in the paid labor force. With World War II, however, the proportion of wives and mothers who worked at paid jobs began to increase, and it continued increasing when the war was over. By 1950, almost a quarter—and by 1974, 42 percent—of all wives worked at paid jobs.

Married women's labor force participation rates are high in the early years of marriage. Around the time of the birth of their first child, some women drop out of the labor force, and stay out while their children are young, especially if they have many children. They seem to start returning to the labor force as their children grow up; labor force participation rates for women in their 40s are quite high. Not all women, however, drop out of the labor force. In 1974 almost a third of all women with children under 3 were in the paid labor force.[17]

Even for women who do stay home while their children are young, lower fertility means a long potential working life. Of the forty years between the ages of 20 and 60, women who have two children spend only about eight and a half years with children under 6. They can spend 80 percent of their adult years working. If nursery schools become more popular, children may be considered old enough to go to school at age 3. Their mothers may then go back to work earlier, if only to part-time work. The mother of two children who decides to stay home with her young children may thus spend only five or six years out of the labor force.

Whatever happens, though, women are likely to spend a substantial portion of their married life in the paid labor force. Even if they stay home until their children are married, they still have thirteen years before the age of 60 that they are likely to spend in working. Thus the success with which husbands and wives fashion a way of living while both work is likely to be quite important in determining the stability and satisfaction of marriage.

Working seems to be generally good for women. Working wives seem to be in slightly better physical health than housewives—although this may be a cause rather than an effect of working. Working mothers exhibit somewhat fewer symptoms of psychosomatic illness than housewives. They are somewhat more likely to be satisfied with their work, although they are also subject to pressures and harassments. Among respondents to a 1973 national survey, 41.5 percent of those employed full time, 42.7 percent of those employed part time, and 46.4 percent of the housewives said that they were "very happy." But when I looked at answers to the question on job satisfaction ("On the whole, how satisfied are you with the work you do —would you say you are very satisfied, moderately satisfied, a little dissatisfied, or very dissatisfied?"), 49.2 percent of the working women and 36.3 percent of the housewives said they were "very satisfied" with their jobs. Perhaps the working women felt pressures on their time and energy that made their general level of satisfaction lower than their level of job satisfaction.[18]

Wives' working is not so clearly good for marriages. Marriages in which the wives work tend to be somewhat less stable and report somewhat less satisfaction than marriages in which the wives keep house.[19] There are, however, a number of possible explanations for their findings. Wives now tend to work when family income is low; these economic difficulties may contribute to marital tension. Wives who work are harassed and pressed for time. When housework, child care, and paid work are combined, the work weeks of working mothers are much longer than those of nonworking wives or of men.[20] They may feel increased pressure and tension, which may in turn affect the marital relationship. There may also be tension between husband and wife over who is to do household chores. Working wives may press for more participation in housework by their husbands; the husbands, knowing a wretched job when they see one, may resist.[21]

In many families, the wife's employment is a departure from tradition and effects a dramatic change in family routines. It is probably not surprising that the event generates some conflict and some dissatisfaction. As more and more wives work, it is possible that more and more married couples will experience conflict and dissatisfaction. On the other hand, increased numbers of working wives may make the two-worker marriage more easily accepted. Young people may choose their partners with the expectation that both will work, and adjustments may be made early in the marriage. When this happens the personal satisfactions or dissatisfactions that each gets from work are likely to be crucial in the marriage, rather than the simple fact of work or no work. Since more work usually brings more money, financial satisfaction is likely to rise. When the wife likes her work, her increased satisfaction is likely to contribute still more to the happiness of the marriage.

Marital Instability

Trends in the marital life cycle seem to be pointing toward marriages that are no less satisfying, on the whole, than marriages in the past. What then should one make of the rising divorce rate? Does it invalidate other predictions? Or is it about to start going down?

The divorce rate is indeed rising. Glick and Norton of the Census Bureau calculate that about 12 percent of the marriages contracted by women born 1900–04 ended in divorce. In contrast, they calculate that between 30 and 40 percent of marriages by women born 1940–44 will end in divorce.[22]

A rising divorce rate appears to signal an increase in marital disruption. The last chapter noted, however, that the proportion of children affected by a parental disruption during their childhood actually went down over the century and began to rise only in the last few years. Death rates went down at all ages, and, probably more important, as family size declined fewer children were born to older parents. The result was that as the century went on many fewer children lost a parent during their childhood. Until the last few years divorce rates did not rise fast enough to balance falling death rates, and thus the total number of marital disruptions affecting children did not increase.

Looking at marital disruptions as they affect adults is somewhat more complicated. All marriages not previously disrupted by divorce are eventually disrupted by death. The proportion of marriages "ever disrupted" is always 100 percent. Variations only occur in how and when they are disrupted. Table 2–2 shows the proportions of ever-married women, aged 45–64, who were living with their husbands at the time of the censuses of 1910, 1940, and 1970. These are stable first marriages; the remaining women were either divorced, separated, widowed, or remarried. The figures are surprisingly similar for the three years.

TABLE 2–2
*Percentages of Ever-married Women
Living with Their First Husbands*

	Age of Women		
Census Year	45–49	50–54	55–64
1910	70.2	64.7	55.0
1940	68.4	64.0	54.9
1970	69.9	65.7	56.6

SOURCE: Appendix, Table A-6.

The data for the three years are not precisely comparable.[23] In this limited sense, however, marital disruption was just as common in 1910 as it was sixty years later. Several different trends probably acted together to produce this surprising result. The death rate fell, making fewer widows. Partially balancing this trend, the differential between male and female death rates increased steadily from 1910 on. The female death rate fell much faster than the male death rate, which must have had the effect of producing more widows at each age level than if the differential had remained constant. A woman can only be a widow, after all, when she lives longer than her husband, and the increasing differential meant not only that more women lived longer than their husbands, but that they themselves lived longer as widows. The combination of falling death rates and rising male-female differentials meant that the proportions of widowed women at given ages fell very slowly over time.

Over the same period, the divorce rate rose from 1930 (and probably earlier) to a high in 1946, fell until 1958, and then began rising again. In 1973 the divorce rate passed the 1946 high, and it is still rising. Women who were between 20 and 30 around 1946 were most affected by the post-war divorce boom. These women were between 45 and 54 in 1970. The proportion ever-divorced was probably higher among these women, there-fore, than among women born a decade earlier or a decade later. Their rela-tively high divorce rate balanced the falling death rate to keep the propor-tion of intact marriages relatively constant. The proportion will probably still be constant in the 1980 census. By 1990, however, the high divorce rate of the 1970s should show up in lower proportions of women over 45 living in intact first marriages, perhaps only half of the 45-to-49-year-olds.[24]

Death and divorce are, of course, quite different events, with quite different effects on people. A relatively constant proportion of intact first marriages among 45-to-64-year-olds should not, therefore, be read as a signal that nothing has changed. It does suggest, though, that relatively large pro-portions of people have suffered and continue to suffer the pain inherent in loss of a marital partner and that large proportions of women have been left alone, even when relatively young. Marital disruption has always been with us.

The Correlates of Divorce

Although the patterns of marital disruption are quite complex, it is still clear that an increasing proportion of marriages are now disrupted by divorce rather than death. Many commentators view this trend with alarm. It is distressing in and of itself, however, only if staying together at all costs is considered an indicator of healthy marriages or healthy societies. Since our view of marriage is considerably more complicated, the reasons for and effects of the rising divorce rate are also important indicators. Some things are fairly clear. The majority of marriages do not end in divorce. The vast majority of divorced people remarry. Only a tiny proportion of people marry more than twice. We are thus a long way from a society in which marriage is rejected or replaced by a series of short-term liaisons.

The future of marriage in the society could be further illuminated by an understanding of the reasons for divorce. If the rising divorce rate indi-cates not that intolerable marriages are increasing particularly but that they are now more often being ended—perhaps because of more liberal divorce laws or more alternatives for women—that is one matter. If, however, rising divorce rates occur because more marriages are intolerable or because less serious tensions are being resolved by divorce, that is another.

The constraints against divorce have clearly been loosening. Until recently, it was almost impossible in many states to get a divorce without considerable expense and usually considerable fraud as well. Many people could not get divorces, however much they might want them. That has now changed in almost all states. The opportunities for a decent life after divorce have also improved. Whether it is better to be married or divorced depends not only on how happy or unhappy the marriage is but also on the nature of life after divorce. If social ostracism and financial destitution follow divorce, even an unhappy marriage looks less bad. Some losses—the partner, perhaps the children—are inevitable after divorce. Others, such as social attitudes and the opportunities for divorced women to support themselves, vary from time to time and place to place. Increased work opportunities for women and increased social acceptability of divorce have made divorce a reasonable alternative to a bad marriage.

Several recent investigations have looked at the effects of loosening constraints—legal, economic, and social—on the divorce rate. The ease of state divorce laws has been found to be related to the probability of divorce.[25] But state divorce laws may be a result rather than a cause of changing societal attitudes toward divorce. They do tend to reflect the demographic composition of their states.[26] A California study of divorce rates before and after the 1969 non-adversary (no-fault) divorce law provides an example of one kind of effect which changing divorce laws can have. The study found that divorces did increase the year following the passage of the new law; but the increase occurred because people waited for passage of the law before filing for divorce. The general trend of divorce in California was not affected by the reformed law; divorce did not go down, but it did not go up either.[27]

The most important predictor of divorce, age at first marriage, is not related to loosening constraints. Teenage marriages are considerably more likely to end in divorce than marriages between older people.[28] The effect persists even when other variables are held constant. Teenage marriages are more likely to involve premarital pregnancies and financial difficulties, but they have other problems as well. Perhaps teenagers make less sensible choices of marital partners.[29]

Another predictor of divorce is low income.[30] Studies which have looked at the components of income and the causes of low income have found, however, that the explanation for the association between income and divorce is quite complex. Sawhill et al. found that serious unemployment and a discrepancy between actual and expected earnings were better predictors of divorce than income per se.[31] This finding suggests that to the extent financial difficulties are unexpected, they may increase marital tension and conflict and thus increase the possibilities of marital breakdown.

If low income were the most important explanation for divorce, however, the divorce rate should have fallen over time as family income increased. Since it did not, other factors must also be at work. One candidate is the economic position of wives. Ross and Sawhill found that when wives' earnings were higher, the probability of separation increased.[32] When the husband provided the largest proportion of family income, when he was most clearly the breadwinner, marriages were more stable. Perhaps deviation from traditional patterns challenges the husband's self-esteem and increases marital tension and marital instability.

The impact of welfare on marital stability is a matter of considerable controversy. Logic suggests that a system which provides welfare support to female-headed but not to male-headed poor families should induce men to leave their families. Some studies support this logic.[33] The effect of welfare is always found to be small, however, and other studies find no effect at all.[34] When welfare mothers in New York City were asked why they separated from their husbands, none gave the availability of welfare as a reason, though some cited financial reasons. Much more important, they said, were drugs, alcohol, other women, and physical abuse.[35]

On the whole, research has little to say about the causes of the rising divorce rate. It seems not to result simply from easier divorce laws or increased welfare payments; both are as much results as causes of rising divorce rates. Society may be changing its attitudes toward the permanence of marriage and its notions on the roles of husbands and wives. It may simply be recognizing that there is no particular benefit to requiring permanence in unhappy marriages.

Remarriage

Remarriage rates, the proportions of divorced or widowed persons who marry for a second time, have followed a pattern similar to that of divorce. The rates rose to a high in 1946, fell until the mid-1950s, and rose again to a new high in the mid-1970s. The general trend is reflected in the

TABLE 2–3

Percentages Remarried of Women Divorced or Widowed

Census Year	Age of Women		
	45–49	50–54	55–64
1910	35.4	28.7	19.2
1940	38.6	31.3	20.8
1970	52.5	45.2	31.7

SOURCE: Calculated from Appendix, Table A-8.

proportions who remarried after being divorced or widowed among women aged 45–64 in 1910, 1940, and 1970. The figures are shown in Table 2–3.

By the late 1960s, over half of all divorced women had remarried within five years of their divorce. Widows remarried less quickly than divorced women, but increasing numbers of widows remarried as well.[36]

In general, the remarriage rate has kept pace with the divorce rate, suggesting that it is not marriage itself but the specific marital partner that is rejected. Very recent data suggest that remarriage rates have leveled off in the past few years, rising less rapidly than divorce rates.[37] This may mean that divorced and widowed people have become more cynical about marriage and are keeping out of it, or it may simply mean that they are waiting longer to remarry, perhaps choosing their new spouses more carefully.

Research on who does and does not remarry is less adequate than research on divorce. What research there is suggests that divorced people are more likely to remarry than widowed people and that those who are younger when they are divorced or widowed are more likely to remarry.[38] Men who are better off economically are more likely to remarry.[39] The effect of women's economic situations on their decisions about remarriage is less clear. One study found that better-off women were more likely to remarry, suggesting that their incomes made them more attractive marriage partners.[40] Another study found they were less likely to remarry,[41] suggesting that women may weigh the decision to remarry more carefully when they are supporting themselves adequately or that men feel threatened by financially independent women. Perhaps the source of the women's income determines its effects. Women on welfare, for example, are less likely to remarry than women not on welfare, and women getting larger welfare checks are less likely to remarry than those getting smaller checks.[42] Higher levels of welfare support and perhaps also increased employment opportunities for women may be part of the reason for the recent leveling off of remarriage rates, assuming that such leveling off has indeed occurred.

Marriage and Society

What, then, of marriage in the United States in the last quarter of the twentieth century? Two conclusions can be drawn from the data. First, marriage is still an exceedingly important part of American life. The popularity of marriage is underlined by the fact that 90–95 percent of Americans marry at least once. It is possible that the proportion of single people can never go much lower (like structural unemployment) because of inevitable imperfections in the system of getting eligible males together with eligible females. And even if the proportion of singles rises slightly, it will still be among the smallest in history. Remarriage rates also testify to the popularity of marriage. Within five years, most divorced people are trying marriage again. Most people manage to keep themselves married, and their marriages are long-term. Very few people marry more than twice.

The importance of marriage in American life is also apparent in people's evaluations of their general well-being. Married men and women are much more likely to say that they are, in general, "very happy" than single, widowed, or divorced men and women.[43] Marriage seems to be especially good for men. Married men are in better physical and emotional health and are more successful economically than single, divorced, or widowed men. Married women are less clearly better off than unmarried women. They are more likely than single women to say they are "very happy," but they also have slightly higher rates of some physical and mental disorders.[44] For both men and women, death rates are lower for the married than for the unmarried at all ages. Again, the advantage to men is much greater than that to women.[45] Nonetheless, marriage seems to make both men and women happier and better off.

Still another indicator of the importance of marriage in American society is the grief and distress that follows divorce or death of a spouse. Even after divorce, which theoretically signifies that the marriage was unsatisfactory, both partners usually feel a great sense of emptiness. Adjusting after divorce is not simply a matter of figuring out how to earn the money or get the housework done. Divorced men and women suffer both from a loss of companionship, often compounded by the fact that many of their friends seem to disappear as well, and from emotional loss. Many divorced people end up under the care of a doctor or psychiatrist.[46]

Taken as a whole, the data on marriage and divorce suggest that the kind of marriage that Americans have always known is still a pervasive and enduring institution. A second conclusion is that marriages are now harder to sustain. The actual amount of marital disruption affecting specific age groups has not increased substantially, but the ratio of voluntary to involuntary disruption has increased. Two trends seem to be producing higher divorce rates. People are more accepting of divorce as a solution to an unsatisfactory marriage. But an increased tendency to end bad marriages probably does not in itself explain the rising divorce rate. The changing roles of husbands and wives, and new opportunities for women to be employed and independent, also seem to contribute to the divorce rate. These changes can create marital tensions and conflicts that not all marriages are able to handle. The inevitable result, in a time when divorce is increasingly acceptable, is more divorce.

But the divorce rate in America falls far short of the level that would characterize a society of casual liaisons rather than permanent families. Some argue that the society may be heading in that direction: that both women and men find more freedom and pleasure outside of marriage; that sexual equality and effective birth control now permit the free and independent life. But more egalitarian marriages are another possible result, and in the long run these new marriages may be as stable and satisfying as the old. Couples will spend less time raising children and more time on their individual lives and their life together. Men and women will do more similar work and will approach each other more equally as partners. Both will have work and friends outside the home and so will place fewer social and emotional demands on the marriage.

Because the pattern is new, however, men and women will have to go through a period of adjustment. Young people should have less trouble, since they will probably choose marriage partners who share their own expectations about what husbands and wives do. People already married may encounter serious difficulties, especially if the wives press for more independence and equality while the husbands prefer traditional patterns.[47] The result may be more tension and conflict, and probably more divorce as well. But it seems unlikely that very large numbers of either young or old people will give up the fight and decide to remain permanently single.

Chapter Three

THE EXPANDED FAMILY: BED AND BOARD

THE EXTENDED FAMILY HOUSEHOLD, populated by a friendly assortment of related people of all ages and their equally cheerful animal friends, is a cornerstone of American mythology. It symbolizes for many people much that was best in the past: sociability, community, the integration of life, a sense of personal responsibility for other people. The alleged disappearance of the large extended family is blamed for much that is wrong with contemporary American family life. Without it mothers are said to be isolated and deprived of help with housework and child care. Its demise has meant that children are in touch with fewer adults and consequently have more difficulty in moving into adult society. The isolated nuclear family, in comparison with the extended family, is overburdened and sterile.[1]

Recent historical studies show the myth of the extended family household to be just that—a myth. The nuclear family, consisting of parents living with their own children and no other adults, has been the predominant family form in America since the earliest period on which historians have data. Families of sisters and brothers almost never shared a common household. Households composed of parents and their married children were never widespread.

Instead, relationships among relatives appear to have been historically what they are now: complex patterns of companionship and help that only occasionally involve sharing bed and board. Recent sociological studies have shown that Americans maintain close ties with many of their relatives and that the American nuclear family is not as isolated from kin as was once thought. At the same time that historians have been exposing the myth of the extended household, sociologists have been showing that contemporary families have very real kinship networks.

Contemporary families, like families in the past, provide bed and board to adult family members who find themselves in situations of economic and social distress. Co-residence is a response to particularly difficult situations and is abandoned when the situation improves. This assumption of family responsibility for members in trouble is still quite prevalent, although perhaps not quite as common now as in earlier centuries. But the decline of family responsibility is only part of what is mourned by those who hold up the myth of the extended family. The other concern is for sociability, friendship, and community, qualities that must have always crossed the boundaries of households. The current state of these larger social networks will be taken up in the next chapter, under the heading of Kith and Kin.

Households in History

The realization that the extended family belongs to myth rather than history has come about largely through the work of several historians who supplement traditional literary sources with quantitative data. Using local and national censuses, wills, and parish marriage, birth, and death registrations, they have reconstructed the family and household arrangements of a variety of European and American communities.

Peter Laslett, of the Cambridge Group for the History of Population and Social Structure, has analyzed the results of studies covering 100 English communities between 1574 and 1821.[2] The studies show that households over the three centuries were predominantly nuclear and relatively small, with no systematic changes during the period. The average household contained slightly under five people. Seventy percent of all households were headed by married couples, and 75 percent included children. Only about 10 percent of all households contained any resident kin—grandparents, siblings of the married couple, and so on. Only 6 percent of the households held three generations: children, parents, and one or more grandparents. Servants and lodgers were considerably more common, especially in the better-off households of the community.[3] Thus, in preindustrial England most households contained only parents and children. Very few households held three generations, and virtually none were extended in the classic sense of the families of brothers and sisters living in the households of their fathers.

It is, of course, true that three-generational households can exist only where one generation lives long enough to see its grandchildren. During the sixteenth and seventeenth centuries, when life expectancy was low and the population stable in size, small household sizes and low proportions of three-generational houses can be explained largely by the birth- and death rates. People may have wanted three-generational families but lacked the three generations. After the population started growing, however, probably in the eighteenth century but perhaps earlier, extended families would have been possible. The household patterns at this time suggest that extended families were rejected on other grounds.[4]

Households in colonial America were generally larger than those of Europe. Average household size ranged from 5.4 people in New York in 1703 to 7.2 in Massachusetts in 1764.[5] In 1790, when the first U.S. Census was taken, the average household in this country had 5.8 people.[6] These household sizes can be accounted for by the high fertility of colonial American women. They are too small to be compatible with substantial numbers of extended households. The evidence suggests that most families in colonial America contained parents and children, sometimes supplemented by lodgers and boarders.[7]

Industrialization brought some changes, although they were not particularly dramatic. The average size of households fell through the entire period of industrialization, from 5.6 persons per household in 1850 to 5.0 in 1890 to 4.1 in 1930. In three towns in the Hudson River Valley in 1855, about 20 percent of the households included at least one relative in addition to the spouse and children of the household. The three towns differed in degree of industrialization. They did not, however, differ much in the proportions of households that included relatives.[8] In 1875 in Rhode Island, 18 percent of the families included live-in relatives.[9] Rhode Island at that point was largely urbanized and maybe not unrepresentative of the urban United States before the turn of the century. These data suggest that industrialism probably did not decrease the extent to which families took in relatives.[10]

During the nineteenth century, families may have taken in relatives when the arrangement provided economic benefits to both parties. Most urban workers at the time, and most farmers as well, received extremely low wages. Thus residential arrangements that enabled them to live or live better on their wages were quite popular. By 1970, only 7.5 percent of American families contained relatives other than parents and children.[11] What probably happened is that when economic pressures became less desperate, co-residence became less attractive.

When they can afford to, Americans seem to prefer to live on their own. Americans still, however, expand their families in response to the needs of young, old, lonely, and financially pressed family members. Several categories of people are likely to need economic and social support in the 1970s. Three are of special interest. Young people, both married and unmarried, are just getting started economically and often have trouble managing financially. Divorced and widowed people are often in social and emotional distress, as well as economic difficulty, and may need the support of a family. Old people too may find themselves socially isolated and economically strapped. The extent to which families take in these people is a good indication of their feelings of responsibility for their troubled members.

Unmarried People

A majority of young adults now seem to live with their parents until marriage. There is, however, a substantial minority that does not. In the nineteenth century, when men and women married relatively late, many young people in their twenties spent a period of time living with another family.[12] By 1970, the practice of living with another family had virtually disappeared among young adults, as it had among teen-agers. Most young men and women who move away from their families live in college dormitories or set up households of their own. Whether or not contemporary young people live with their parents depends on their student status, their marital status, their own income, and the incomes of their families. Table 3–1 shows the proportion of 18- to 24-year-olds who live with their parents or other relatives. Single people not enrolled in college are most likely to live at home. A large proportion of unmarried college stuents also live at home, as do many widowed, divorced, and separated young people.

Other data show that young adults are most likely to live at home when their own income is very low. Most young married couples who lived with their parents in 1970 had incomes under $2,000. Young unmarried people were most likely to head their own households when they made more than $8,000 per year. Families that have young adults living with them tend to have above average family incomes, probably because

TABLE 3–1

Percentages of 18- To 24-Year-Olds Living with Parents or Other Relatives

College Students, 1971	Percentage Living with Relatives
Male students (32% of males 18–24)	39
Married, with spouse (16% of students)	4
Not Married (84%)	45
Female students (21% of females 18–24)	37
Married, with spouse (12% of students)	7
Not Married (88%)	41

All 18- to 24-year-olds, 1970	Percentage Living with Relatives
Males	46
Married, living with spouse (28% of males 18–24)	7
Single (67%)	64
Separated, widowed, and divorced (5%)	37
Females	39
Married, living with spouse (43% of females 18–24)	5
Single (49%)	67
Separated, widowed, and divorced (8%)	53

SOURCES: CPR, P-20, No. 245, "Living Arrangements of College Students: October 1971"; CPR, P-20, No. 241, "Social and Economic Characteristics of Students: October 1971"; 1970 Census, *Persons by Family Characteristics*, Table 2.

the head of a family who has children over 18 is older and has more work experience than the average family head.[13] There are other reasons beside low income for young adults living with their parents, of course, but income is a major one.

The importance of income in determining living arrangements is also shown by a five-year study that compared young people who left low-income parental homes during the period of the study with those who did not. Those who moved were more likely to have increased their income in the year before they moved. They were also more likely to have improved their own well-being by moving; that is, their own income after moving was greater than their share of family income.[14] The differences were not large and explain rather little of the decision to move out. It is interesting, however, that the income of the parental family had no relationship to whether or not young people moved out. They left home if it was to their own financial advantage regardless of whether it helped or hurt the parental family. The altruism in these cases seems to have flowed from parents to children rather than vice versa.

Young Married People

One way for young married people to make ends meet during the years when their earnings are low is to live with their parents. Virtually no young married people do so, however. Table 3–1 shows the low proportions of 18- to 24-year-old married people who lived with parents or relatives in 1970. The arrangement was most common among female college students, and only 7 percent of that group lived with their parents. Young married men are most likely to live with their parents when their incomes are very low. Even then, however, most establish and head their own households. Seventy-five percent of 18- to 24-year-old men with incomes below $2,000 headed their own households in 1970. Among older married men, almost none live with their parents, even among the very poor.[15]

It is possible, of course, that young married people receive economic help from their parents. Surveys of consumer finances suggest that this happens to a considerable degree.[16] But parental help for married children does not usually include sharing bed and board. Perhaps the norm that married couples should have their own households is sufficiently strong to govern the behavior of both parents and married children. Married children may prefer to be hard up in their own homes rather than well-off with their parents. Parents in turn may be willing to provide the financial help to make such separation possible.

Widowed and Divorced People

Relatively large proportions of men and women who are divorced, separated, or widowed while their parents are still alive seem to spend some period of time living in their parents' home. Table 3–1 shows that almost half of the separated, widowed, or divorced 18- to 24-year-olds were living with parents or other relatives at the time of the 1970 census. These figures, which account only for young people actually living with parents when the census was taken, undoubtedly underestimate the total proportion who move in with their parents for some amount of time after the marital disruption and before remarriage. If people normally live with their parents for only a year or so before they established their own households, the actual proportion would be closer to three-quarters.[17]

Among older divorced, separated, or widowed people, the proportions living with parents and relatives are not so large, as Table 3–2 shows. The proportions of widowed, divorced, or separated people who live with parents or other relatives are highest among younger people and are considerably higher for men than for women. The age and sex differences result

TABLE 3–2

Percentages of Separated, Widowed, or Divorced People Living with Parents or Other Relatives, 1970

	Male	Female
Age 25–34:		
Separated	36	20
Widowed	22	14
Divorced	34	20
Age 35–44:		
Separated	24	12
Widowed	13	9
Divorced	24	12
Age 45–64:		
Separated	17	17
Widowed	11	13
Divorced	17	14

SOURCE: Calculated from 1970 Census, *Persons by Family Characteristics*, Table 2.
NOTES: Data for other marital statuses and comparisons with 1960 are given in Appendix, Table A–7.
Bernard, 1975, presents similar data for 1974. There appears to have been a decrease in the proportion of divorced and separated people living with family between 1970 and 1974.

from a combination of circumstances. Older men and women are less likely to have living parents or parents who can provide support. They must rely on other relatives. The majority of older women, for example, live with their children rather than with their parents.

The differences between men and women among 25- to 44-year-old separated or divorced people probably depend on child custody. Women usually have custody of the children after a disruption, and women with children are inclined to establish their own households whenever possible. Among 25- to 34-year-old divorced women, about 15 percent of those with children live with parents or relatives, compared with about 31 percent of those without children. Among 35- to 44-year-old divorced women, about 6 percent of those with children live with parents or relatives, compared with 25 percent of those without children.[18]

Men who have custody of children are also more likely to establish households of their own than men who are alone, although the numbers are too small and too inferential to draw firm conclusions. But if the differences are real for men as well as for women, then many people who move in with relatives must do so to avoid being alone. They are not looking particularly for help with child care or the other mechanics of life. Instead, they are looking for companionship and protection against loneliness.

No data are available on how long those people who do live with their parents stay. If they spend the entire time between divorce and remarriage in their parents' house, then the census figures give an estimate of the proportion who ever live at home as well as the proportion living there at a given time. If most people stay only part of that time, however, the proportions who go home for some period are much larger. For people over 25 the average time between divorce and remarriage is about five years.[19] If the average person who lives at home does so for only half that period, then the number counted at the time of the census is only half the number who have ever lived at home.

Most people who live with their parents probably do so for relatively short periods of time. Thus, the proportion of separated, divorced, or widowed people who are taken in by parents and relatives is probably much larger than it appears in census surveys. Perhaps as many as half of those who lose their spouses take advantage of their parents' hospitality.

Old People

The aged are a topic of increased concern in contemporary America. The reason is not hard to discover. An increasing proportion of the population is now over 65, and indeed over 75. The age of 65 commonly defines old age, since it is the age at which most firms and offices ask people to retire. Since the average man who has reached age 65 can expect to live another thirteen years and the average woman another seventeen years, however, it is questionable whether those over 65 should really be thought of as old.[20] A large proportion are healthy, vigorous, and active, perfectly capable of caring for themselves and rightfully insulted at being considered "social problems." [21] Some do have difficulty adjusting to a life without work, but most, especially when a life without work does not imply a life without money, do reasonably well.

In looking at the living arrangements of old people, it is well to keep in mind that only a fraction are likely to be in need of care by other people. Those over 75 are more likely to be physically disabled and are, therefore, of more concern. The widowed are probably more likely to feel socially isolated and alone. They are not necessarily in any difficulty, but are somewhat more likely to be. These two categories, therefore, the over-75 and the widowed, are most likely to need help.

Table 3–3 shows the proportions of men and women over 65 who live in families. Since a census "family" by definition contains two or more related persons, everyone who lives in a family is living with at least one relative. The proportion living in families is thus a reasonably good summary measure of the proportion living with relatives.[22]

TABLE 3–3
Percentages of Old People Living in Families, 1970

	Male	Female
Age 65–74: All marital statuses	82	64
Married	97	97
Widowed	30	35
Single	32	40
Age 75+: All marital statuses	71	51
Married	94	93
Widowed	37	40
Single	33	38

SOURCE: Calculated from 1970 Census, *Persons by Family Characteristics*, Table 1.
NOTES: "Married" combines categories of spouse absent, spouse present, and separated.
Data for other marital statuses and for 1960 are given in Appendix, Table A-8.

Table 3–3 shows that virtually all married older people live in families. Most of the couples live in households of their own. They may be near their children and see a good deal of them, but the actual living arrangements are separate. A substantial minority of single and widowed people do, however, live with family. Most of the widowed people live with their children, while most of the single people live with brothers and sisters. Most of those who do not live with family live in households by themselves. Even among over-75 widowed women, relatively small numbers live with roommates or in rooming houses.[23] Women are somewhat more likely than men to live with family. Between ages 65 and 75 single people are more likely to live with family, while over-75 widowed people are slightly more likely to do so. Widowed parents are probably more likely to move in with their children when they are older and less able to take care of themselves. Single people, however, may have shared living arrangements with their brothers and sisters for a substantial portion of their adult lives. As they become older, some of the brothers and sisters may die, leaving the others on their own.

Table 3–4 shows the proportions of people over 65 who live in homes for the aged, hospitals, and other institutions. The increase in the proportion of old people living in these homes has caused concern in recent years. Old people in homes can be lonely, cut off from the world, and poorly cared for. Homes for the aged are sometimes seen as a device by which children abrogate responsibility for their aging parents and leave them to the tender mercies of the institution.

TABLE 3–4

Percentages of Old People Living in Homes for the Aged
or Other Institutions, 1970

	Male	Female
Age 65–74: All marital statuses	2	2
Married	1	1
Widowed	5	3
Single	11	6
Age 75+: All marital statuses	7	11
Married	3	4
Widowed	12	12
Single	17	17

SOURCE: Calculated from 1970 Census, *Persons by Family Characteristics*, Table 1.
NOTES: "Married" combines the categories of spouse absent, spouse present, and separated.
See also Appendix, Table A-9.

A comparison of Tables 3–3 and 3–4, however, shows that a much larger proportion of old people live with family than in homes. Almost no married couples live in homes for the aged, with the exception of a very small proportion of those over 75. Only 2 percent of all those aged 65–74 live in institutions. Single males are most likely to live in homes for the aged when they are 65–74, and even among that group, three times as many live with family as live in institutions. A large proportion of those over 75 live in homes for the aged, which is consistent with their generally greater debility. Single people are most likely to be in institutions, perhaps because they are less likely to have relatives who can take them in or visit and help them in households of their own. Three times as many widowed people live with family as in institutions. Some of those who are in institutions may have had no children and thus be in the same boat as single people. Others may be seriously ill and in need of a great deal of medical attention. Considering all these possibilities, the proportions of old people put in nursing homes by children who could care for them but will not must be relatively small.

These facts suggest that people do feel responsible for aging family members and very often take them into their homes. Unfortunately, almost nothing is known about the living situations of old people who live alone—the majority of single, widowed, and divorced people over 65. Some undoubtedly live near children or other relatives who visit and watch out for them. Others undoubtedly do not.

Changes Over Time

Even though the proportions of old people living with family are quite high, they may be lower than in the past. The argument is made that families feel less responsibility than they did for aging members, that they are less likely to provide them bed and board and more likely to leave them on their own or place them in homes. Unfortunately, data are not available to evaluate this argument with any degree of certainty. Detailed data on living arrangements by marital status, age, and sex are available only from the censuses of 1960 and 1970. Only changes that occurred during that decade can be documented precisely.

Between 1960 and 1970 the proportions of people who shared bed and board with their families dropped slightly in all categories. Fewer unmarried young people lived with parents; fewer divorced, separated, and widowed people moved in with parents and relatives. Larger proportions of people in these categories lived alone, as did a larger proportion of people over 65. For all categories of people, changes over the decade were small. They were, however, consistent and suggest a real change over the decade in how people lived.[24]

Gross data on family relationships, which are available from 1940 to 1970, suggest that a trend toward independent households has been apparent at least since 1940.[25] Among young adults, aged 20–24, the proportion living with parents and relatives declined between 1940 and 1970 —from 47.7 percent in 1940 to 28.4 percent in 1970 among young women.

An increase in the proportion of women living with husbands accounted for half the decline. The rest was accounted for by an increase in those living alone or in college dormitories.[26]

Among women aged 25–34, the proportion living with parents or relatives also went down—from 20.8 percent in 1940 to 8.3 percent in 1970 —and the proportions living either as heads of families or alone more than doubled.[27] Similar, but less dramatic, trends occurred among women aged 35–64. The proportion of 35- to 64-year-old women living with parents or relatives went from 10.5 percent in 1940 to 5.6 percent in 1970, while the proportion living alone went from 14.5 to 18.1 percent.[28] These data, unlike the data for 1960 and 1970, are not broken down by marital status. The changes in the living arrangements of 25- to 64-year-old women probably resulted, however, from the increased tendency of women whose marriages had been disrupted to establish their own households rather than to live with others.

Among people over 65 of all marital statuses, the proportion living as parents of household heads dropped for men from 10.4 percent in 1940 to 4.2 percent in 1970, and for women from 22.2 percent to 11.9 percent. Among single, separated, divorced, and widowed women over 65, the proportion living as the "parent" or "other relative" of the head fell from 41 percent in 1940 to 24 percent in 1970; the proportion of women over 75 in the same category fell from 48 percent to 28 percent.[29]

With little data available on living arrangements before 1940, it is hard to say whether the changes between 1940 and 1970 are part of a general trend. In mid-nineteenth-century rural England, 47 percent of widowed and separated old people lived with their children and in mid-nineteenth-century Hamilton, Ontario, 44 percent of the widows over 60 lived with relatives. A study of living arrangements in Buffalo, New York, in 1855 found that about 50 percent of widows over 60 lived with their children; the proportions were about the same for native American, Irish, or German women.[30] These proportions are not very different from those found in the United States in 1940.

Taking in relatives has, however, declined somewhat over the last three decades. What this means depends on one's explanation of why it is happening. One plausible interpretation starts with the assumption that people prefer to live in their own households when they can afford to and when they are relatively healthy and active. From this assumption, the increasing proportion of old people living on their own might reflect better health and better economic conditions. An alternative assumption is that people dislike living alone and find life alone depressing and lonely. They live alone because they have no children or relatives willing to take them in. If this assumption is correct, the increased proportion of old people living on their own might result from the increasing wickedness of American children or from decreasing family sizes.

It is hard to know whether wickedness is increasing or decreasing. But it is true that people who were over 65 in 1970 were members of the generation born around the turn of the century that had low marriage rates and high rates of childlessness. Since about 10 percent never married, and since 15–20 percent of those who did marry had no children, almost a quarter of the old people of the 1970s have no children—wicked or not —to take them in. During the next decade or so, even fewer old people will be able to live with children since even more of them will have had none. Only around 1990 will that situation change.[31] But even then, those old people who had only a few children may have difficulty finding one who is able and willing to take them in.

In summary, although few extended families have ever existed in America, families have always expanded to take in needy members. Fewer old people and people in disrupted marital situations now live with their families than did thirty years ago. Whether this indicates less need, more wickedness, or more care arrangements not involving bed and board depends on the larger social context.

Do changes in living arrangements reflect changes in the amount of social contact people have and the amount of care they receive from others? Are people who live alone suffering from loneliness and depression? Do smaller households cut their members off from adult companionship and adult responsibilities? The answer to these questions is not necessarily yes. Changes in living arrangements can occur within a context of considerable companionship and shared responsibility. Where people live, how often they move, how much free time they have, and how much inclination they have to visit must all affect their social relationships. Neighborhoods, communities, and kin networks are probably more important to the lives of healthy people than living arrangements. Unfortunately, not much is known about them. The following chapter will attempt to summarize what is known.

Chapter Four

THE EXPANDED FAMILY: KITH AND KIN

NUCLEAR FAMILIES need not expand their households to establish ties with the larger society. They can also maintain close relationships with relatives and friends outside the household. Family members can visit, exchange services, and belong to organizations with people who are not in their own nuclear family.

These outside relationships are important complements to family ties, since no family can provide for all the social and emotional needs of its members.[1] Friends and neighbors can enrich family life and can also provide a safety valve for families. By supplying companionship and shared activity, they can avert the dangers of one marital partner's relying completely on the other. They can also help people get over the traumas of marital difficulty or marital breakup.

Even when their families are intact, women and children probably need groups of friends, neighbors, or relatives for protection against the confining and isolating aspects of the nuclear family. (Men in most societies belong to work groups as well as families. Men are neither as isolated nor as vulnerable as women and children.) In some traditional societies, groups of women work together and develop strong supportive bonds; women's work groups are important, for example, in most hunting-gathering societies and in many primitive agricultural societies.[2] Women's groups do seem to accentuate the separation of men's and women's worlds and in that sense may reinforce sexual inequalities. But they also strengthen the power of women in their own spheres and may afford them a stronger bargaining position when they deal with men.

Children's groups may operate in similar ways. In many societies and subcultures, even very young children spend most of their time with other children rather than with adults.[3] Spending time with other children gives children some freedom of action that they lack when under the close supervision of adults. Being able to say that "everyone else is doing_____" also gives children some leverage with their parents.

But children may need more of an independent base than that provided by their peers. Other adults may be better able to protect children than children's groups per se. Children who have extensive contacts with adult neighbors, friends, relatives, and teachers are to some extent in the public eye. Parental abuse or neglect can be noticed, and even if the parents are not brought to the attention of the law, they may feel the deterrent effect of public opinion.

Yet another potential function of family and neighborhood groups is in furthering political and economic activity. Groups of friends and neighbors have the potential for organizing political and economic interests and for united action vis-à-vis local government. Confederations of neighborhood groups can wield enough power to affect decisions made by larger units of government.[4]

Much criticism of modern life focuses on its isolation and lack of community. Urbanization and mobility are often cited as the main causes of community decline.[5] But there may not have been an actual decline in the social relationships and community feelings of most citizens. Specific studies of social contacts, organizational memberships, and community participation are available only for the last few years and are spotty even for that period. A historical perspective must, therefore, rely on inferences drawn from other sorts of information.

Four sorts of data provide insight into the probability of social activity. The first is the size of kin networks. If a woman has four sisters, one of them is more likely to live close by than if she has only one sister. If a child has twelve aunts and uncles, he has a better chance to encounter a more varied array of adult occupations and personalities than if he has four. Larger kin networks seem at least to increase the probability that relatives see, like, and help each other.

A second consideration that might affect the quality of social life is the size of neighborhoods and workplaces. Relatives are not the only source of friends; neighbors and work colleagues may be fully as important. The latter are probably more likely to become friends when neighborhoods and workplaces are neither too small nor too large. Of course, the exact size of "too large" is a complicated determination. The characteristics of the participants must be taken into account, as well as the size of the unit and the potential for small subunits within seemingly enormous cities or firms. Data on size can, however, give some sense of what is possible. A third source of information on potential social activity is the location of work in relation to home. When living and working places are nearby, community life is more apt to exist.

A final influence on the potential for social life is geographical and job mobility. Since social life takes time to develop, transiency may be a serious barrier to social life and community feelings. People who move in and out of neighborhoods may make fewer close friends and participate less in community activities than people who stay put. Similarly, men and women who move from job to job have fewer opportunities to establish and build social ties.

Despite common perceptions, data on scale and mobility suggest that opportunities for sociability and community may be as prevalent today as they were in the past. The first part of this chapter will look at these historical trends; the second part will examine contemporary data on social activity and participation.

Family Size

Family size, which affects so many aspects of family life, also affects the size of the kin network. The relationship is easy to see. The great-grandparents of today, born around 1880, had on the average six brothers and sisters. People born around 1910 might easily have had twenty aunts and uncles (some unmarried) and forty cousins, as well as five brothers and sisters, two parents, and four grandparents. In contrast, a child born in the 1970s is likely to have two brothers and sisters, eight to twelve aunts and uncles, and perhaps sixteen cousins. The decline in average family size has meant a dramatic decline in the number of close kin.

Whether this decline in numbers has actually affected the quality and quantity of relationships among relatives is not known. It is possible that people are close to only one or two brothers and sisters however many siblings they have and that having only two brothers and sisters is enough to generate close relationships. The same may be true of aunts, uncles, and cousins. If people maintain only a few close ties, then a relatively small number of relatives is sufficient.

Studies of contacts with relatives have not, as far as I know, investigated whether the number of relatives that people have affects the amount of their contact with them. The studies have found—as one would expect

—that contact between relatives is greater when they live in the same town or within a very short distance. Ties seem to be stronger between relatives, especially siblings, of the same sex and between relatives who have similar occupations and social status.[6]

If these circumstances generally determine relationships, family size is important mainly as it influences the probability of relatives being geographically, socially, and emotionally close to each other. If a person has two siblings, there is a high probability (75 percent) that at least one of them will be of the same sex. The probability that they will spend their lives in the same state is lower, perhaps 30–40 percent.[7] Adding the requirement that the siblings be socially and emotionally congenial reduces the probabilities for strong ties even more. Therefore most people from small families are unlikely to have a same-sex sibling available for a close relationship. In larger families, congenial siblings would be more likely to live within visiting distance and thus more likely to maintain close ties.

The same calculations could be made for aunts, uncles, and cousins. Most Americans, however, consider their brothers and sisters their most important relatives after their parents. The most important change brought about by smaller families, then, is probably the decreased probability that a person will be close to a brother or sister.

Community Size

One of the most striking changes in American life over the last century has been the increased size of communities where people live, a result of population growth and urbanization. Increased urbanization is the villain of many pieces on community and social life. In fact, however, the changes and their effects are not clear.

Friendship and neighborliness must depend on the density, size, and homogeneity of neighborhoods. Friendships should occur more often where the population is dense enough to increase the probability of families finding others who share their interests and live close by. Thus, communities that are too isolated or too small are not so conducive to friendship and social activity. On the other hand, dense urban areas seem, in many cases, to breed fear, alienation, isolation, and loneliness. Community size is, in fact, one of the best predictors of whether people say they are satisfied with their community.[8]

Unfortunately, little can be gleaned from the data on metropolitan residence and city size about the proportion of the population that lives in isolation from friends and neighbors, and whether it is increasing. Neighborhood boundaries seldom coincide with political boundaries. Many large cities contain within them small, close neighborhoods, where people find friends and a sense of belonging. Suburbs also vary considerably in the extent to which they are real neighborhoods, bound together by ties of friendship and shared interests. And rural areas vary in the distance between farm houses and in the difficulty of covering those distances.

Census figures do allow some comparisons between the sorts of communities in which Americans now live and those of a century or so ago. Perhaps the biggest change is in the proportion of Americans who live on farms. In 1880 probably 40 or 50 percent of all Americans lived on farms. In 1930, 25 percent of the population lived on farms, and by 1970, the proportion had fallen below 5 percent.[9] Since most American farming families actually live on their farms rather than in rural villages, the move off the farm must have lessened the isolation of families and brought them into closer contact with potential friends and neighbors.

This would not necessarily happen, of course, if people moved from the farms into the large cities. But that was not the case. Moving was most common among sons of farmers, who left the farms when they were ready to establish their own households. Most of these young men either stayed in rural areas or moved to small cities of less than 50,000 people.[10] The larger cities were, of course, growing. Between 1880 and 1910 the proportion of the population who lived in cities of more than 100,000 people nearly doubled. After this turn-of-the-century growth spurt, however, the trend leveled off. In 1940, 28.9 percent of the population lived in cities of over 100,000 and in 1970, 27.8 percent.[11]

In 1970 two-thirds of the population of the United States lived neither on isolated farms nor in large central cities. Table 4–1 shows the distribution. The majority of Americans lived in metropolitan areas, most of these in towns or small cities near a central city, rather than in the city itself. Nearly a third of the population, however, lived outside metropolitan areas, in small self-contained cities, towns, and villages. Between 1970 and 1974, more people moved out of metropolitan areas than moved in, and thus the proportion living in small towns and villages increased.[12] The growth of small cities, towns, and villages, like the decline of the farm population, has been a persistent trend of the last century.

In 1880, 57 percent of the population lived either on farms or in large cities; in 1970, 32 percent. The proportion of the population that

TABLE 4–1
Distribution of Population, 1970
(Percentages)

On farms	4.1
In villages and rural areas, outside metropoliton areas, population less than 2,500	14.3
In towns, outside metropolitan areas, population 2,500–10,000	5.5
In small cities, outside metropolitan areas, population over 10,000	7.1
In small suburbs and small towns within metropolitan areas, population less than 25,000	26.9
In large suburbs and small cities within metropolitan areas, population 25,000–100,000	13.9
In core cities of metropolitan areas, population greater than 100,000	27.8

SOURCES: Percentages calculated from 1970 Census, *Number of Inhabitants*, Table 5; farm population, from 1970 Census, *Detailed Characteristics*, Table 189. Categories are defined to be as similar as census categories allow to those used by Verba and Nie, 1972, in their study of political participation.

lives in what are most often considered socially isolating environments has, therefore, dropped considerably. It is not necessarily true, of course, that small cities, towns, and villages are social and neighborly; nor is it true that all farm areas and big cities are lonely. Nonetheless, those characterizations are probably more true than not, and the changes that have taken place in the distribution of population seem more likely to have enhanced social networks than to have destroyed them.

The shift is not so favorable for community political participation. As part of their 1967 study of political participation in America, Verba and Nie looked at political activity in different kinds of places. They found that "communal activity," people working together with others on local problems and organizing groups to deal with local issues, was more common in isolated villages, towns, and cities outside metropolitan areas. Community activity was less common in suburbs, especially large suburbs, and in central cities. Local participation of all sorts—voting in local elections and initiating contacts with local officials, as well as community work —was also higher outside metropolitan areas than in. The suburbs scored worst of all on this scale, with central cities generating more respectable amounts of political participation.[13] If these patterns have been true over the century, the concentration of the population in suburbs has probably been accompanied by a decline in political activity. Verba and Nie did not, however, look separately at farmers since there are now so few of them. If the political participation of farmers is typically less than that of people in rural villages, which seems likely, then the movement of population off farms would increase political activity and counter the suburban pattern.

Workplace Size

Just as community size may affect relationships among neighbors, so the size of workplaces may affect relationships among workmates. The modern work environment is often described as incompatible with friendly social activity, because of the size and regimentation of the places where people work. As with community size, however, the issue is complex. Workplaces can certainly be too small to permit social activity. A man or woman who works alone, for example, has no opportunity for social inter-action; a man or woman who works with only two or three other people has less chance of finding a friend at work than if more people were around. On the other hand, like cities, workplaces can be so big that they hinder social interaction. Factories or offices with more than a hundred or so employees are probably too large for everyone to know each other. If they are organized so that workers are isolated either physically or through intense competition, smaller subgroups of friends or companions may not form.

The biggest change in the work force over the century has been the decline in the proportion of agricultural workers. Since a large proportion of American farmers work (or at least used to work) their farms alone or with only family help, this decline implies that fewer contemporary work-ers are isolated from other workers than in the past. The proportion of women who work solely at housework has also declined. Housework, like farming, is usually done alone, so the movement from housework into paid jobs represents another substantial decline in the proportion of adult workers who are cut off from social activity with other adults during the working day.

Manufacturing industries are more likely than others to be "too large" for social activity, and it is these industries that most often come to mind as alienating. By 1880, industrialization was well developed in America, with manufacturing employing 22.1 percent of the paid work force. The proportion employed in manufacturing is surprisingly similar in contemporary America—26 percent in 1967.[14] The 1880 census and the 1972 Census of Manufacturers report data on the number of employees per manufacturing establishment that, although not precisely comparable, give an idea of the changes that have taken place in workplace size.

The average size of a manufacturing establishment has more than quintupled since 1880, from eleven to fifty-nine employees. Average firm size has increased for all the major industries. No industries in 1880 even approached the 1972 average size of iron and steel plants, automobile plants, and aircraft factories, which employed over a thousand people each. But even in 1972, the average plant employed only about sixty people, a number that is probably small enough for most workers to know each other. In many manufacturing industries, in sawmills and machine shops, for example, the average plant is much smaller.[15]

For the economy as a whole, workplaces are smaller, on the average, than those in manufacturing. Table 4–2 shows the proportion of workers in private firms of various sizes in 1972, based on social security data reported by employers. The proportions have not changed dramatically since 1956, when comparable figures were first published, although the proportion employed in agriculture has gone down and that employed by government has gone up.[16]

TABLE 4–2

Percentage Distribution of Workers by Type of Work and Size of Firm, 1972

Employed in agriculture	4.3	
Self-employed	6.5	
Employed in non-agricultural, private firms	72.9	
Size of firm:		
1–3 employees		3.7
4–7 employees		4.8
8–19 employees		9.0
20–49 employees		10.7
50–99 employees		7.7
100–499 employees		17.0
500+ employees		18.2
not known		1.9
Government employees	16.3	

SOURCES: Figures on self-employment from Ray, 1975; on labor force, employment in agriculture, and employment in government, from *Monthly Labor Review*, January 1975; on firm size, from *County Business Patterns, 1972*, Table 1c.

When a representative national sample of workers was asked in 1972, "About how many people work for your employer at the location where you work?" 25.9 percent answered 1 to 9 people and 24.1 percent answered 10 to 49 people. Only 14.2 percent reported that their workplaces employed 1,000 or more people. When this same sample of workers was asked to give the number of people "you see every day and with whom you have to work closely in order to do your job," 18.4 percent said they had no identifiable work group. Only 12.3 percent said their work group included twenty or more people.[17] It appears, then, that about a fifth of all American workers are essentially alone on the job and that another fifth work in places that employ 500 or more workers. But most Americans seem to work in groups of from two to twenty people.

A century ago fewer workers were in large factories, but more were isolated on farms. Factories and offices, even large ones, at least allow the possibility of forming friendships and social groups, whether or not they actually develop. Farming seems much less likely to do so.

Location of Home and Work

One of the most characteristic and most criticized features of contemporary American life is the separation of home and work. Within metropolitan areas, large numbers of people live in one place and work in another. For such people, there may be little overlap between home life and work life. Work friends may live in other parts of the city and may, therefore, be less often available for social activity. Moreover, the separation of home and work may detract from the sense of belonging to a community and may explain the relatively low levels of political participation in the suburbs.

Data on the location of home and work are not available over time and are scanty even for recent years. It seems safe to assume, however, that a century ago almost everyone lived close to where they worked. Many, most notably the farmers, lived and worked in the same place. Most people probably lived within walking distance of work, and a vast majority must have lived in the same town or city where they worked. In contrast, only 16 percent of the workers interviewed in a 1972 survey reported that they lived less than two miles from their work.[18]

More detailed data are available on living and working patterns in specific metropolitan areas in 1970. One analysis of the 1970 data for ninety-eight metropolitan areas found that 35.1 percent of all the workers both lived and worked in the central city, while 26.3 percent both lived and worked in the suburban ring. Commuters made up 23 percent: 15.3 percent lived in the suburbs and worked in the central city, while 7.7 percent commuted from the central city to the suburban ring. The proportions of both kinds of commuters were up somewhat from 1960.[19]

Not all of those who live and work in the suburban ring live and work in the same town, so 61 percent is probably an overestimate of the proportion living and working in the same town. On the other hand, large proportions of those who both live and work outside of metropolitan areas must do so in the same town. The data are not good enough to draw firm conclusions, but I would estimate that at least half of all American workers live and work in the same town or city, a tenth commute into central cities, and the remainder live in one town and work in another.[20] These figures do not suggest a complete separation of work and home life. But still, few Americans live and work in the same neighborhood; few can walk to work.

Geographical Mobility

As indicated earlier, the best predictor of community satisfaction among Americans was community size, with people in larger cities distinctly less satisfied. Length of residence in the area was considerably less important.[21] Nevertheless, the mythology of modern times includes the belief that contemporary life is characterized by widespread geographical mobility, and that this has resulted in the decline of family, neighborhood, and community bonds.

Recent historical studies cast doubt on the notion that modern America is peculiarly transient. A number of historians have recently published studies of geographical mobility in nineteenth-century cities. Michael Katz' study of Hamilton, Ontario is a good example.[22]

Katz first reports on the experience of one Hamilton man who left a diary of his everyday life. William Benson noted sixteen different residences in his 54 years, eight in Scotland and Ireland and eight in Canada. Benson was apparently not atypical. Katz calculated "persistence rates" for Hamilton and he found that only about 32 percent of the 1851 population of Hamilton were still there in 1861. This rate of mobility, high as it is, is an underestimate, since people who moved in after 1851 and out before 1861 were not recorded at all.

Steven Thernstrom found high—although not quite so high—transiency rates in Boston. Between 1840 and 1850, and between 1850 and 1860, only 39 percent of Boston residents stayed in the community for the entire decade. Geographical mobility in Boston was higher during the nineteenth century than the twentieth. Between 1958 and 1968, for example, 46 percent of the population stayed put for ten years.

Other nineteenth-century urban communities also show a good deal of transiency. For example, only 32 percent of the population of Philadelphia remained in the city from 1850 to 1860; 44 percent of the 1880 population of Omaha were still there in 1890. Interestingly, persistence rates in rural areas were strikingly similar. Thernstrom gives persistence rates for twenty-one rural areas for time periods between 1800 and 1905. The rates range from 21 percent in Grant County, Wisconsin, 1885–95, to 59 percent in East Central Kansas, 1870–80.[23]

The nineteenth century in America was clearly a time of tremendous mobility. However, the majority of moves were short-distance, and the majority of movers were young people. The 1960s and 1970s may not be all that different. About 20 percent of the population of the United States moves every year. But the figure is misleading. Only 4 percent move to another state. Moreover, the movers tend to be young people. Thirty-nine percent of men 20- to 24-years-old move every year, which means that most members of that age group would move at least once in four years and over half would move twice. In contrast, 60.7 percent of the population aged 35–44 in 1974 were living in the same house in which they had lived in 1970. Most of those who did move stayed in the same metropolitan area, but the census does not indicate whether or not they remained in the same neighborhood.[24]

A five-year longitudinal study of about 5,000 American families found that 35 percent of the sample families moved during a five-year period.[25] Newly formed families and families that experienced divorce or death moved much more than stable families. Movers were disproportionately young, and disproportionately families who rented rather than owned their homes.

About half of the American people seem to live in the same state all their lives. In 1970, 55 percent of those 55- to 64-years-old and 48 percent of those over 65 were living in the state in which they were born. The proportions living in the state of their birth rose between 1960 and 1970 for the age groups over 45 and fell for the age groups under 45.[26]

Since data on lifetime mobility are not published for earlier census years, it is impossible to know whether there has been a change over time in this particular measure. The historical studies suggest that twentieth-century Americans are about as mobile as nineteenth-century Americans. If mobility is destroying community and social life in America, it has been doing so for a long time.

Job Mobility

Changing jobs must have the same sort of effect on work-based social relationships that changing neighborhoods has on community relationships. Unfortunately, data on job changes have not been collected as systematically and conscientiously as data on residential mobility, and changes over time cannot be documented. Michael Katz looked at some indicators of occupational change in Hamilton, Ontario, in the mid nineteenth century. The diary of William Benson, covering the period between 1821 and 1874, records a remarkable thirty job changes, among such diverse occupations as porridge maker, weaver, apprentice-baker, cook on a boat, farmer, and storekeeper.

Twentieth-century Americans certainly change jobs less often than William Benson. One national study gathered information on about 2,500 male heads of household. About a third of the household heads reported that they had worked for the same employer for at least fourteen years; another third changed jobs at least once during the four years of the study, about half of those voluntarily and half involuntarily. The remaining third did not change jobs during the study but had changed jobs sometime during the ten-year period between 1958 and 1967. Those who changed jobs during the study were disproportionately young, nonwhite, and poorly paid. Another study looked only at older men: about 5,000 men who were between 45 and 59 in 1966. Between 1966 and 1969, one fifth of these older men changed employers, a lower proportion than that found among younger men over a similar time period.[27]

The rate of job change is lower than the rate of residential change for age groups over 35. About 45 percent of 35- to 44-year-old men move during a four-year period, and about 30 percent change jobs. About 35 percent of 45- to 54-year-olds move, and about 20 percent change jobs. About 30 percent of 55- to 64-year-olds move during a four-year period, and about 15 percent change jobs. Young people are more mobile in both respects, although their residential mobility is much greater than their job mobility.

Friends, Neighbors, and Kin

Changes in family, community, and workplace size and in residential and job mobility do not clearly indicate what changes, if any, have actually occurred in relationships among friends and neighbors. According to the surveys, however, contemporary Americans are by no means isolated from friends and relatives. In a 1974 national survey, 57 percent of the respondents said they spend a social evening with relatives at least several times a month. About the same number see friends and neighbors at least once a month. A third of the respondents spend time with relatives, neighbors, or friends at least once or twice a week.[28]

Comparison of the 1974 survey with similar surveys in 1959 and 1971 suggest that rates of social participation have not changed much in fifteen years. This is hardly a long-term trend but may indicate that the various pressures for and against social activity balance each other out. The last fifteen years have seen a dramatic increase in the proportion of women who work outside the home. Since it is usually women who maintain ties with relatives and neighbors, working outside the home might be expected to divert their energy from kin and neighborhood ties and thus decrease their families' social activity. That social participation has not changed over fifteen years suggests that this does not happen. Social occasions with friends and relatives may have to be more carefully planned when both adults in a family are working. But changed work patterns do not seem to have cut families off from social activity.

Organizational Membership

Organizations provide a formal structure for social activity that can supplement the informal network of visiting and shared activity with friends and neighbors. A large proportion of Americans do belong to organizations. The most popular are church groups, followed by labor unions and school service groups like the PTA. Fraternal groups like the Masons and Elks, sports teams, and professional societies also have large memberships.[29]

Organizations are probably important to people as a source of friends and as a vehicle for social activity. They are also important, however, in the opportunities they offer for political and economic cooperation. A wide variety of intermediate organizations have developed in response to the need for cooperation in the political or economic sphere—labor unions, producer and consumer cooperatives, community action groups.

Surveys done over the last fifteen years show no startling trends in organizational membership. Labor-union membership has gone down, as has membership in farm organizations—trends that coincide with changes in the distribution of occupations.[30] Membership in school-service groups has gone up but will probably now decline as a smaller proportion of the population has school-age children. The churches report relatively stable membership, about 60 percent of the population.[31] Women's organizations also report enrolling a relatively stable proportion of the female population.[32]

Membership in credit unions, electric power cooperatives, and rural telephone cooperatives rose between 1965 and 1972.[33] The proportion of farmers who belong to farmer cooperatives, both marketing and farm supply, also rose between 1950 and 1970.[34] Consumer coops, from cooperatively owned supermarkets to food-buying clubs, receive increasing media attention, which may or may not reflect higher membership. Whatever the trends, though, most contemporary Americans do not belong to organizations that exercise cooperative economic power. Even labor unions, the most important, enroll only a minority of workers, most of whom are not active.[35]

Political groups also enroll only a small proportion of Americans. Verba and Nie [36] report that 8 percent of their survey respondents listed themselves as members of "political groups, such as Democratic or Republican clubs, and political action groups, such as voters' leagues." The League of Women Voters, which may or may not be typical of political clubs, reports a steady increase in membership from 1940 on, greater than would be expected from population growth alone.[37] In Detroit area studies, approximately the same proportion of respondents (2–3 percent) reported themselves as members of political clubs in 1959 and 1971.[38] Thus, the only clear statement to make about membership in political organizations is that it is low.

Membership in political organizations may not, however, be a particularly good indicator of participation in cooperative political activity. Forty-seven percent of the respondents in the Verba and Nie study reported that they regularly vote in local elections. This is not a difficult political activity, to be sure, but it at least suggests some personal involvement in a local community. Thirty-two percent of the respondents said they were active in at least one organization involved in community problems, and 30 percent reported working with others in trying to solve some community problems.[39]

Sects, Class, and Intentional "Families"

A few groups exist that are quite different from either the informal social groupings of daily life or traditional voluntary organizations. They involve strong emotional ties between members, usually based on family or religious or ethnic characteristics, and command strong loyalties. Such groups were common in traditional societies. The clan and tribal secret societies compelled loyalty and provided a secure sense of identity.[40] Today, such organizations are relatively rare. People still define themselves as members of church, clan, racial, and ethnic groups, which sometimes inspire strong feelings of loyalty and commitment. Most of these groups, however, are too large for members to know each other personally and too diverse for members to feel toward each other the emotional ties of brotherhood and sisterhood. Only a few real brotherhoods and sisterhoods exist: Amish, Hutterite, and other small sect communities; small fundamentalist churches in isolated homogeneous towns; small beseiged ethnic neighborhoods in large cities, where clan and ethnic ties may be precipitated by a need for united opposition to the outside world; consciousness-raising groups, which combine ideological loyalty to the feminist movement with more particular loyalty to sisters in the group; blood sisters and brothers in large, close families; a few isolated utopian communities; army buddies in the trenches.

Brotherhoods and sisterhoods depend on real or ideological kinship, which is lacking in most contemporary lives. Brotherhoods and sisterhoods cannot readily be created on a permanent basis, as the experiences of utopian communities show. Even for those who "belong" the groups have costs as well as benefits. The most important costs are in limited opportunities. Brothers and sisters leave their communities to acquire new knowledge, to learn a trade, to see the world, to make a future. The narrowness and isolation of brotherhoods and sisterhoods is both their strength and their weakness. The contradiction is probably not solvable. To the extent that the groups open themselves to the outside world to provide broader opportunities for their members, they lose their sense of identity and purpose. History suggests that most of them eventually dissolve as communities.[41]

For most Americans, brotherhoods and sisterhoods run counter to cherished American notions of individual freedom and opportunity. Brotherhoods and sisterhoods exclude as well as include, often on the basis of characteristics that the polity has defined as irrelevant: race, national origin, religion, family. They create a "them" as well as an "us" and deny to outsiders that equality of respect that Americans believe is everyone's due. Brotherhoods and sisterhoods place loyalty to the group not only above the welfare of the individual but also above adherence to the laws of the larger polity. They are probably doomed to extinction.

Social Activity and Society

Descriptions of scale and mobility and even data on social contacts and organizational membership are far from satisfactory for evaluating the real feel of social life in contemporary America. At best, they give a sense of the potential for social activity: whether families, workplaces, and neighborhoods are large enough to provide a choice of friends; whether people stay put long enough to become part of a neighborhood; whether formal organizations and expectations of informal visiting exist. They do suggest that social activity is still possible—a conclusion that contradicts some writings on transiency. But statistics and surveys say almost nothing about whether Americans feel close to a family or group of friends that they can depend on to be available, friendly, and helpful. They say nothing about how much people care about each other and about the places where they live and work compared to Americans a century ago. Nor do they say whether or not contemporary people may need each other even more in these times of smaller families and an increasingly bureaucratic economy and polity.

Most community studies, which provide a fuller sense of the texture of people's lives, reveal a surprising amount of visiting, social exchange, and neighborliness even in conditions that would seem to preclude it. Gans' study of Levittown, for example, noted a good deal of shared activity. Stack's study of poor blacks in an urban housing project, a completely different setting, also documented an enormous, sometimes overbearing, amount of visiting, sharing and exchange.[42] Barbara Garson noted that companionship and cooperative activities to make jobs more pleasant occurred in a variety of workplaces. Studs Terkel's interviews with workers also describe camaraderie and cooperation.[43] All these reports suggest that Americans are amazingly resourceful in finding friends and buddies in spite of architectural or bureaucratic obstacles.

But these studies, impressive as they may be, do not change the fact that rather little is known about an extremely important aspect of American life. Changed patterns of family and work life may well have changed people's perceptions and feelings about their families and neighborhoods in ways that survey data and even community studies have not documented.

The general agitation about the decline of the family and the demise of community seems to assume that these two institutions once provided protection against the twin dangers of individual vulnerability and political alienation. That the family and the community, from all the historical evidence, never fulfilled these roles—for families have always been small and nuclear, and communities in America always transient—does not mitigate the need for concern. Friendship may well be the key, and friendship is something about which almost nothing is known.

PART
II

Commitments in
Conflict

Chapter Five

DILEMMAS OF FAMILY POLICY

THE MYTH of the decaying American family is often publicly used to bolster arguments for legislative action. The 1973 and 1974 hearings of the Senate Subcommittee on Children and Youth provide good examples. Not all of the witnesses before the subcommittee based their testimony on the troubles of the contemporary family in comparison with families of earlier days, but some did. A child psychologist with considerable experience in government said, for example:

> I agree with many others who feel that a variety of historical, economic and social factors as well as current pressures make family life in America more difficult today than it once was.
>
> I refer here to the decline of the extended family, to the extremely important phenomenon of the ever-increasing numbers of working mothers, to the increased mobility which has come to characterize the American people, to those types of urbanization and suburbanization that tend to isolate American families one from another. . . .
>
> All of these phenomena have taken away supports that families once relied on.[1]

Other witnesses—and the chairman—also pointed to the "decline of the extended family" as a problem of contemporary families. Many noted rising divorce rates and increasing proportions of working mothers as signs of increased disruption in the lives of children.

Pointing to a new problem before proposing a new policy is probably good politics. Americans have gotten along without a "family policy" for two centuries; the argument for adopting one now is that the family is suddenly in desperate straits. But what if the facts indicate that the "problem" is not new at all? The data presented in Part I show that many of the arguments made by advocates of new family policies are based on incomplete or inaccurate information. The extended family is not, in fact, declining; it never existed. Family disruption has not increased but has only changed in character. The proportion of children living with at least one parent has gone up, not down. The increased proportion of children living in single parent families results to a great extent from mothers keeping their children instead of farming them out. Mothers have changed the location and character of their work, but there is no evidence that this harms children. Nor is there any evidence that contemporary families have fewer neighbors and friends to call on for help and companionship now than in the past.

In short, American families are "here to stay." But what does that imply about public policy: about day care; children's allowances; divorce reform; Aid to Families with Dependent Children; the Equal Rights Amendment; the innumerable bills, large and small, that come before legislatures; the innumerable cases, important and not, that courts confront under the rubric of family law? These policies are obviously very complex and to evaluate them would require careful scrutiny of technical details, relationships to other programs, political feasibility, and so on. A general description of the state of American families cannot help much with these issues. It may help, however, in thinking about the responsibilities of people for each other and of one generation for others.

Two persisting and partially contradictory themes characterize the family in America. First, families are the units in which one generation brings forth the next and raises it to maturity. Society exercises its collective responsibility for the preservation of the species through millions of families, in which collective responsibility is translated into individual responsibility: men and women raising and caring for their own children. Families are not the only conceivable societal institutions for raising children, but they seem peculiarly suited for delivering the prolonged care and emotional intimacy that totally dependent human infants need to survive. Whatever the biological necessity, however, Americans seem deeply committed to the notion that families are the best places to raise children.

Second, families are places where people can share intimate and unconditional affection and love. The unconditional nature of family love —home is where you go and they have to take you in—seems to provide security and satisfaction that people seldom find elsewhere. People do not continually have to guard their behavior with family members; they can express their fears and their inadequacies without anxiety that the relationship will be destroyed. The persistence of marriage and family ties in America is witness to the importance of these noncontractual, non-meritocratic, slightly archaic relationships.

Because the family bears the primary responsibility for the next generation, the society as a whole has a legitimate interest in some aspects of its life. If the society, indeed the species, is to continue, individuals and families must accept the responsibilities of raising the next generation; and society, not unreasonably, has a collective interest in seeing that they do so. On the other hand, since the family is also the place where people express their most intimate selves, the society also has a responsibility to protect family privacy. Tension between these two stances is a persisting feature of relationships between society and the family, expressed most often over the issue of legal regulation of family formation and dissolution.

Regulating Families and Households

In Puritan New England the family was the basic unit of both church and state. God chose, so the Puritans believed, "to lay the foundations both of State and Church, in a family, making that the Mother Hive, out of which both those swarms of State and Church issued forth." [2] To ensure that the base would be solid, both state and church maintained a close watch over the family. They also made every effort to see that everyone, especially young people, lived in a family under the rule of family government. In 1636, Massachusetts ordered every town to "dispose of all single persons and inmates within their towne to service, or otherwise"—that is, to require them to live in families. [3] Connecticut and Plymouth Colony had similar laws.

The strict laws regulating the Puritan family were gradually abandoned, often because they were impossible to enforce. The requirement that all young men live in families, for example, had to be abandoned around the end of the eighteenth century; towns needed the labor of unattached young men but could not always find families willing to house them. [4]

The change was considered unfortunate, but one of the necessary costs of progress. Marriage and divorce regulations have also floundered before the apparent determination of men and women to marry or not marry as they please, whatever the law. Attempts to forbid the marriages of minors as a way of preventing breakup-prone teenage marriages are met with evasion and fraud and perhaps a rise in illegitimacy.[5] Divorce law reform is often precipitated by the realization that aggrieved spouses make a mockery of restrictive divorce laws, inventing grounds for divorce to satisfy the existing laws.[6]

In general, regulation has been recognized as a notably ineffective way of dealing with family problems. Family government was an early casualty of people's refusal to conform to laws that restricted their freedom to form the kinds of families and households they wanted. As time has gone on, other attempts to regulate marriage and divorce have fallen before the demand that they conform with reality.

The practical argument for liberalizing family regulation is sometimes joined by the argument that family formation is one of the important rights of individuals which government has no business interfering with. The U.S. Supreme Court took this line in two important recent decisions on birth control and abortion. In the Connecticut birth control case, the court referred to marital privacy as "a right of privacy older than the Bill of Rights," asking the rhetorical question, "Would we allow the police to search the sacred precincts of marital bedrooms for telltale signs of the use of contraceptives?"[7] The right of privacy in family formation was affirmed in the abortion case.[8] The law now recognizes a fundamental right to have children as well as a right not to have them.[9]

State regulation of family and household formation has not been finally laid to rest, however. The trend toward liberalized divorce seems inexorable, but arguments are still made that it is weakening the family and, therefore, tearing at the fabric of society. The right to abortion will probably continue to be affirmed, but it remains a controversial issue. In other areas regulation of marriage and household formation is still being upheld. The Supreme Court of Minnesota in 1971 upheld that state's prohibition of homosexual marriage, affirming the state's right to regulate marriage. The court said, "The institution of marriage as a union of man and woman, uniquely involving the procreation and rearing of children within a family, is as old as the book of Genesis" and went on to say, "The due process clause of the Fourteenth Amendment is not a charter for restructuring it by judicial legislation."[10]

A much older case, but one that still articulates U.S. law on the subject, upheld the constitutionality of bigamy statutes, even against members of the Mormon Church.[11] In this case too, the court reaffirmed the right of states to make regulations designed to buttress traditional marriage contracts. In still another important case, local regulations governing household formation were upheld by the Supreme Court. The case challenged a zoning ordinance in a Long Island town which defined "family" in such a way that groups of more than two unrelated people were prevented from living in the town, since the town was zoned for single-family dwellings. In its opinion the Court said that the case involved no "fundamental right" guaranteed by the Constitution. It concluded that the zoning ordinance was a reasonable exercise of state power.[12]

All these cases raise complicated issues that are not easily resolved: bigamy laws and the status of women, for example; zoning laws and neighborhood planning. But common to all these cases is the state's alleged interest in protecting the family and its right to regulate family and household formation.

There are several aspects of family life over which legal regulation has, in recent years, been declining. "Family government" is no longer mandated by law; contraception and abortion are no longer forbidden. The passage of non-adversary divorce laws in most states means that decisions over the dissolution of marriage are, like decisions over entering into marriage, now made by the marital partners. There is a tendency among many to distrust government regulation of the family, and arguments are sometimes made that legal regulation of family life should come to a complete halt.

There are, however, societal commitments which may require regulation of some aspects of family life. The first is society's responsibility to its young and old dependent members. Society may oblige its adult members to "pay back" for the care they received as children either by assuming responsibility for aging parents or by raising and caring for the next generation. These responsibilities may require limited state intervention in families and may also require state transfer of resources from the working-age generation to the old and the young.

Two other commitments also come into play in assessing the role of the society vis-à-vis the family. One is American society's developing commitment to sexual equality. Family life was considerably simpler when sex roles were rigidly stereotyped. That day is past, but its passage does not mean that family roles have now ceased to exist or to be of legitimate interest to the society. It does mean that society's stance toward family members, especially women, is now considerably more complicated. To some extent, the rights of women can be strengthened by simply respecting family privacy and the right of men and women to live as they wish, with or without the traditional strictures of the marriage contract. Sexual equality may also require, however, more active intervention in family affairs, in ways that must be reconciled both with family privacy and with the protection of children.

Another commitment of American society, one that also causes complications, is to equality of opportunity for children. Americans have long believed that people ought to have an equal chance to get ahead and to be whatever they can be. One massive intrusion into the lives of children, compulsory schooling, has been partially justified by this goal. Society has stopped short, however, of further intrusion into family life despite the abundant research that emphasizes the crucial importance of early family experiences. But the arguments for intervention continue to be made, and it is at least possible that the centuries-long increase in pressures for greater equality may force the society to face some of these issues.

Family privacy, family responsibility for children, sexual equality, and equality of opportunity are principles to which American society is strongly committed, at least in its rhetoric. Many of the issues facing the society today involve conflicts between these principles. In this sense the problems cannot be "solved." Instead specific situations must be explored; and principles reconciled when possible, weighed when not. We now turn to some of these issues.

Chapter Six

SEXUAL EQUALITY AND FAMILY RESPONSIBILITY: HUSBANDS AND WIVES

WHEN the feminist Lucy Stone married Henry Blackwell in 1855, the couple composed a "protest" against the notion of marriage embodied in the law:

> While we acknowledge our mutual affection by publicly assuming the relationship of husband and wife, yet in justice to ourselves and a great principle, we deem it a duty to declare that this act on our part implies no sanction of, nor promise of voluntary obedience to such of the present laws of marriage as refuse to recognize the wife as an independent, rational being, while they confer upon the husband injurious and unnatural superiority, investing him with legal powers which no honorable man would exercise and which no man should possess.[1]

Stone and Blackwell went on to specify the laws they opposed: laws that gave to the husband control of the children, of the wife's property and earnings, and even of the wife's person. They opposed, in short, the idea codified in Blackstone's *Commentaries on the Laws of England* that "by marriage the husband and wife are one person in law: that is, the very being or legal existence of the woman is suspended during the marriage."[2]

Since the time of the Stone-Blackwell "protest," the legal unity of husband and wife has been abandoned, and some steps have been taken to recognize the individual identity of married women. Enough remnants of traditional sexual roles remain, however, that some feminists still protest against legal marriage. On the other side of the issue, courts and lawmakers have been reluctant to recognize those rights of women that they think might jeopardize the stability of the family or the peace and harmony of the home. It is still an issue in many states, for example, whether a married woman is entitled to use her own name and maintain her own legal residence.[3] Courts and legislatures have appealed to the importance of the family and the peace and harmony of the home as reasons for not disturbing traditional definitions of marital power. But questions of sexual equality, both inside and outside of marriage, are without question on the policy agenda for the next few years. That women have been discriminated against and that the discrimination must be remedied are ideas that now command widespread acceptance and need hardly be argued.[4] What these remedies should be, however, is a topic of great controversy.

There are three alternatives: to try to halt progress toward sexual equality in order to save the family; to proceed toward sexual equality, abandon the family, and develop substitute institutions for raising children; or to work toward reconciling family responsibilities with sexual equality. The myth of family decline, which suggests that as women have been liberated the family has degenerated, has contributed to a phrasing of the issue as one of women's rights versus the family. If this construction were true, then the first two alternatives would be the only ones available. The persistence of the family over the century, however, suggests that the third alternative—reconciling women's rights and the family —is both possible and preferable. Working out the reconciliation will not be easy, however, as a glance at some of the major issues will show.

The Economic Status of Women

All societies that have been studied by anthropologists and historians allocate the care of young children to women.[5] The division between the sexes of other tasks varies tremendously. Both men and women have important and valued roles in economic production in hunting and gathering societies, for example. Although the men hunt, the women provide the basic source of nutrition through the vegetable foodstuffs they gather. In many West African tribes women manage trading and do most of the farmwork as well. Thus economic dependence of women on men, the characteristic feature of American society today, is not a universal phenomenon.[6]

There is also some evidence that women in preindustrial Europe were considerably more self-sufficient economically than their contemporary counterparts. They probably did a greater variety of work and pursued more of the occupations now classified as male.[7] But whatever the status of married women in preindustrial times—and it may well have been equal only in the sense that men were willing to share the burdens of unpleasant work and economic deprivation—married women were surely economic dependents in the early nineteenth century. By law, they could hold no property. In fact, they were excluded from all good jobs and many poor ones.

The first important step toward sexual equality in the economic sphere came with the passage of the Married Women's Property Acts in the mid-nineteenth century. These laws, which were passed by all American states, took from the husband and gave to the married woman a good deal of control over her property and earnings. Under the new laws, married women could make contracts, become independent parties to suits, retain and control any property they brought to the marriage, work at paying jobs without their husbands' permission, and retain their earnings.[8] For women from wealthy families, ownership of the property they held before marriage provided them a good measure of economic independence. For most women, though, the vital issue was control over the financial resources which the family acquired after marriage. Since for most families the husband's earnings are the most important source of income, the issue comes down to whether wives have a claim on their husbands' earnings.

Under the laws of most states, both spouses retain control over their own earnings. Women's earnings are their own property, but they have no claim of ownership on their husbands' earnings, even if their unpaid work as housekeepers or helpers contributes substantially to their husbands' earnings. Thus women who do housework in return for support must depend on the generosity of their husbands; they have only minimal rights to spend their husbands' earnings on their own. If a couple divorces, the wife must depend on the benevolence of her husband or the judge to consider her unpaid housework as a contribution to the family.

To remedy this situation, several states have passed "community property" laws.[9] Under these laws, all property and earnings acquired during a marriage, including the earnings of both husband and wife, become common property. But until the early 1970s, the husband controlled community property. A few states still give control to the husband, but others have, since 1971, revised their laws to give wives more control. Under one of the new laws, wives are given control over their own property and earnings, husbands control over their own property and earnings, and couples joint control over the property—house, car, and so on—that they hold in common. In another state both spouses are given control over all community property, and the consent of both is required to sell or rent common property.[10]

The Married Women's Property Acts were an important step forward, despite their limited recognition of wives' contributions to their husband's earnings. They at least established the principle that married women had some rights to property and income, rights that are gradually being expanded. The second important step toward economic independence for women occurred more gradually, as married women began to exercise their legal right to hold paying jobs. During World War II married women were encouraged to support the war effort in munitions factories and to replace men who were needed for fighting. Many stayed in the labor market after the war, and by 1974 nearly half of all married women were working outside the home. The vast majority of married women work at some time or other.[11]

Any job that pays money, no matter how little, gives a person some degree of economic independence. In addition, federal legislation over the last decade has made equal pay and equal job opportunities for men and women legal requirements. Although the legislation has been directed at all, not just married, women, it has already had some effect on the economic status of wives vis-à-vis husbands and has considerable potential for greater effect. Employers are now prohibited from discriminating against women in hiring, training, promotion, and pay.[12] The courts, in enforcing this legislation, have generally placed the burden of proof on employers to show that hiring or promotion policies that result in unequal representation of women or minorities are required by business necessity.[13] A good example is the court's opinion in a case brought by a woman against Southern Bell Telephone and Telegraph. The company refused to consider her application for the job of switch operator, solely because she was a woman. The company argued that the job was "strenuous" and that women could not do it. The court decided, however, that the company could not prove its case simply by claims; it would have to carefully spell out exactly what the job required and then prove that "all or substantially all women would be unable to perform safely and efficiently the duties of the job involved."[14] The courts' requirements that employers prove the business necessity of discriminatory practices have opened up most jobs to women. If the trend continues—and there is no reason to believe it will not—sperm donor and wet nurse may become the only sexually segregated jobs allowed by law.[15]

Legislation is also on the books forbidding "wage differentials based on sex." [16] Courts deciding cases brought under the Equal Pay Act have been strict on employers. The burden of proof is on employers to show that wage differentials by sex are justified on sexually neutral grounds, such as merit or seniority.[17] Moreover, the courts have been willing to look into the actual content of jobs held by men and women rather than accepting at face value job titles applied by companies.[18]

Job opportunities and wages of women are still far from equal to those of men. Employers are reluctant to change, and male workers are often unenthusiastic about the prospect of having female colleagues. Litigation is all too often necessary before employers will obey the law, and litigation is costly and time consuming. Nevertheless, all the necessary legislation exists and the courts have been reasonably clear about what the law requires: nondiscriminatory hiring, promotion, and pay. It forbids consideration of the marital or parental status of women if similar consideration is not taken of the marital or parental status of men. (Issues of parental status are quite complicated, however, and the law in this area is far from clear. These issues are taken up in a later section.) When the existing legislation is actually enforced, economic independence for women will become more common. Women will not only be able to hold jobs, but they will be able to hold as good jobs and make as much money as their husbands. (The obstacles raised by maternity and child care will be discussed later.) If men and women are distributed randomly through jobs, there should be as many marriages in which the wife makes more than the husband as those in which the husband makes more than the wife. If this actually occurs, the economic position of women will be drastically different from what it has been in the past.

Equal Economic Status and the Family

It is hard to predict the effect, if any, of sexual economic equality on the family. History provides only limited evidence. American families did not wither and die after the passage of the Married Women's Property Acts. Nor have they suffered much since married women began holding paid jobs in increasing numbers. Americans still seem to consider marriage and children overwhelmingly important, and family ties have persisted despite a number of important steps toward sexual equality. But it is not really safe to conclude from this evidence that sexual equality in the economic sphere will have no effect on the family.

It seems at least possible that women whose work is substantially equal to their husbands' in prestige and income will expect more equal participation in housework and child care and more say in decisions on important purchases and on moving. The existing research on two-worker families gives few hints as to what changes in the family are taking place. Researchers have found that among families with two working adults some divide household tasks more equally and share household decisions somewhat more often.[19] The differences are very small, however. Time-use studies show that the major burden of housework still falls on women. Full-time employed women (thirty hours or more per week) spend an average of 4.8 hours per day on household work, while their husbands spend 1.6 hours per day, and other family members totaled together spend another 1.6 hours.[20]

Studies that simply compare employed and nonemployed mothers do not really get at the potential effects of economic equality. In most contemporary two-worker families the wife works less and earns less than the husband.[21] This inequality of economic power means that in most families traditional notions of husbands' and wives' roles are not challenged by economic facts. Even in families where both adults are professionals, the husband usually earns more. Wives of blue-collar workers may have white-collar jobs, but still earn on the average much less. Thus the effects of economic equality on families have not been studied, since economic equality so seldom exists. Studies of divorce suggest that couples are slightly more prone to divorce when the wife's income is high relative to the husband's.[22] It is certainly possible that increased economic equality will generate marital tension, especially among husbands whose only experience has been in families with traditionally defined roles.

Whether the tension is temporary or permanent is one of the most important unanswered questions. Americans are strongly committed to marriage and families as their preferred arrangement for living and raising children. It seems unlikely that substantial numbers will reject marriage completely. Women who are economically independent may well marry later.[23] They are likely to know what their expectations are and to choose like-minded partners. Most women who discover their economic independence during marriage will probably find that their families eventually adjust. Those couples who do not may divorce, but if they are like most Americans, they will remarry. In short, assuming that most Americans want families, which seems true, and further assuming that they are not hopelessly stupid in choosing spouses nor hopelessly recalcitrant in working out relationships, then the conclusion is that the marital tension that results from improved economic status for women will eventually return to normal as people sort out themselves and their relationships.

Family Status and Employment Status

The question of what to do about child care may provide the most serious source of tensions in marriages and may also pose the most serious obstacles to economic equality for women. None of the equal employment legislation deals directly with these issues, and there is no consensus on how to deal with them. The problem is this: Most families want children. If women continue to carry the major responsibility for home and children, they will accumulate less work experience and fewer job skills than men. The resulting wage and status differentials pose a problem for a society committed to sexual equality. They also pose a problem for individual men and women, especially for those women who became accustomed to their own income and their own job status before marriage. If economic equality were achieved and if women could earn as much as men, the decision that one partner should give up his or her income to assume family responsibilities would be much more difficult than it now is.

Individual families now most often resolve the conflict by choosing either children or job continuity for the woman. A small percentage of women choose not to have children so they can pursue their work. Another small percentage have children but hire care for them even in infancy, choosing work over child care, though not over maternity. In a much larger percentage of families one parent, almost always the mother, stays home to care for the children more or less full time, for more or fewer years. These families ask one partner to give up work continuity and the associated economic benefits in order to raise their children. A few families work out a fourth solution, in which the burden of the choice falls on the husband as well as the wife. These rare families share child care, either by both reducing outside work commitments or by working different shifts and expanding total working hours so that each spouse holds in effect two full-time jobs.

None of these individual solutions is a completely satisfactory model for the society as a whole. Widespread childlessness is perhaps the least satisfactory, and certainly the least likely. The population problem notwithstanding, the society will not survive if it has no children. Since people's desire to have at least one child seems to be strong and deeply rooted, any policy to encourage childlessness is likely to be strongly resented and impossible to implement. It can be argued, of course, that in a time of overpopulation, it is reasonable for people to make a choice between children and careers. But society would be compromising its commitment to sexual equality if only women had to make this choice. Thus any policy that forces the choice must also deal with distributing the burdens of the choice equally between men and women.

Day Care

Hiring child care seems somewhat more feasible than doing without children. Universal free day care is, in fact, the solution proposed by many feminists. Day care would lead to overall economic equality between the sexes only if all women used it. Under that condition, all child care would be done by hired caretakers, and all women would work continuously. Continuous work, plus vigorous enforcement of equal pay and equal opportunity legislation, should result in substantially equal economic status for women. They would be financially independent, and their status within the family would be, on the average, equal to that of their husbands.

Universal continuous work and use of day care by all women, however, would probably require coercive legislation. A few societies, like the People's Republic of China and the Israeli kibbutzim, do require women to work and leave their children in day care. These societies, however, are motivated not only by ideological commitment to sexual equality but also by a pressing need for women's labor in the tasks of economic development. The United States is in a quite different economic situation and has a strong commitment to the idea that families have a right to choose the kind of care their children will receive. Although it is possible to construct ideological arguments about why all women should be required to work and leave their children with hired caretakers, it is farfetched to imagine that these arguments will ever be accepted.

In fact the proponents of day care make no such argument. Instead, they argue that free day care should be available to any woman who wants to work. The availability of free day care might provide a strong incentive for women to work, but the incentive would be strongest for two groups of women: those who really like the jobs they would hold, mainly well-educated professional women, and those whose families are most hard pressed economically. Families in which one partner's earnings were relatively high and the other's job possibilities not very interesting—now the normal situation in the middle class—might well ask one partner to stay home and care for their children, at least while the children were infants.

This disproportionate use of day care by the rich and the poor, which would probably result if day care were financed from public funds and made available to everyone, poses two sorts of problems.[24] If well-educated professional women benefited disproportionately from the day care system, it would provide yet another example of our system of taxation robbing the poor to pay the rich. Such a situation has ample historical precedent but is nonetheless unfortunate.

The use of day care by those who are economically hard pressed presents more complex issues of rationality and choice. (They are the same issues posed by a system available only to the poor or a system of sliding scale payments.) One fact to consider is that day care is not much more efficient a way of caring for children than is parent care. It would be more efficient, of course, if each day care worker took care of twenty children (like the public schools) or even ten. But day care workers seem to think that a caretaker ought to be responsible for only two infants, three or four toddlers, or five to seven 3- and 4-year-olds.[25] This works out to an average of four children for each day care worker. Since the average family that has any children under 6 has 1.35 of them, the system would require a third as many day care workers as there are mothers of small children. This is an economy, of course. But the overhead costs of the system might well eat up much of the savings, and the overall ratio might be more accurately assumed to be two mothers for every day care worker. If day care workers were paid about the average wage of women workers in other fields, the total cost of day care would be equal to half the total earnings of the women whose children were being cared for. If day care workers made above the average wage, which, of course, the professionals are advocating, or if the mothers of the children they cared for made less than the average wage, which if users were disproportionately the poor they would, or if the families using the system had more than the average number of preschool children, then the cost of the system might approach the aggregate earnings of the mothers. If the goal is to ease the financial difficulties of poor one- or two-parent families, day care is an inefficient way of achieving it.

It is very difficult, therefore, to argue for a free public day care system on grounds of economic efficiency. One can only argue other grounds: that it is good for children to be in day care, that it is good for all adults to work for pay, that it is good for people who are cooped up with small children eight hours a day to do something else part of the time. A few people do argue that it is good for children, especially disadvantaged children, to be in day care. Most psychologists and day care professionals only argue, however, that it is not harmful—and their evidence supports only this modest claim.[26]

A second argument is that it is good for everybody to work for pay— so good as to justify the enormous public expenditure that a free day care system would entail. Certainly, it is good for people who enjoy their work and want to work to do so. But it is much harder to argue that it is better for someone to work on factory assembly lines, to do routine office work, or to clean other people's houses than to take care of his or her own children. Many women, rationally, now prefer the job of child care to the other jobs they might hold. Men might express the same preference, if their own jobs were not interesting and if their wives' earnings could support the family.

In families where both parents do work for pay, they often do so primarily for the money. If day care were free, they would have an even stronger financial incentive to work. But public day care is not really "free"—it is paid for by taxes. If society is mostly interested in alleviating the poverty of poor families, it could simply transfer funds to them, or it could pay them for caring for their own children rather than paying someone else to care for them. Indeed, it seems to me quite illogical to pay people out of general taxation for taking care of other people's children but not for their own.

The third argument for day care—that it is not good for anybody to be cooped up in a house all day with children and no adult contact—is the most persuasive. This problem can be solved, however, in a variety of ways other than full time day care. Neighborhood play groups or community centers staffed by student or elderly volunteers can provide mothers with a few free hours at a very low financial cost and at a very real benefit to the community.

Thus, the arguments do not seem to me sufficiently powerful to justify a massive transfer of public funds to families of small children in which both parents want to work. Some of the families in this group are already privileged and need no further subsidy. But more generally, I can see no particular reason to prefer women who want to work over women who want to care for their own children to the tune of $3,375 in tax money a year.[27] There must be simpler and cheaper ways to achieve equal status for women, ways which are more tolerant of family choices. There must also be simpler ways of helping families, especially one-parent families, cope with the problems that come from the loss of income.

Maternity and Child Care Leaves

An alternative approach to resolving the tension between sexual equality and family responsibility is suggested by the behavior of most working mothers—they drop out for child care and then return to work. This pattern reflects the fact that many women prefer (or think they ought to prefer) caring for their young children to the paid jobs they would otherwise hold. They drop out of the labor force when their children are born and stay home caring for them while they are young. They then return to work when the children are old enough to go to school. Some return part time when children are nursery school age. Others wait unitl children are 6 and go to school all day. Still others stay out of full-time work until children are old enough to care for themselves after school.

When women have a small number of closely spaced children, as most now do, the period that they are out of the labor force is not particularly long, relative to their total working lives. If women have two children, two and a half years apart, they are out only eight and a half years, even if they do not work until the youngest child is 6. This is about 20 percent of a normal working life and may not seem to be a particularly great handicap. But many women find that it is. And they are backed up by research on differences in average wages between men and women that shows that differences in years of work experience and interrupted work patterns account for an important part of the wage gap.[28] More subjectively, women often encounter difficulties in beginning or resuming careers after raising children. Some find it hard to get a good job even when children are older because of employers' real or imagined fears about absenteeism and turnover.

Both economic equality and parental care of children could be pursued if nondiscriminatory maternity and child care leaves and opportunities for reduced work commitments for parents were widespread. Legislation could be directed toward requiring or encouraging employers to hire, promote, and pay mothers on the same basis as other workers and to accommodate their special needs through special policies for short- and long-term leaves. Such legislation, though attractive in many ways, raises important questions about who should bear the costs of children. The policies do involve costs, which, although assessed on employers, actually fall on the general public.

The courts have already taken one step in the direction of putting the burden on employers, in the case of a company that refused to accept job applications from women with preschool children.[29] The company argued that its actions did not discriminate against women per se, showing that a large majority of the company's employees were women; it further argued that its refusal to hire women with preschool children was a reasonable business decision. The district court ruled in the company's favor, but the U.S. Supreme Court reached a different decision, ruling that a policy that treated women with preschool children differently from men with preschool children was discriminatory on its face. The court did not completely reject the company's argument, however. The majority opinion said that "the existence of such conflicting family obligations, if demonstrably more relevant to job performance for a woman than for a man" could be cited as a "bona fide occupational qualification" and thus a permitted defense for refusing to hire women. Thus the step taken was a small one. It remains to be seen whether subsequent decisions will require that mothers be treated the same as fathers.

The issue is not clear-cut. The first question is whether mothers of preschool children do perform more poorly on the job than fathers of preschool children. Most of the data on absenteeism and turnover, the problems most often raised by employers, show that women's records are no worse than those of men in similar jobs.[30] But it seems at least possible that the rates for parents of preschool children would differ. Women do bear more of the responsibility for children than men, and probably more often than men stay home with sick children or in place of a sick baby-sitter, take the children to the doctor, and so on. If a company could prove such differences, a court might permit discriminatory treatment of women. Under the current law, however, an employer would have to prove that "all or substantially all" mothers of preschool children were unable to perform their jobs satisfactorily, a proof that few employers would be able to offer. It seems likely, then, that employers would be required to treat parents equally, and that in so doing they would suffer some costs due to increased absenteeism.

To avoid these costs, a company might pursue a policy of preferring nonparents over parents of both sexes in hiring and promotion. There is no law prohibiting discrimination against parents, and this might be a sensible policy for employers to follow. No research that I know of has looked at the question of whether parents are more reliable workers than nonparents. On the one hand, parents have home responsibilities that may well interfere with their work. On the other hand, parents may be more motivated to work hard and make money. Parents of young children are also unlikely to be either very old or very young, ages when job performance suffers. If the pluses and the minuses of being parents do indeed balance out, employers may continue hiring parents and nonparents equally. The costs of hiring people with preschool children would then be absorbed by the company. They might be taken out of profits, a course that experience has shown to be unlikely. They might also be spread among employees in the form of lower wages, or passed on to consumers as higher prices. The result, in short, is a transfer of part of the cost of having children from parents to the society as a whole.

The issue of costs is raised even more sharply with regard to maternity (actually delivering the baby) and child care leave. A comment by a dissenting district judge in the *Phillips* case, described above, put the problem of maternity leave succinctly: "Nobody—and this includes Judges, Solomonic or life tenured—has yet seen a male mother." [31] Policies covering maternity leave, whether designed by employers or government, are necessarily relevant only to women. In order to bring maternity leave under sex-neutral purview, Equal Employment Opportunity Commission guidelines require that maternity be treated as a temporary disability: that compliance with the Equal Employment Opportunity Act requires that "disabilities caused or contributed to by pregnancy, miscarriage, abortion, childbirth and recovery therefrom are, for all job-related purposes temporary disabilities and should be treated as such under any health or temporary disability insurance or sick leave plan available in connection with employment." [32] Under these guidelines, pregnant women should be able to take sick leave and collect disability pay on the same basis as other sick and disabled employees.

Putting the guidelines into effect raises several sorts of problems. The first is practical: how to determine when a pregnant women is disabled and when the new mother is recovered.[33] If the determination is to be made by the woman and her doctor, the company will need some assurance that maternity leave is kept distinct from child care leave and is granted only for those periods when the woman is physically disabled. If the determination is made by the company and set as a certain number of weeks before and after delivery, the woman will need some mechanism for requesting either more or less leave, as her needs require. If only leave is at issue, the woman may want to work longer than the employer has determined.[34] If disability pay is at issue, employers and insurance companies may want women to quit later and return earlier than individual needs may dictate.

Assuming that the practical issues can be solved, and they have been by many companies and government agencies, other issues arise. One issue concerns fairness between men and women. Only women carry and deliver babies, which will probably mean that women will receive more disability leave and more disability pay than men. Is this fair to men, especially if the disability insurance premiums they pay are equally high? Moreover, pregnancy is usually (it is hoped) a voluntary disability, in contrast to other types of disability normally covered by leaves or disability insurance. It can be argued that in fairness to men, other sorts of voluntary disabilities should also be covered. One court used alcoholism as an analogy to maternity—a voluntary disability that ought to be treated like maternity.[35] The similarity is perhaps not completely obvious, but the issue is nonetheless a real one.

Another concern is the cost of maternity leave and disability pay. Treating maternity as a temporary disability inevitably requires the subsidization of parenthood by nonparents. Disability pay is normally financed by insurance. If maternity is defined as a disability the cost of the premiums must go up. If employers pay the premiums, the cost will be recovered by lower wages or higher prices. Even if employees pay the premiums, some transfer of cost will be required. One could try to charge higher premiums to women than to men, but that distinction is probably illegal. The most likely course is to raise premiums for everyone or to subsidize plans with state funds with the result that nonparents would partially subsidize the cost of parenthood. A recent U.S. Supreme Court decision allowed the state of California to exclude normal pregnancies from disability coverage, on the grounds that the increased costs to the state outweigh the interests of individual women in obtaining insurance against the risk of pregnancy. A number of cases are now in the courts, some brought on statutory rather than constitutional grounds, which may well be decided differently.[36] If the court does require employers to bear these costs, the latter will eventually be passed on, and the general public will be subsidizing parenthood more than it now does.

Even more difficult issues are raised by the question of child care leave—time off to care for babies and young children. The actual physical disability resulting from having a baby is of short duration—only a few weeks before and after delivery for most healthy women. Only this short-term condition can logically be called a physical disability and dealt with under disability policies. But most women who have babies want a longer leave, not to recover physically but to care for their children. Child care leaves, although sometimes defined as maternity leaves, are really quite different. Only pregnant women can have babies. Child care, however, can be done by anyone—father or mother, hired hand or relative. Child care leave, therefore, involves a preference on the part of the employee, not a physical disability. Moreover, child care leaves could conceivably involve quite long periods of time and raise very tricky issues about the length of permitted leaves. An argument could conceivably be made that child care leave should be allowed during the period that children need intensive adult care, and that they need such care until they start school. Under this definition, child care leave could last eight and a half years for a two-child family or eleven years for a three-child family. I do not believe that anyone argues for paid leave for anywhere near this length of time.

A number of other issues arise beside that of pay. Only one of these seems easily resolvable. That issue concerns the sex of the parents: Fairness surely demands that if a mother can obtain child care leave a father should be able to do so as well.[37]

But none of the other issues is easy. Is it practical to require an employer to hold a job for someone for eight to ten years (or even five and a half years, if one lowers the age of needing care to 3 and only two children are involved)? Child care leave might be considered analogous to the leave that employers grant to men in military service, but the duration, if nothing else, provides an important distinction. Many employers might find such a policy impossible to implement. Small research firms provide an extreme example; their activities and technology change rapidly. Even firms that were lucky enough to be in business ten years later might find themselves with absolutely no need for a person they are required to rehire.

Questions of fairness and cost also arise. The cost issues are similar to those for maternity leave. Fairness issues arise from the voluntary nature of child care leave. If leave to care for children is legitimate, why not leave to fish, garden, or go to movies?

Similar issues can be raised concerning proposals that would require employers to provide part-time and flexible-hour jobs equal in pay and promotion potential to full-time standard-hour jobs. But in this case, the costs to employers would probably be quite small. Part-time workers do raise the costs of benefits and limit an employer's opportunity to require overtime, but in many jobs their productivity seems to be at least as high as that of full-time workers.[38]

Resolution of the issues raised by maternity and child care requires answers to two very fundamental questions. First, is parenthood to be defined in law as a special status, requiring privileges not granted to non-parents? Second, are more of the costs of raising children to be borne, partially or wholly, by the society as a whole? Society now pays for schooling: Should it do more? Answers to these questions will probably develop slowly, as specific problems and policies are dealt with. But let us for a moment make a few assumptions about what the answers may be, in order to move into a somewhat different area of argument.

Let us assume that the society decides that the benefits of sexual equality are worth the cost of more public assumption of responsibility for children. Let us assume, which seems reasonable, that laws are passed requiring employers to treat maternity as a temporary disability and to provide part-time and flexible-hour jobs. Let us further assume that employers are forbidden to discriminate against parents, part-time workers, and workers who have taken child care leaves in hiring and promotion. The society either subsidizes the cost of these policies, directly or through tax breaks, or agrees that employers can pass the costs on in higher prices. But let us also assume that the society decides to continue allocating the major responsibilities for the cost of children to parents, that it rejects paid child care leave, wages for mothers paid by the government, and free day care for all children.

Let us assume, in short, that some of the costs of children are transferred to the state but that most remain with the parents. To be consistent with sexual equality this public decision cannot require that *mothers* pay the cost. It thus raises the question of whether public policy, short of transferring the costs of raising children to the state, can induce an equal division of costs between male parents and female parents, which sexual equality would seem to demand.

Equal employment opportunity legislation can have important but limited effects. Employers can be forbidden to discriminate against women in hiring and pay, they can be required to grant parental leaves equally to men and women, and they can be required to hire and pay male parents and female parents equally. These measures should serve to increase the bargaining power of women within the family since they will accord women substantially equal earnings potential. They should also permit men and women to divide child care in nontraditional ways, if both can take leaves or reduce work commitments for the same costs. But these measures cannot require or even encourage husbands and wives to actually work out equitable arrangements. They do not necessarily even focus attention on the questions.

To make men and women conscious of the possibilities for sexual equality within marriage requires focusing attention on the marriage roles themselves. Men and women are stubborn creatures and cannot be forced to conform to any particular notions of what husbands and wives should do, especially if those notions conflict with their experience. But there may be legislative and legal actions that can stimulate questioning and perhaps change behavior. The extension of the Fourteenth Amendment into family law or the adoption of the Equal Rights Amendment may generate such action.

Sexual Equality and Family Roles

Marriage is essentially a civil contract between two adults. Like other contracts, marriages must meet certain state requirements in order to be valid. Like other valid contracts, the obligations accompanying a valid marriage can be enforced in state civil courts.

But marriage is a very peculiar sort of contract, because the terms are not set by the parties to the contract. Instead, the obligations of husband and wife within marriage are defined by state statute and by common law as interpreted by the courts. All states have statutes that require husbands to support their families. In return, wives are expected to care for the homes and families. All states designate the husband as the "head of the family."

Couples can alter some of the terms of the contract concerning property. If a couple draws up a premarital agreement on property, the courts will enforce that agreement. The courts have not been willing, however, to enforce premarital agreements that alter the terms of the contract in other respects. Such cases do not often come up, and how the courts would deal with one today is an interesting question. *Graham* v. *Graham*,[39] decided in 1940, dealt with a suit by a man against his former wife, claiming that she had broken the terms of their pre-marital agreement. That agreement stated that the wife would pay the husband $300 a month, in return for which the husband agreed "to give his wife his constant society, to travel with his wife wherever she wished and as frequently as she wished and not to return to work."

In deciding against the husband, the court said:

> Even if the contract is otherwise within the contractual power of the parties it is void because it contravenes public policy. Under the law, marriage is not merely a private contract between the parties, but creates a status in which the state is vitally interested and under which certain rights and duties incident to the relationship come into being, irrespective of the wishes of the parties. As a result of the marriage contract, for example, the husband had a duty to support and to live with his wife and the wife must contribute her services and society to the husband and follow him in his choice of domicile. The law is well settled that a private agreement between persons married or about to be married which attempts to change the essential obligations of the marriage contract as defined by the law is contrary to public policy and unenforceable.

Marriage obligations usually become subjects for litigation only when the marriage is about to be dissolved. Because support obligations are regularly defined only in divorce actions, the U.S. Supreme Court's recent refusal to review a Georgia court's decision upholding an alimony law is important.[40] Georgia law provided alimony for women but not for men. In deciding that the law was not a denial of equal protection the court supported the traditional allocation of responsibilities within marriage.

The principles expressed in the Equal Rights Amendment, however, require complete revision of the laws governing marriages. Opponents of the ERA have made much of women's loss of support rights, while proponents have argued that women have no real support rights to lose. It is certainly true that courts will not enforce support rights within an ongoing marriage. The classic case on the issue is a catalogue of horrors. A woman sued her husband for support, and both parties agreed on the facts. The woman did housework, worked in the fields, and raised and sold chickens. The husband owned the land worth $84,000 (in 1953) and had savings of $13,000 and bonds worth $104,000. The husband had given the wife no money for furniture or household goods in four years, had not taken her to a movie in twelve years, refused to buy her a kitchen sink or a car, and would not pay for fixing a furnace that had been defective for five or six years. The court refused to intervene, claiming that as long as necessities were provided "the living standards of a family are a matter of concern to the household, and not for the courts to determine." [41]

The legal right that wives do have to purchase necessities and charge them to their husbands is of little practical value since merchants seldom extend credit to wives without their husband's consent. Moreover, a recent decision of a district court in New Jersey weakened that right further. A hospital sued both the husband and wife for the payment of charges incurred when the wife had a baby. The court decided that these medical services were "necessities" and that the husband had a responsibility to pay for them. The court went on, however, to argue that times have changed since the original common law doctrine of support was formulated:

> Judicial notice must be taken of the efforts of the Women's Liberation movement to end all inequity between the sexes. . . . We recognize that under the common law the rights of women have enjoyed a slow but almost uninterrupted expansion. We at the same time recognize the inescapable logic that the expansion of such rights involves, in fact demands, an equivalent expansion of the responsibilities of women who have been given their rights.[42]

The court then held the wife liable for the entire bill.

These cases indicate that wives will not lose much if they lose their rights to be supported. The courts have always been reluctant to intervene in ongoing marriages. Even after divorce or separation, the courts have hesitated to award alimony to women who are young and healthy enough to get jobs; alimony will usually be awarded only when the wife (and in some states the husband) gives evidence of her need and of her spouse's ability to pay.[43] The divorce laws of many states explicitly state that maintenance awards should be based on need and take into account potential as well as past opportunities for self-support. These considerations seem to apply even in states without explicit laws, since by no means do all divorced women receive alimony or child support. One study found that only 41 percent of divorced and separated women —all of whom had been divorced or separated within the previous seven years—were receiving alimony or child support. The average yearly payment to these women in 1973 was about $2000.[44]

Revising the support laws to conform with principles of equal treatment will probably have little practical effect. It might, however, have an important and positive symbolic effect. Under traditional conceptions of marriage, reflected in support laws, husbands expect to support their wives and wives expect to be supported. This expectation probably diminishes the importance that women place on preparing themselves for work and on finding themselves secure jobs wth prospects for advancement. A revised support law would announce something to the effect that both spouses are liable for the support of their children and that each is liable for the support of the other if the other is incapable of self-support. Such a law might begin to change the expectation of both men and women that women are incapable of supporting themselves. It might make women more protective of their employment possibilities and less willing to sacrifice them. It might possibly induce them to bargain more with their husbands about responsibility for child care and about deciding which spouse will reduce work commitment to care for the children.

A revised support law would also presumably have to say something about housework. Many couples will undoubtedly choose to arrange their lives so that one spouse works more outside the home while the other does more housework and child care. There are a number of possible variations: The spouse who earns less does proportionately more of the household work. Or, each spouse contributes financially according to ability, contributes to household work according to available time, and shares in family resources according to need. Or, one spouse agrees to assume financial responsibility in return for the other's assuming household responsibility; each shares equally in family resources. Or, one spouse takes time off from paid employment with the understanding that the other can do so at a later time. Household work and family resources are equalized over the two time periods.

The law should make some provision for these situations, if only to guide judges in devising settlements after divorce. The law might state, for example, that "if one spouse were a wage earner and the other performed uncompensated domestic labor for the family, the wage-earning spouse would owe a duty of support to the spouse who worked in the home." [45] Or the law might provide that housework and child care should be compensated at a rate and in a manner agreed on by the two spouses. This latter formulation need not require any actual transfer of cash, but it would suggest that both spouses ought to agree on who will do how much domestic work and on the value of that work to the family.

The main value of such laws might be to reverse the legal presumption that the husband works for pay and the wife does the housework, and establish the presumption that division of labor and support responsibilities are to be mutually discussed and decided. Writing this presumption into the law might encourage husbands and wives at least to think about their own division of responsibilities and might encourage some wives to press for a more egalitarian redefinition of responsibilities. The law might go even further toward encouraging husbands and wives to work out mutually satisfactory definitions of marriage roles. One possible measure would be to require men and women to file a marriage contract as a prerequisite for obtaining a marriage license. The required contracts would not have to be long or particularly detailed but would cover the general areas of financial arrangements, division of labor, and support responsibilities. Being required to file a contract would force prospective spouses to think about marriage roles, at least to the extent of reading the variety of standard contracts that would undoubtedly be put forth by civic organizations and commercial publishers.

The idea of filing a marriage contract might meet with considerable resistance, especially among the romantic young who enter most marriages. Extremely detailed marriage contracts that state, for example, that the husband shall get breakfast on Mondays, Wednesdays, and Fridays and the wife shall care for children born on even-numbered days of the month certainly conflict with an atmosphere of mutual trust in the marriage.[46] But in many situations, especially second and third marriages, contracts specifying the financial and time obligations of each partner to both new and old families may be necessary. In other situations, contracts could be simply statements of principles that the spouses agree to respect.[47]

The law might go even further and recognize marriage contracts as legally enforceable. Such a measure would give teeth to contracts between spouses and would allow both husbands and wives a way of changing their spouses behavior short of divorce. The proposal does have problems, however. Traditional marriage contracts have never been enforceable in court: Wives cannot sue for support nor husbands for services. Courts have been reluctant, probably rightly, to intervene in disputes within the home, fearing the exacerbation of domestic bitterness that could result from husbands and wives confronting each other in court. These problems would not be solved by redefining marriage contracts. They might, in fact, be compounded, especially if implicit as well as explicit contracts could provide the basis for suit. The traditional marriage contract at least sets expectations. Revised support laws mean that expectations can conflict: "I'm doing housework and she owes me support." "He doesn't need to do housework. He's sitting around not getting a job and I'm not going to support his laziness from my hard-earned money." The disadvantages of making marriage contracts legally enforceable probably outweigh the advantages. The issue should, however, be raised when state legislatures are in the process of redefining support laws.

Work, the Status of Women, and the Family

The pursuit of sexual equality is likely to be one of the dominant themes of the next decade. Considerable progress has been made in the areas of equal pay and equal employment opportunities. Further progress requires facing the issues of maternity, child care, and housework. There are three possible approaches. The first is to leave things as they are, with women mainly responsible for housework and child care. The inevitable result of that approach is that women will never achieve economic equality with men. If they drop out of the work force during the years that their children are young, they will suffer from falling behind men in experience and training. If they do not drop out, they will be rightly perceived by employers as having family responsibilities that men do not have that interefere with their job performance. They will find it harder than men to be hired or promoted. This approach, therefore, implies continuing sexual inequality. It is not likely to be acceptable either to women or to society as a whole for very long.

The second approach is to transfer all or part of the costs of having and raising children from women to society as a whole. By freeing women from the burdens of child care, these policies would permit them to work continuously and theoretically to advance economically at the same rate as men. Free public day care is an example of a policy that transfers the costs of child care from women to the general public. Policies that would require employers or insurance companies to absorb the costs of hiring mothers also transfer costs to the public. Requirements that employers treat maternity as a temporary disability, grant nonprejudicial maternity and child care leaves, and hire and promote mothers on a nondiscriminatory basis, all involve costs. If the costs are not directly subsidized by public funds, they are likely to be passed on by employers either to workers or to consumers. In any event, the result is a transfer of the costs of having children from women to the society as a whole.

This approach has considerable appeal. It does, however, require that society reassess the division of responsibility for children. It also has serious practical problems. Free day care for all children of working mothers would be tremendously expensive and quite inefficient. Child care leaves, to be truly egalitarian, would presumably involve pay to parents on leave. This policy too would be very expensive. It therefore seems unlikely that the public will agree to the massive programs that would be necessary if equality for women were pursued only through this approach.

The third approach is to concentrate on equalizing the division of home and child care responsibilities between husbands and wives. This approach is probably a necessary complement to the second, since not all the costs of child care could be socialized even if the public were willing to spend large sums of money. Equality between husbands and wives cannot be legislated. Several steps might, however, encourage it. Equal pay and equal employment opportunities can increase the bargaining position of women within marriage. Requirements that child care leave or reduction of hours be available equally to fathers and mothers can permit husbands and wives to allocate responsibilities in nontraditional ways. Revised support laws can further encourage husbands and wives to strike mutually acceptable bargains about who will do what.

A combination of the second and third approaches will not automatically reconcile women's rights with family responsibilities. The various measures should, however, begin a process in which husbands and wives work out their family roles. Many may decide that they prefer more or less traditional family roles, but at least opportunities and encouragements will be available for more egalitarian definitions. Pushing the issue any faster would require state intervention in the family of an extremely intrusive type, for example requiring mothers to work and to send children to day care centers. I think this would be too high a price to pay. I suspect most Americans would agree. A policy of making opportunities available and relying on people's good will to take advantage of them seems to me more sensible and more appropriate.

Chapter Seven

FAMILY PRIVACY AND FAMILY RESPONSIBILITY: ADULTS AND CHILDREN

UNLIKE WOMEN, whose powerlessness is mostly cultural and only minimally physiological, children are inherently much less powerful than adults. They are less smart, less experienced, and less skilled than adults, not because adults have deprived them of opportunities to learn but because development takes time. The welfare of children depends on adults who can protect them from other adults and from the hardships of adult life. But since the protectors are themselves adults, children may need protection against their protectors.

Although the family has historically been the most important protector of children, it appears that in different periods in Europe and North America, the family provided different levels of protection. At one time, the family was a loosely bound unit, which left children on their own a good deal of the time; the protective family is a relatively recent development. The role of the state has also changed over time. The state has long concerned itself, to some extent at least, with orphans, foundlings, and children of the poor. But the state's protective role grew considerably around the end of the nineteenth century in the United States, with the development of the juvenile justice system. At that point, state intervention to protect children from injurious or simply deviant parental care became more common and more accepted.

Because children are cared for in families, the exercise of collective responsibility for children can involve the invasion of family privacy. Since American families continue to perform and protect their function of caring for children, the tension between family privacy and the protection of children poses a difficult dilemma for public policy.

Children by Themselves

No society can survive if it provides no adult care for children. Human children simply cannot care for themselves and must rely on adults. Even the Ik of Uganda, described by Colin Turnbull as so pressed by economic circumstances that they show no altruistic impulses, manage to take care of children under three.[1] But some societies provide little more than minimal care, including some European societies of only a few centuries ago.

In his classic book on the history of childhood, *Centuries of Childhood*, Philippe Ariès describes the transition in continental European society from an era in which children were pretty much left to take care of themselves within the community to an era when nuclear families kept close watch on and close control over children.[2] In the earlier period infants were treated with considerable indifference. They were not considered people and often were not even named until they had survived the major crisis periods of infancy. They were often left alone, wrapped tightly in their swaddling clothes, while their mothers worked in the fields. Their nutrition was often poor and their safety seldom well-protected. Whether as cause or result of maternal and societal indifference, large numbers of infants died.

Those who managed to survive infancy were, according to Ariès, portrayed and treated as little adults. They participated in all the festivals and games of the adult society, a society that was itself childlike. They were dressed as miniature adults. They were initiated early on into adult work and began working as apprentices as early as age 7 or 8. Although the attitude of adult indifference was clearly disastrous for infants, the welfare of older children is less easy to evaluate. Ariès himself makes very clear his preference for the integrated world before "childhood" was invented over the later world of family protectiveness and formal schooling. He sees the protective family and the schools as depriving children of the freedom they enjoyed when they participated fully in adult societies: "The solicitude of family, Church, moralists and administrators . . . inflicted on him [the child] the birch, the prison cell—in a word, the punishments usually reserved for convicts from the lowest strata of society." [3]

Others evaluate the change somewhat differently. One fifteenth-century observer, for example, saw the practice of early apprenticeship not as healthy integration into the community but as evidence of a lack of parental care for children. He believed that parents put children into service "because they like to enjoy all their comforts themselves, and that they are better served by strangers than they would be by their own children." [4] Other writers argue that the early period was characterized by considerable physical and sexual abuse of children.[5] One example is the experience of the young Louis XIII of France, who must surely have been treated better according to the standards of the time than more ordinary mortals. The diary kept by Louis' physician reports that he was whipped frequently and made to perform sexually for adults.[6]

The evidence relied on by writers investigating the history of childhood before the eighteenth century is shaky, but it appears that infants and probably also older children in pre-eighteenth-century Europe were not all that well off.[7]

The Family as Protector

Ariès dates the growth and consolidation of the nuclear family as the main protector of children from the seventeenth century. Other historians quarrel with the date.[8] Historians also quarrel over interpretations of why the new developments occurred and what effects they had on the welfare of children. These quarrels are of more than academic interest, since they raise issues that must be considered in formulating policy. Consider, for example, that in eighteenth-century France there occurred both a dramatic decline in infant mortality and a dramatic change in the extent to which mothers cared for their children. Breast-feeding increased, swaddling decreased, fewer children were sent out to wet nurses, and there are more indications of parental affection and playfulness.[9]

The conventional historical explanation is that declining infant mortality caused these changes in maternal behavior. Because infants were more likely to survive, mothers could afford to make more of an emotional investment in them. But it can also be argued that these changes in maternal behavior came about for quite different reasons. For example, improvements in economic conditions may have freed women from heavy field work and increased the time they could give to their babies. Better maternal care may in turn have caused the dramatic decline in infant mortality. If this latter explanation is correct, it suggests that the growth of close relationships between mothers and children was essential to improvements in the welfare of children and not simply incidental.

Whatever the explanation, however, it appears that sometime during the seventeenth century, the family in continental Europe became closer, more private, and more focused on the welfare of children than it had been in earlier periods. Houses included more rooms with separate functions, so that family members had some privacy. Manners changed to protect the privacy of the family against outside intrusion. Families spent more time at home and less in the public life of the streets. Parents became increasingly concerned about the health and education of their children.[10]

In England, the small, private, child-centered family may have emerged earlier, and the white settlers of North America established such families right from the time of settlement. New England seems never to have had the high levels of infant mortality characteristic of Europe, and its history shows no evidence of widespread maternal neglect. Demos estimates that 75 percent of the children born in seventeenth-century Plymouth survived to age 20,[11] a low figure in comparison with the 90 percent of the twentieth century, but high in comparison with the figures for Europe.[12]

Demos found no evidence that New England babies were regularly put out to nurse, and some evidence that nearly all were breast-fed. New England babies do not seem to have been swaddled, which, considering that they were also breast-fed, suggests that they were not left alone for long periods of time. Colonial mothers do not seem to have worked in the fields, as European mothers were often forced to do. Instead, they probably worked in or near the home, on the production of goods for domestic use and perhaps on gardening—activities that are compatible with caring for and minding small children.

Older children in colonial New England were not so closely bound to their parents. They began apprenticeships sometimes as early as age 10, in preparation for the occupation they had chosen. As apprentices, they normally lived with the master who taught them. Children were sometimes sent to live with other families for other reasons as well: Morgan suggests that parents relied on other adults to discipline their children.[13] The growth of formal schooling meant that children were away from parents during school hours, but it also meant that they were less often apprentices in other families. Children lived with their own families and were dependent on them for support and protection.

The family, as indicated, continues to be the main protector of children in the United States and is recognized as such by both tradition and law. All states have laws requiring parents to support their children. Parents have wide-ranging authority over children. They may decide where children live, whether they work, and how they are raised. Parents may discipline and correct their children subject only to very broad restraints. They may call on the juvenile courts to back up their authority over children who are "incorrigible, ungovernable or habitually disobedient and beyond the lawful control of parent or other lawful authority." [14]

The rights of parents over children once extended to life and death. They are not now nearly so wide-ranging. Nonetheless courts and law makers have been most reluctant to intervene in the relationships between parents and children. The emergence of the family as protector of children has been accompanied by an emphasis on the privacy of family relationships and a distrust of those who would intrude.

The State as Protector

Even during the periods of strongest emphasis on the role of the family, governmental bodies have exercised some independent control over children. From the time of the Elizabethan poor laws, local agencies have had the power to remove the children of the poor from their parents and bind them out as apprentices. Apprenticeship was seen not only as a way of reducing the costs of the welfare authorities, but also as a way of protecting children from the tendencies toward dependency and poverty that their families were thought to pass on to them.

In the nineteenth century the notion of *parens patriae*—that the state had the ultimate responsibility for guarding the interests of children and legal incompetents—expanded considerably. The juvenile justice system is perhaps the best example of the expansion of the role of the state as protector of children. The system was given the mandate of preventing as well as punishing deviant behavior by juveniles. It thus had jurisdiction over neglected and dependent children as well as delinquent children and broad discretionary powers in disposing of juvenile cases.

The allegedly benign motives of the child welfare reformers have been called into question by recent scholars. Whatever their motives, however, the reformers had unquestionably important effects. First, they questioned whether families, especially poor immigrant families, were capable of raising children to be competent, well-behaved adults. Second, they established the principle that the state could intervene in families to prevent criminal behavior by children as well as to punish it. Third, they permitted parents to abrogate their responsibilities for their children on the grounds of inability to cope with difficult behavior.[15] The juvenile court system was established to deal with children who were being raised by their families to lives of poverty and crime, traits the reformers saw as almost equally reprehensible.

The power of the state to intervene in cases of child neglect is far-reaching and poorly defined. All states have statutes that allow the courts to determine that a child has been neglected and to take appropriate action. The Missouri statute in force in 1972, for example, stated:

> The juvenile court may, upon petition filed as provided in other cases of children coming under the jurisdiction of the court, terminate all rights of parents to a child when it finds that such termination is in the best interest of the child and one or more of the following conditions are found to exist: . . .

(2)   When it appears by clear, cogent and convincing evidence that for one year or more immediately prior to the filing of the petition

(a)   The parents have abandoned the child;

(b)   The parents have willfully, substantially and continuously or repeatedly neglected the child and refused to give the child necessary care and protection;

(c)   The parents, being financially able, have willfully neglected to provide the child with the necessary subsistence, education or other care necessary for his health, morals or welfare or have neglected to pay for such subsistence, education or other care when legal custody of the child is lodged with others;

(d)   The parents are unfit by reason of debauchery, habitual use of intoxicating liquor or narcotic drugs or repeated lewd and lascivious behavior, which conduct is found by the court to be seriously detrimental to the health, morals, or well being of the child.[16]

Most state statutes identify neglected and dependent children along with delinquents as subject to the jurisdiction of the juvenile or family courts. They are subject to the same court actions: They may be placed on probation or removed from their homes and placed in a training school or charitable institution.[17] The blurring of dependency and delinquency arose in the mid-nineteenth century out of the zeal of reformers to prevent rather than merely punish crime. The nineteenth-century tendency to see poverty, especially among immigrants, as a cause of crime and almost a crime itself, reinforced the resolve of the child savers to use the strong arm of the state to protect children against the evil influences of their environment, including the evil influences of their parents. That the jurisdiction of the juvenile court includes both dependency and delinquency results from those historical attitudes toward poverty and crime and from the nineteenth-century preoccupation with assimilating and controlling the immigrants.[18]

The historical legacy of the nineteenth-century reformers is still apparent in contemporary proceedings concerning child neglect. Charges of neglect of young children are most often brought by representatives of welfare agencies. Thus, cases of neglect that come to the attention of the courts most often arise in poor, urban, minority families. This has led some to question whether there is, in fact, more child neglect in poor families or whether the system is simply discriminating against the poor. Questions have also been raised about how much children actually benefit from the kind of remedies available to the juvenile justice system. This question is especially important in deciding whether the state should increase its role as protector of children, for example, by strengthening and attempting to enforce child abuse laws.

Contemporary Balance

Contemporary family law places explicit legal limits on the powers that parents can exercise over their children. Parents, for example, have lost "ownership" of their children's bodies: A murder or assault that would be a crime if the victim were a stranger is also a crime when committed by parents against their children. Courts can also overrule the wishes of parents who deprive their children of medical treatment, even if the parents' refusal is grounded in religious beliefs. Parents cannot sell their children. They must support, educate, and take care of them or be subject to criminal penalties.[19]

On a variety of issues, however, contemporary legal opinion seems to favor strengthening the power of the family and limiting the power of the state to intervene in the family.[20] One issue arises because of the limited alternatives open to courts once they determine that a child is dependent or neglected. The courts can leave the child in the family, while, it is hoped, providing the family with services aimed at improving the situation of the child. They can send the child to a state training school, or they can place the child in a foster home. At one time, dependent, delinquent, and neglected children were all sent to state institutions. Now only delinquents—both children who have committed crimes and "status offenders" like truants, runaways, and uncontrollable children—are regularly institutionalized. Even for delinquents, however, the efficacy of state training schools is being questioned. No studies systematically compare institutional with noninstitutional treatments, but research has shown that state training schools do a rather poor job. A large proportion of training school graduates are convicted of later crimes. Many observers consider the training schools to be breeding grounds of crime and poverty.[21]

Few dependent or neglected children are placed in institutions. If cases are serious enough to justify removal from their own homes, most of the children go to foster homes. Evaluating the quality of foster care is a difficult business. An adequate study would compare foster care with care in their own families, which would require the random assignment of some dependent and neglected children to foster care and of others to their own homes. This sort of study has never been done and, indeed, for political and ethical reasons, cannot be. A few studies have looked at the conditions of children in foster care, however. They find that a fairly large proportion of children in foster care, perhaps 40 or 50 percent, show symptoms of poor adjustment and emotional distress.[22] These are higher rates than one would expect in a random population of children. But, of course, children in foster care are not a random population of children. They have been removed from their homes by a court order, often supported or even requested by their parents. Their homes are, therefore, not places that are likely to produce healthy, happy children. Whether the children would have been less or more disturbed if they had remained in their own homes is an open question.

Since there is a question, though, about whether foster care might do more harm than good, other problems with the foster care system seem to be leading some lawyers and judges to advocate less reliance on removing children from their homes and more effort in improving conditions in the home. One problem is fairness. In a study attempting to examine judges' decisions in removal cases, three experienced judges were given files on ninety-four children and asked to decide whether the children should be placed in foster care or not. The judges agreed on a decision in only about half the cases and agreed hardly at all in their reasons for the decisions.[23] Judges' decisions in foster care cases thus seem to be fairly arbitrary. They may remove children from parents more often when parents are poor or otherwise deviant, without any real assurance that the child will benefit. When the child is removed over the objections of the parents, the rights of the parents may be violated, if not the rights of the children.

These considerations have led some states to establish rules protecting the rights of parents to a fair hearing in custody cases, including neglect proceedings.[24] A number of other proposals have also been made —for example, that parents be entitled to counsel in neglect cases and that removal of children from their parents be considered the alternative of last resort for the courts.[25] Since adequate information about the effects of foster placement on children is not likely to be available in the next few years, the law may move toward emphasis on the rights of parents in cases concerning neglected children. With the shortcomings of the state as protector of children so apparent, the trend will most likely swing back toward reliance on the parent as protector.

It is possible that there will also be a move toward protection of the rights of parents over their children's education. The issues involved are complex. Just as there is no objective way of determining whether foster care or family care is best for children, there is also no objective way of deciding what children should be taught. The question becomes one of who should decide. Are social workers better judges than parents of what is good for children? Are teachers and professional educators better judges than parents of what children should be taught?

Most of the recent court cases that have considered the rights of parents over their children's education have involved claims by parents that the schools violate their freedom of religion. In several jurisdictions, for example, parents have objected to the inclusion of sex education or "family life" courses on religious grounds. The courts have generally held that these courses are not an essential part of the school curriculum [26] and that students should not be required to attend over their parents' objections. The right of the schools to offer the courses has, however, been upheld.[27] In cases regarding subjects that are an essential part of the curriculum, like English and biology, the courts have had to balance the rights of teachers against the rights of parents. Several cases have upheld the prerogative of English teachers to choose reading material for their classes from books not explicitly proscribed by the school board.[28] These cases have not challenged the right of the school board, presumably acting in the interests of parents, to forbid teachers from using specific books or teaching methods, as long as the teachers know the regulations ahead of time.[29]

The most important recent case, *Wisconsin* v. *Yoder*, on the rights of parents over their children's education involved compulsory schooling. The state of Wisconsin brought action against a group of Amish parents who refused to send their children to public high school, in violation of the state's law requiring school attendence until the age of 16. The parents appealed, on the ground that state law interfered with their constitutionally protected right of free exercise of religion. The case went to the U.S. Supreme Court, which reached a guarded decision in favor of the Amish parents.[30]

In its opinion, the court articulated the right of parents to direct the religious upbringing of their young, quoting an earlier court opinion that had upheld the right of parents to establish and send their children to parochial schools: "The child is not the mere creature of the State; those who nurture him and direct his destiny have the right, coupled with the high duty, to recognize and prepare him for additional obligations." [31] The court then went on to hold that public high school education indeed threatened the Amish way of life and also that the vocational training that the Amish gave to their teenage children was appropriate education for them. The court found no compelling reason for the state to require Amish children to attend public high school. It therefore decided that the religious objections of the Amish parents were sufficiently important to override the compulsory schooling law.

The *Yoder* decision, although emphasizing the rights of parents, was qualified in a number of ways. The court emphasized that the way of life that the Amish sought to uphold was "not merely a matter of personal preference, but one of deep religious conviction." The court rejected the idea that an argument by parents not based on religious grounds would carry the same weight. The court also emphasized the self-sufficiency and lawful behavior of the Amish, which were important in establishing that the states had no real reason to require high-school education. The Amish trained their children well in farming; there was little danger that Amish children would end up in jail or on welfare. Wisconsin had no grounds for arguing that the Amish were not good citizens, and this was an important element in the case.

Thus, it is by no means clear that the *Yoder* decision would be extended to less self-sufficient or less law-abiding religious groups. It is quite obvious that it will not be extended, at least in the near future, to nonreligious groups. Nonetheless, *Yoder* provides an important statement of the rights of parents over their children's upbringing. It seems to me to be another example of a faintly discernible tendency in the law to limit the role of the state as protector of children and to re-emphasize the role of parents.

The Persistent Dilemmas

Strengthening the rights of parents is a reasonable strategy for balancing the power of the state over children. Government agencies, whether run by teachers, social workers, or lawyers, habitually try to extend their authority, a tendency that needs to be regularly checked. But strengthening the rights of parents does nothing for the children who need to be protected against their parents. Some parents physically abuse their children, and some neglect the physical and emotional needs of their children. Legal measures that make it more difficult for courts to remove children from parents may mean that more children will be left with parents who do not care about them. It can be argued that foster care is so bad that leaving children with parents is in most cases the lesser of two evils. It can further be argued that if it is just as difficult to improve foster care as it is to improve parental care—which may or may not be the case—one might as well focus on the rights of parents. These arguments do not leave one completely sanguine about the situation.

The issues in education are just as difficult as those in parental neglect. Consider the parents who object to sex education for their children. If sex education is helpful in achieving satisfactory adult sexuality and preventing unwanted pregnancies—effects that have not yet been established empirically but that may result—then parents who keep their children out of sex education classes are depriving them of important potential benefits. Likewise, if a high-school education is necessary for children to be able to take advantage of intellectual or occupational opportunities, then the Amish who keep their children out of high school are depriving them of these opportunities.

Justice Douglas dissented from the decision in *Yoder* on precisely these grounds. He argued that the court's decision could confine children, perhaps against their will, to the traditional Amish religion and the traditional Amish way of life. Douglas wondered whether an Amish child might not want to be "a pianist or an astronaut or an oceanographer," occupations that would require him or her to break from the Amish tradition. "If a parent keeps his child out of school beyond the grade school," Douglas wrote, "then the child will be forever barred from entry into the new and amazing world of diversity that we have today." Douglas concluded that the court should have determined the children's preferences before reaching a decision in the *Yoder* case.

Even consultation with the child, however, cannot resolve the dilemma inherent in cases like *Yoder*. Should children make decisions about their future before they really understand the implications of their decisions? Should children be required or even allowed to make decisions that they might later regret? The questions raised by the powerlessness of children cannot be resolved by emphasizing the rights of parents as opposed to the state.

Another kind of unresolved dilemma is presented by cases in which parents cannot agree on the upbringing of children. The most common are those in which the custody of children is contested by the two parents after divorce.

With divorce rates high and rising, more and more families encounter the judicial system in its function of determining custody. Since between 20 and 30 percent of the children born during the 1970s are likely to be participants in a parental divorce,[32] the legal principles that develop around custody have far-reaching effects. Because of the number of divorce cases, the trend toward no-fault divorce, and challenges to traditional custody assumptions, judges are being forced to formulate and articulate new procedures and assumptions.

In earlier centuries, all the property of a marriage was considered in law to belong to the husband. After divorce, or more commonly annulment, all marital property including the children was routinely awarded to the husband. As new definitions of marital property developed, this procedure fell into disfavor. Instead, divorce was construed as resulting from a wicked action by one spouse against the innocent other, and the children went to the innocent party. Part of the punishment for causing the divorce was losing the children.

This notion has been tempered by customs and statutes that require courts to consider "the best interest of the child." In applying this standard judges have almost always awarded custody to the mother.

Judges seem to assume that mothers are uniquely suited to taking care of children, especially young children. Fathers who claim custody are normally required to prove not that they would provide for the best interest of the child but that the mother is unfit and incompetent.[33]

Several recent developments have made custody decisions more difficult. States are moving toward no-fault grounds for divorce, granting divorces to marriages that are "irretrievably broken" without allocating blame or guilt.[34]

The new formulation of divorce laws obviously precludes custody decisions based on guilt or innocence. The Uniform Marriage and Divorce Act, which has served as a guide for many states, explicitly rules out guilt or innocence regarding the divorce as a basis for custody decisions. The Equal Rights Amendment, or successful challenge under the Fourteenth Amendment, would make custody decisions based on sex unconstitutional. Thus courts will be faced with more difficult decisions and will have available fewer objective guidelines than they have had in the past.

The multiplicity of interests that must be taken into account are well illustrated by the section on child custody in the model "Uniform Marriage and Divorce Act" proposed by the American Bar Association.

Section 402. (Best Interest of Child.) The court shall determine custody in accordance with the best interest of the child. The court shall consider all relevant factors including:

(1)   the wishes of the child's parent or parents as to his custody;
(2)   the wishes of the child as to his custodian;
(3)   the interaction and interrelationship of the child with his parent or parents, his siblings, and any other person who may significantly affect the child's best interest;
(4)   the child's adjustment to his home, school, and community; and
(5)   the mental and physical health of all individuals involved.

The court shall not consider conduct of a proposed custodian that does not affect his relationship to the child.[35]

Needless to say, such guidelines are of little real help to judges faced with difficult custody decisions. Consider, for example, the tenuous evidence that a judge was forced to rely on in a 1973 District of Columbia case. The court first stated that although the children were relatively young (9, 7, and 5), the District of Columbia law did not permit an automatic assumption that the mother should receive custody. The court was thus forced to carry out an investigation of the relationship of the children to each parent. Each parent called a clinical psychologist to testify; both psychologists, as one might expect, testified that their clients had a warm and affectionate relationship to the children. The court noted that the father took the children to the beach and attended PTA meetings, which the mother did less often. The court had to decide which psychologist to rely on, and how to interpret the psychological test evidence presented by one. It had to deal with such questions as whether the mother's reasons for not accompanying the family to the beach were persuasive. Custody was finally awarded to the father.[36] With such uncertain evidence, the court must have relied on the personal characteristics of the parties and their expert witnesses, which other judges might have reacted to quite differently.

One way of resolving difficult custody decisions is to ask the children their preferences. The Uniform Marriage and Divorce Act states that children's preferences should be considered, and two states have laws that make the preferences of older children determinant.[37] But having to make a decision to live with one or other of their parents forces children to reject one of them. The pressure that the decision puts on children and the guilt they feel afterward may be considerable. Sometimes children may actually be better off if their preferences are not decisive, if they are not forced to bear the responsibility of choosing between their parents. The dilemma remains.

The Rights of Children

At present, childhood ends at different ages depending on the area of concern. Sixteen-year-olds have certain kinds of legal autonomy: In most states they can drive, leave school, and get married. By age 21, all legal protections and restrictions of childhood are removed, and a person has full adult status. Childhood ends, then, between the ages of 16 and 21 according to the law.[38]

More age distinctions, allowing minors to make certain kinds of decisions at lower ages, might be made. At puberty (which could be defined as age 12), for example, children might be allowed to make certain kinds of decisions about who they will live with and what they will do.

A child over 12 might be allowed to petition the court to appoint some adult other than a parent as a legal guardian.[39] This would give teenagers a limited right to run away from home. They could live with relatives or in an adult-supervised youth hostel when they were not getting along with their parents. Teenagers could also be given the right to ask for a particular guardian in custody cases. Moreover, they could be allowed considerable say in their own education and given a legal right to choose courses, schools, or nonschool educational experiences.

Children over 7 could also be given certain kinds of legal rights, although their rights might not be as extensive as those given to children over 12. Seven has been the traditional "age of reason," when Christian churches consider children old enough to know the difference between right and wrong and hence old enough to sin. Seven also seems to mark the end of a transition period in the cognitive development of children; at age 7 most children are capable of moderately complex logical operations.[40] Thus, 7 might be chosen as the age—somewhat arbitrary to be sure—when children can claim a right to voice their preferences about such things as custody and schooling and have their preferences listened to by adults.

Giving children more rights to speak and decide for themselves in various kinds of cases does not, however, solve the problem of children's rights. Indeed, the rights of children now recognized in law include the right not to be forced into self-reliance, the right to be supported by adults. They also include the right to make mistakes, embodied in the notion that children cannot be obliged to abide by contracts made with adults, whereas the adults can be held to their promises. The law may well have gone too far in emphasizing the dependency of children, but the remedy should surely not require throwing children back on their own resources.

Areas of particular concern ought to be the position of children in an aging society and in the small families that are so characteristic of contemporary society. Children today make up a smaller proportion of American society than at any other time, with the exception of the Great Depression. This fact must affect the place of children in the society and the stance of the society toward children. Medieval society quickly incorporated children into adult institutions; but at the same time medieval society was ubiquitously childlike—boisterous, rowdy, sociable.[41] The majority of the population was, in fact, made up of children. A society older in age may be more mature in style, emphasizing restraint, control, and compromise.

An older society could attempt to turn children into adults as quickly as possible, to mobilize education, law enforcement, and public opinion to civilize and restrain youth. Alternatively, an older society might see children's life and joy as a precious diversion and counterpoint to adult sobriety. The society might pamper children and encourage them to be as different as possible from the adults they entertained. At some point of course the children would have to become adults, a transition that if abrupt could be extremely difficult.

Children in an "old" society are in danger on the one hand of being toys for adults and on the other hand of being pressured into premature adulthood. These dangers may, ironically, be compounded by the fact that American society is moving toward a time when virtually all children will be planned for and wanted. It is at least possible that these carefully planned, carefully spaced children are in more danger from parental possessiveness and exaggerated parental expectations than were those who arrived more casually. Parents may formulate their reasons for having a child—to complete their lives, to ensure their immortality—in ways that practically guarantee that the child will be pampered, fussed over, and expected to develop in particular ways. Even when their reasons for having children are not made explicit, parents of small planned families are, I suspect, more likely than others to see their infants as playthings and their children as the raw material for producing replicas of themselves.

The dangers that very small families may pose for children also need to be investigated. Most of the research on family size, as Chapter One explained, suggests that children benefit from the increased parental attention that they receive in small families. However small families may also mean that children are more vulnerable to their parents. Children in larger families may be more able and more inclined to band together to protect themselves against adult cruelty or indifference. Moreover, the presence of older children in the home may temper the actions of parents against younger children, if only because they might tell the neighbors.

Chapter Eight

EQUAL OPPORTUNITY AND FAMILY RESPONSIBILITY

WHEN RICHARD NIXON vetoed the Child Development Bill of 1969, which would have provided money for child and family services, including day care, he explained his action with a warning that federal provision of services for children would lead to the "collectivization" of child rearing and the demise of the family. His message partly echoed the arguments of those who, seeing the impending death of the family all about them, are preparing a last ditch stand against its enemies. But Nixon was also expressing a notion of responsibility for children: that families have the sole responsibility for children in America; that the government has no right to interfere; and that parents have no call on societal resources as supplements to their own.

This is probably a fairly common perception of family responsibility. But, in fact, the division of responsibility for children has long been more complicated. By providing free public education for children, the society assumes control over a substantial portion of children's time and takes on considerable responsibility for them. Conceptually too the issue is complicated. The society might be thought of as having a collective responsibility to ensure its own survival through generational continuity. In addition, because each individual in the society was cared for and taught as a child, each might be said to have a responsibility to "pay back" that care.

Paying back can go in two directions: People can take care of their parents in their old age, and they can continue the network of responsibility by caring for the next generation. In traditional societies, responsibility went in both directions, at least theoretically. Children were supposed to take care of their parents in their old age; parents saw children as an investment in their own future well-being and had many children in order to increase the odds that one would actually pay off. Modern American society has greatly attenuated this bond of responsibility between children and their aged parents. Adults are expected to provide for their own old age, through insurance programs encouraged and partially subsidized by the society. At the same time, children have come to be seen as something that people should have only if they can afford the time and money that children require. Appreciation of the problems of overpopulation and control over reproduction have encouraged people to think carefully about having children.

All this has obscured notions of responsibility for the next generation and recompense to the last. But if generational continuity is the basic mandate of the species, then each person, either individually or collectively, has some responsibility. Traditionally this responsibility has been mitigated by chance; people who had no aged parents or no children had no additional responsibility. In modern times, however, generational responsibility has been partly collectivized, for the old through Social Security and for the young through public education.

An argument for greater collective assumption of responsibility for children can be made on the grounds that since children are an investment made by the whole society, including those who by choice or chance have no children, the whole society ought to contribute, if only financially, to their care and education. A further argument can be made on the basis of society's alleged commitment to equal opportunity for children. Most Americans seem to believe that everyone ought to have an equal chance to be successful and happy in the society. Because of the unequal distribution of resources among adults, equal opportunity would seem to require some transfer of resources to partially equalize the environments of children. Balancing these arguments are the American commitments to family privacy and family responsibility for children. One of the strongest arguments against government aid to children and families has been the fear of government intrusion. Families are protective of both their rights and their responsibilities for their children; the question is whether this protectiveness ought to yield to other societal goals. The last chapter dealt with one set of issues, concerning the protection of children. This chapter looks at the allocation of financial resources and responsibilities.

The Economic Situation of Children

A discussion of whether more money ought to be transferred to children from other groups in the population logically begins with the economic conditions of families that have children. One way of describing these conditions is by comparing a distribution of children by family income with a distribution of people in general.

Table 8–1 presents such a distribution. It shows, for example, that 7.9 percent of all the people in the United States live in families with income under $3,000 and that 5.6 percent of all children live in these poor families. The table also shows that families with children are more equal in income than families generally. Fewer children, for example, fall into the very low income category—17.1 percent of children, compared with 20.8 percent of all persons, live in families with incomes below $6,000. At the upper end of the scale, fewer children than persons generally live in families with incomes above $25,000—8.8 percent of children compared with 9.7 percent of all persons. The differences in the two distributions are not great, however.

The distribution of persons and children by family income is only one part of the picture. How well a family's income supports its members depends not only on the amount of income, but also on how many people the income must support. A measure of income that was adjusted for family size would, therefore, give a better sense of the resources actually available to children. Per capita income is one such measure. It has the problem, however, of making too large an adjustment for family size. There are some economies in living together, particularly in the cost of housing but also in food, transportation, and so on. To take these economies into account, the Department of Labor has devised measures of family "needs" that can be used as a standard for measuring family income

TABLE 8–1
Persons and Children
by Family Money Income, 1973
(percentages)

Income	Persons	Children
Under $3,000	7.9	5.6
$3,000–$5,999	12.9	11.5
$6,000–$8,999	13.9	13.6
$9,000–$11,999	15.0	16.2
$12,000–$14,999	14.0	16.1
$15,000–$24,999	26.2	28.3
$25,000 +	9.7	8.8
Median Income	$12,040	$12,600

SOURCE: Calculated from CPR, P-60, No. 97, "Money Income in 1973," Tables 27 and 24. Persons in families and unrelated individuals were combined and categories were collapsed to make this table.

adequacy. The needs standard is based on estimates of the cost of food for men, women, and children of different ages. The estimated food costs are then multiplied by a factor of about three, which is assumed to represent the costs of housing, clothing, health care, and other family needs. The department has worked out a number of alternative budgets. The needs standard that is used in defining poverty levels is very low and is based on "a nutritionally adequate food plan ('economy' plan) designed by the Department of Agriculture for 'emergency or temporary use when funds are low.'" [1] In 1974, for example, the estimated needs of a non-farm family of four headed by a male were $5,000. A female-headed family with two children was estimated to need $3,946.[2]

The adequacy of a family's income can be evaluated by dividing their income by their needs; this ratio could be used as a means of ranking families.[3] The Census Bureau does not publish such a distribution. It does, however, publish data on the proportion of people who fall below the "low-income" level, defined as the point at which family income is equal to family needs. The proportion falling below the low-income level, although not a perfect measure of income adequacy, probably gives a good sense of how well off various groups in the population are relative to each other.

Table 8–2 shows the proportion of people of different ages and in different family forms who fell below the low-income level in 1974. The table shows that the proportion living in poverty is greatest at both extremes of age. Young children are more likely to be in poverty than older children, and children in general are more likely to be in poverty than adults in their working years. These proportions do not mean that children are poor while their parents are rich: Everyone in a family is presumed to have the same level of income adequacy. Instead, they suggest that many families have no children at home and that the adults in these families are better off than either the adults or the children in families with children. The proportions suggest that families with very young children are worse off then families with adolescent children, a finding that might seem contrary to common sense. What seems to happen, however, is that family income increases rapidly enough to more than cover the increased costs of older children. Husbands earn more and wives often go to work, which together result in adolescent children being below the poverty level less often than younger children. The data on families confirm these findings. Families without children are less likely to be in poverty than families with children. Families with adolescent children are less likely to be in poverty than families with young children.[4]

The most striking differences that appear in Table 8–2, however,

TABLE 8–2
*Proportion of Population
Below Low-Income Level, 1974*

All persons	11.6
Persons by age:	
Under 3 years	17.4
3–5	16.5
6–13	16.1
14–15	14.1
16–21	12.3
22–44	8.2
45–54	7.0
55–59	8.9
60–64	10.1
65+	15.7
In families with male heads	
Adults	5.4
Children under 18	8.7
Children under 6	9.3
In families with female heads	
Adults	24.8
Children under 18	51.5
Children under 6	61.4
Living alone	
Under age 65	22.3
Age 65 +	31.8

SOURCE: CPR, P-60, No. 99, "Money Income and Poverty Status, 1974," Tables 15 and 19.

are related to whether the family head is a male or a female. Of all the children in female-headed families 51.5 percent are living in poverty; the proportion is almost six times that for children living in male-headed families. Female-headed families with children are considerably worse off than female-headed families without children, as is shown by the difference between adults and children. Those female-headed families without young children—families made up, for example, of two sisters living together or of a grown child living with his or her mother—are relatively well off and tend to bring the average up.

The Old and the Young

Interestingly, the economic status of old people has improved much more since 1960 than the economic status of children. Table 8–3 shows the proportion of old people and children below the low-income level for various years since 1960. The table shows that between 1967 and 1974, the latest years for which comparable data for all groups are available, the proportion of persons below the low-income level decreased by 21 percent. The proportion of aged persons below the low-income level decreased relatively more, by 47 percent. Children did less well. The proportion of all children in poverty went down by 5 percent between 1967 and 1974.

TABLE 8–3
Percentages below Low-Income Level, 1960–74

	All Persons	Persons Over 65	Related Children in Families	Related Children in Female Headed Families
1960	22.2	NA	26.5	68.4
1965	17.3	NA	20.7	64.2
1967	14.7	29.5	16.3	54.3
1969	12.1	NA	13.8	54.4
1971	12.5	21.6	15.1	53.1
1973	11.1	16.3	14.2	52.1
1974	11.6	15.7	15.5	51.5

SOURCES: CPR, P-60, No. 98, "Characteristics of the Low-Income Population: 1973"; CPR, P-60, No. 99, "Money Income and Poverty Status, 1974."

The differences are largely attributable to differences in government transfer payments. Since public transfers now amount to 10.7 percent of national income and provide more than half the income of families with total income below $5,000, these payments make a substantial difference. In 1973, $51 billion was paid out in Social Security payments, most of it to old people. Only $7 billion was paid out by Aid to Families with Dependent Children (AFDC).[5] The total amount of AFDC funds paid out in 1973 averages only $700 per child in female-headed families.

Between 1965 and 1973, the average monthly payment under Social Security to a retired worker rose 98 percent. During the same period, the average monthly payment under AFDC to a recipient family rose only 42 percent. The Consumer Price Index rose 41 percent.[6] As a result, the relative income position of the aged has improved, while the relative income position of children in one-parent families has deteriorated. In 1967 the income of white female-headed families averaged 57 percent of the income of white male-headed families; the income of black female-headed families averaged 52 percent of the income of black male-headed families. By

1973 the situation of female-headed families had worsened. The average income of white female-headed families was 49 percent, that of black female-headed families only 44 percent, of the income of male-headed families. In contrast, the relative income position of the aged improved over the period 1967 to 1973. Families with heads over 65 had incomes of 51 percent of the median family income in 1967 but 55 percent of the median family income in 1973. The improvement in the position of the aged and deterioration in that of female-headed families is consistent with trends in transfer payments.

A commitment to equal opportunity implies a focus on children; what then explains the greater public effort to relieve the poverty of the aged? Several explanations come to mind. The first is that the men who make laws are old or at least closer to being old than to being children.

Second is a corollary of the fact that the biological imperative may be more compelling with regard to children. Parental care of the young evolved in many animal species. The pattern is clearly beneficial to the survival of species in which newborns are not fully enough developed to survive. No animal species, in contrast, exhibits care of the old by the young. Care of those past the reproductive age gives no particular advantage to a species and seems not to have evolved.[7] Human families do care for their aged, but with less feeling of necessity than that which accompanies care for the young. Public responsibility for the aged thus can be seen as assumption of a family responsibility that was never felt very strongly or performed very well. Care for the young, on the other hand, is seen as a fundmental family responsibility.

A third reason for greater societal concern with the old than the young may be the notion that Social Security is an insurance scheme and that the aged who receive Social Security have previously contributed to the fund. No such notion of insurance has been formulated with regard to children. Instead, aid to the young has been thought of either as charity or as investment, conceptions that may not be as appropriate to contemporary society as the insurance notion.

Family and Community Charity

American and British notions of responsibility for the poor, including poor children, find their early antecedents in the English poor laws: the 1601 Act for the Relief of the Poor and the 1662 Act for the Better Relief of the Poor of This Kingdom. The 1601 law provided as follows:

That the churchwardens of every parish, and four . . . substantial householders there . . . shall be called overseers of the poor of the same parish: and they . . . shall take order from time to time, by and with the consent of two or more justices of peace . . . for setting to work all such persons, married or unmarried, having no means to maintain them, and use no ordinary and daily trade of life to get their living by: and also to raise . . . (by taxation of every inhabitant . . . and of every occupier of lands, houses . . . or saleable underwoods in the same parish . . .) a convenient stock of flax, hemp, wool, thread, iron or other necessary ware and stuff, to set the poor on work: and also competent sums of money for and towards the necessary relief of the lame, impotent, old, blind, and such others among them, being poor and not able to work, and also for putting out of such children to be apprentices. . . .[8]

The poor laws established that the primary responsibility for the poor lay not in the parish but in the family. The act stated:

That the father and grandfather, and the mother and the grandmother, and the children of every poor, old, blind, lame, and impotent person, or other poor person not able to work, being of sufficient ability, shall at their own charges relieve and maintain every such person. . . .[9]

The law established the obligation of adults to support themselves by work and of children to support themselves through apprenticeship. The public responsibility (assigned to the parishes rather than to the central government) was to provide work for the able-bodied and public charity for those who could not work.

The poor laws gave the parishes substantial control over the lives of the poor. The children of the poor could be apprenticed and taken away from their parents for long periods of time. Moreover, charity recipients could not move freely; parishes had the right to send the dependent poor back to the parishes from whence they came. Financial support was accompanied by substantial interference in the lives of the poor.

These principles were carried over into the poor laws of the American colonies. During the seventeenth century, the new colonies enacted their own relief statutes. Each community was responsible for its own poor. The community could enforce family responsibility, either by assigning the poor to live with families or by assessing relatives for the amount of poor relief. The community's main goals were to deter poverty, to put able-bodied adults to work, and to remove children from unwholesome families. The community tried, however, to keep families together, sometimes by outdoor relief and sometimes by placing whole families in institutions for the poor.

Because relief was carried out locally, the colonial towns could differentiate the poor they cared about—town residents—from those outside their area of jurisdiction. Since towns had the power to exclude nonresidents, the poor who remained were well-known to the townspeople. Those responsible for relief could easily distinguish the deserving poor who were victims of misfortune from the "rogues and vagabonds." [10] Thus relief might be described as a function of the "larger family," i.e., the town, which supplemented and enforced the obligations of the smaller family, i.e., the close relatives of the poor. The poor were normally cared for in their own homes or the homes of other townspeople, rather than in institutions, thus emphasizing the family bases of relief. [11]

In the mid-nineteenth century, public attitudes and practices toward the poor changed dramatically. The poor were increasingly immigrants, strangers to the community. They more often lived in cities that were too large for all citizens—rich or poor—to know each other personally. The cities determined to reform the poor, now seen not as neighbors but as a distinct deviant class. They began to rely increasingly on institutional relief, workhouses for adults and reform schools for children. The dependent poor were no longer cared for in families. The administrative machinery for their relief was likewise no longer located in a familylike town but in an impersonal city bureaucracy.

Most state statutes continued, however, the tradition that the relatives of the poor were responsible for at least part of their support. The state agencies that administered relief had the power to require the responsible relatives to reimburse the state for the care of the poor. Even though the state was seldom able to collect much from the relatives, often near poverty themselves, the principle that relatives were responsible for the financial support of the dependent poor remained embodied in law. The principle of financial responsibility contrasted sharply with the state's notion of who should be responsible for the physical care, training, and instruction of the poor. The poor were sometimes removed from their families and neighborhoods, which were considered bad influences, and placed in public institutions. Welfare officials were especially concerned to remove children from morally deficient families and bad companions and to place them in reform schools where their prospects could be improved.

Luckily, the vogue for institutional relief of the poor did not last long in America, although vestiges of the old attitudes remain in the treatment of neglected, dependent, and delinquent juveniles.[12] By the early twentieth century, the federal and state governments had begun to enact other programs for the relief of various categories of the poor. In 1909 the first White House Conference on Children argued that needy children were best taken care of in their own homes by their own mothers and that states should provide financial assistance to needy women with dependent children. Another important category of the poor that attracted public attention was the aged. In the early twentieth century, reformers formulated a variety of proposals for the relief of the aged, and in 1923, Montana enacted the first old age assistance law.[13]

The real transformation of relief from a family and local responsibility to a public one came, however, during the depression of the 1930s. The Social Security Act of 1935 signaled the first major effort by the federal government to relieve poverty. Unemployment Compensation and Old Age and Survivors' Insurance were contributory insurance schemes, which are discussed in a later section. But the Social Security Act also established more conventional relief programs. Old Age Assistance, Aid to the Blind, and Aid to Families with Dependent Children provided for federally assisted relief for other categories of the poor who were unable to support themselves. These programs established the principle of broad public responsibility for the poor. Since they were programs for grants to the states, state laws specified most of the operating details.

Three general characteristics of state welfare laws illustrate changing conceptions of public "charity." First, the Social Security Act authorized the states to impose residence requirements of up to a year for relief recipients, which virtually all of them did. Thus the old colonial poor law tradition of helping poor neighbors and punishing poor strangers was continued. Second, virtually all state laws included provisions for requiring contributions from relatives. State welfare was to be a supplement to that provided by those primarily responsible—the spouse, parents, children, grandparents, and grandchildren of the needy. Third, the states established their own payment limits. The executive committee that originally drafted the Social Security Act had proposed that states be required to provide a level of subsistence compatible with decency and health. Congress rejected this provision, however, and states were permitted under the act to provide as high or as low a payment level as they wished.

Residence requirements were declared unconstitutional by the Supreme Court in the 1969 case of *Shapiro* v. *Thompson*.[14] The court held that state residence requirements denied the equal protection of the laws to migrants. State discrimination against migrants was held to be impermissible because it infringed upon the right to travel, which the court had defined in 1966 as "so elementary" as to be "a necessary concomitant of the stronger Union the Constitution created." [15] Only a compelling state interest could justify infringement of a constitutional right, and the court found that no compelling interest existed. Thus *Shapiro* meant that communities could no longer distinguish between residents and recent migrants in their welfare systems.

Requirements that relatives contribute to the support of those receiving public assistance are now in a somewhat ambiguous legal situation. The Supreme Court of California, in the 1964 case of *Department of Mental Hygiene* v. *Kirchner*, held that the daughter of a mental patient was not responsible for the cost of the patient's care.[16] In reaching its decision, the court held that a California statute that stated that "the husband, wife, father, mother, or children of a mentally ill person or inebriate . . . shall be liable for his care, support and maintenance in a state institution of which he is an inmate" violated the constitutional guarantee of equal protection of the laws. The court argued that the care and control of the insane were the responsibility of the state as a whole, since it operated state institutions for the insane partly to protect the citizens of the state from actions by the insane. Equal protection, the court held, demanded that no class of citizens be singled out to bear disproportionately this state responsibility: "A statute obviously violates the equal protection clause if it selects one particular class of persons for a species of taxation and no rational basis supports such classification . . . Such a concept for the state's taking of a free man's property manifestly denies him equal protection of the laws."

The California court's interpretation of relative responsibility statutes has not been widely accepted. The U.S. Supreme Court vacated the judgment in *Kirchner* and asked the California court to determine whether its decision was based on California statute or the U.S. Constitution. When it reconsidered, the California court determined it had based its decision on the California Constitution alone and thereby precluded review by the Supreme Court. In subsequent decisions, the California court appeared to retreat from Kirchner, and distinguished cases in which relatives' duties to support were prior to state assumption of responsibility:

> In a line of decisions since Kirchner imposition of liability upon the estate of the recipient of welfare, upon the recipient's spouse, and, where the recipient was a minor, upon his parents, has been upheld as constitutional. In each of these cases, it was found that the person

upon whom liability was imposed owed a preexisting duty of support to the recipient of the public assistance. . . . Such a preexisting duty of support provides a rational ground for classification of those who must bear a disproportionate amount of the costs of the welfare program.[17]

Other state courts have also upheld relative responsibility laws. The most recent important federal welfare program, however, the Supplemental Security Income program, imposes no liability for support on relatives other than spouses.[18]

Decisions regarding the support obligations of male partners or husbands of mothers entitled to AFDC also serve to limit private responsibility. In 1968 the U.S. Supreme Court struck down state statutes that denied AFDC to women living with men they were not married to.[19] The court ruled that these substitute fathers were not legally responsibile for the support of children not their own and that it could not be assumed that the resources of the mother's male companion were made available to the children. In a later case the court ruled that even men legally married to the children's mother could not be assumed to be supporting the children.[20] Only if the mother's husband legally adopted the children could the assumption be made that he was supporting the children, and AFDC benefits be denied.

These decisions have tended to severely limit the extent to which states can require private charity from family members in place of public relief. They have also severely limited the supervision that the state can exercise over the living arrangements of welfare recipients, since residence requirements and man-in-the-house rules are unconstitutional. The states still, however, have discretion over benefit limits. The Social Security Act requires states to define a standard of need as a basis for benefit levels. They are then permitted, however, to use a variety of measures, as the Supreme Court said in an important welfare case, to "reconcile the demands of its needy citizens with the finite resources available to meet those demands." [21] The court reaffirmed the right of states to establish welfare policy responsive not only to the needs of the recipients but also to the demands of the tax-paying citizenry.

The Supplemental Security Income program, however, sets standard benefit levels for its aged recipients throughout the country. National standards for AFDC are one of the major goals of welfare reformers. If they were enacted, they would change considerably the character of welfare.[22] Taxpayers might still think of welfare as charity, but their control over it would be much less than the notion of "charity" normally suggests.

Perhaps welfare should now be seen as an investment that society makes in its young, or as a kind of social insurance. These principles too have historical precedent.

Investment in the Young

Public schools have long been an important feature of the American scene. The colonists, although they relied heavily on informal education, set up schools where children could be taught how to thwart the "olde deluder." It was not until the nineteenth century, however, that publicly supported common schools became widespread. Horace Mann's efforts in Massachusetts also affected other states, and by the time of the Civil War almost all the states had common school systems. During the late nineteenth century many states also established public secondary schools. At the same time they made attendance at their common schools compulsory.

As public education spread, the arguments offered as to why it was a good thing multiplied. The arguments almost invariably had to do with the country's need for an educated citizenry. Workers needed education to participate in the complex new industrial economy. Voters needed education to be able to choose wisely among competing candidates and parties. Immigrants needed education to become part of American life.[23] Legislators and the general public seemed to accept the idea that schooling was an important investment in the future of the country and that funds spent on schooling would pay off in future benefits.

The idea that education was a good investment not only for individual citizens but also for the society retained its popularity well into the twentieth century. During the "War on Poverty" of the 1960s education was seen as a major weapon. Reformers worked to increase the amount of money spent on public elementary and secondary education. They worked for publicly financed postsecondary programs, both in specific skills and in general education. Perhaps most important for current debates on family policy, they advocated and achieved a commitment of public funds to preschool education. The Head Start program was perhaps the most popular of the Great Society inventions. It was seen as a way of preventing some of the health problems, behavioral problems, and learning problems that barred many disadvantaged children from success in school. If these problems were solved, poverty—at least to some extent—could be nipped in the bud.

Recently, however, questions have been raised about how good an investment education actually is. A number of studies have shown that spending additional money on schools does not noticeably improve the performance of students on standardized tests or in the pursuit of economic gain.[24] Evaluation of Head Start and other preschool programs have not shown any dramatic long-term changes in students, at least by standard measurements.[25]

Many of the large studies of schooling have emphasized the importance of family background characteristics in determining both school achievement and later economic success.[26] These findings have led to the suggestion that investment in families would be the most productive form of investment in the young. A few programs to train parents in better parenting have been tried experimentally with good results.[27] The findings on the relationship between family economic status and children's achievement have also been interpreted as evidence that aiding families financially would be a sound investment in the future of their children.

Investment arguments are among the most persistent and the most popular in the history of public support for both education and families. The power of the argument, however, depends on the investment's producing the desired outcome. Poor results in education have led some to advocate more investment in families, but they have also led to considerable cynicism about large-scale investment in any social program. The investment argument may have been too overworked in the past to have much contemporary political appeal.

Social Insurance

Since the depression of the 1930s, social insurance has become the largest item in the public social services budget. The principles underlying social insurance may well become the backbone of future policy.

The Social Security Act, passed in response to severe economic deprivation, contained some provisions for simple relief, including Aid for Families with Dependent Children. The two most important programs established under the act were, however, social insurance programs: Old Age and Survivors' Insurance (Social Security) and Unemployment Compensation. Both programs were to be financed through contributions by potential beneficiaries rather than through general taxation. Employers were required to pay a tax on their payrolls into a state unemployment compensation fund, from which workers would draw benefits when they were involuntarily unemployed. Most of the tax burden probably falls on the insured workers, however, since employers seem to consider their own share as part of their total wage package. Thus Unemployment Compensation tends to spread the risks of unemployment among all workers.

Social Security is financed through a payroll tax levied in part on workers and in part on employers. The Social Security fund pays out retirement benefits to workers and survivors' benefits to spouses and children of workers who die. Both Unemployment Compensation and Social Security are, with some exceptions, compulsory, which is their most important feature. High-risk people cannot be excluded; low-risk people cannot opt out. Thus the fund receives sufficient contributions to meet payments, and the risks are spread widely enough that no one pays exhorbitant rates.

Social Security has long had a good press. Its popularity cannot be explained solely by its being billed as insurance rather than relief. Public opinion polls reveal that many people do not understand that paying Social Security tax while they are employed entitles them to Social Security benefits when they are old. A large proportion of poll respondents, especially in the early years of the program, believed that Social Security was and should be a benefit going only to those who needed it.[28] However, as more and more people have paid Social Security taxes and received benefits, the notion that Social Security is an insurance program became more widely accepted and probably contributed to the popularity of the program.

Two features of Social Security make it look like insurance or forced savings. First, the Social Security tax is explicitly identified as a payroll deduction distinct from the federal income tax. Second, Social Security benefits are based on earnings during the years Social Security taxes were paid. People who earn more during their working years and therefore pay higher Social Security taxes receive higher benefits during their retirement. These two features give Social Security the character of forced savings, in which people put away money during their working years to provide for their old age. The insurance notion comes in because people receive benefits from retirement until death, no matter how long or short a time that is. Thus what any individual person puts in is not directly related to what he or she takes out. The worker is in effect insured against a long life. Disproportionately large benefits to long-lived workers are balanced by disproportionately short benefits to workers who die earlier.[29]

But Social Security is not insurance pure and simple. If it were, the contributions of one generation would finance the retirement income of that generation; aggregate benefits to a generation of retired workers would equal the returns from the aggregate contributions of that generation during its working years. But Social Security has never worked that way. Benefits began soon after the passage of the act and were paid to a generation of workers who had made only minimal contributions. Social Security benefits to retired workers were substantially subsidized by contributions of younger workers. Benefit levels were and are set on the basis of what retired workers need to live on under changing economic conditions. Although variations in the benefits individuals receive correspond to variations in their earnings while they were working, benefit levels are not set to correspond to actuarially determined yearly returns on the worker's investment. Congress does not look only at actuarial calculations when it raises benefit levels; debates instead focus on changes·in the cost of living and changes in need.

Social Security is, therefore, an insurance scheme more in appearance than in fact. Perhaps the appearance is convincing because it could be an insurance scheme. People contribute before they collect, and benefits could be set equal to returns on contributions.

But insurance schemes need not incorporate the chronological sequence of premiums followed by benefits. Health insurance plans pay benefits regardless of how much recipients have contributed up to the time they receive benefits, as do fire, theft, casualty, and other insurance programs. These plans work, not because people are willing to be forced to save for a foreseeable time when they will need money (like their old age) but because they are willing to pay to protect themselves against unforeseeable and potentially disastrous risks. The risks are spread by the device of setting premiums high enough to finance the expected risks, which can be predicted quite accurately on an aggregate (although not on an individual) basis. These principles—forced savings and risk spreading— may be applicable to the problem of equalizing opportunity for children.

Lifetime Insurance

There are a number of periods in people's lives when they are unable to support themselves by work. Two of these periods, old age and temporary unemployment, are recognized as times when social insurance is necessary to tide people over. Another period during which people cannot support themselves is childhood; this period, too, might be sensibly covered by social insurance programs.

With American life expectancy at about seventy-five years, and with the average working life slightly over forty years (age 20 or 25 to age 65), the average person's productive contributions during working years must "finance" almost an equal number of years of dependency. Americans think as a matter of course about putting money away during working years to pay for retirement years, but they seldom think about paying for childhood's dependent years. But thinking in terms of the total lifetime would not be at all silly. Suppose payments to the Social Security system were approximately tripled, to cover twenty dependent years of childhood as well as about ten retirement years. The additional money could be thought of as paying back the money spent for childhood care. In turn, the money could be "loaned" to the next generation of children, probably in the form of tax credits to their families.[30] The loan to the child could be used to buy food, clothing, and shelter and also to pay for the care provided either by a mother or by a paid caretaker.[31]

Such a scheme would have two major advantages. First, it would help families even out their income over the life cycle. Many families now experience serious economic pressure when children arrive because either one parent must quit a paid job to care for the children or the family must pay for care by others. The "loan" to the child would, in effect, pay for this care. If the loan were calculated to reflect changes with age in the child's needs (for example, increasing food costs and decreasing care costs), and if a sensible procedure for financing college education were also developed,[32] families' income would be spread over the lifetime in a way that better reflected family needs and earnings potential.

The second big advantage of a lifetime insurance scheme would be increased equality of opportunity for children resulting from spread risks. The contributions of adults to the insurance scheme would logically be a percentage of income, calculated so that the aggregate collected would cover aggregate payments. "Loans" to children would presumably be the same amount for each child, since they could not be varied to reflect unknown potential contributions. The risk of being rich or poor as adults would be spread evenly among children. The scheme could thus have a fairly powerful effect on equalizing the resources available to children and providing all children with an environment conducive to survival and growth.

Schemes for payments to children have long been debated under the label of "children's allowances." Opponents of children's allowances worry about their tendency to encourage people to have more children; this argument becomes less pressing when the payments are thought of as loans, since each person who receives a loan and who survives to adulthood will pay it back. (There may be a cash flow problem, however. The scheme would work best when the population was stable, since at any given time the number of dependents would be less than the number of working-age people and the number of young children would be relatively small.)

A second argument is that childless people should not be asked to subsidize people who choose to have children, presumably for their own pleasure. If contributions to the scheme are thought of as paying back loans, however, this argument too becomes unreasonable. A third argument made against children's allowances is that spending public money for children would lead to public intrusion into child-rearing practices, Nixon's "collectivization." If children's allowances are thought of as either charity or investment, an argument for public supervision over the spending of the money is not unreasonable. If, however, they are thought of as insurance payments, the precedent of nonintervention established for Social Security payments to the aged would be expected to govern.

A lifetime insurance scheme also provides a sensible framework for thinking about minimum wages and minimum incomes. Critics have rightly pointed out that setting minimum wages by the device of establishing the needs of a family of four is not sensible, since most people at any given time do not live in families of four.[33] But setting minimum wages at a level to meet the needs of an adult plus "putting away" for retirement and "paying back" for childhood might be a useful way of thinking about minimum wages and incomes.

There are, of course, enormous practical difficulties in establishing a lifetime insurance scheme. Figuring out a fair way of getting it started would not be easy, since the adults who would make contributions in the beginning years would not have received benefits. Moreover, the scheme would involve the transfer of an enormous amount of money, if the payments to children were set high enough to actually affect their environments.[34] The sum is so large that the program is unlikely to even be considered a possibility for national legislation. In lieu of such a scheme, it may be more practical to think about more limited schemes. The most needy group of children are those in single-parent families, and that group should perhaps be the first priority.

Single-Parent Benefits

As Table 8–2 showed, children in single-parent families are the most economically disadvantaged group in the population. Most children in these families are living with one parent only because of the divorce or separation of their parents. Only 18 percent are living with a widowed mother or father; most of the rest presumably have two living parents. In theory, only the children of widowed parents should suffer severe economic deprivation, since only in families broken by death has the number of adults capable of earning money decreased. The children of divorce and separated parents should continue to be supported by two parents. Their standard of living should go down only to the extent that they lose the benefits of economies of scale in family living.

But these economies are not trivial. The low-income threshold for a family made up of husband, wife, and two children was set at $4,505 in 1973. The low-income threshold for that same family if the parents separated and the mother had custody would equal that for a female-headed family with two children, set at $3,556, plus that for a man living alone, set at $2,396, for a total of $5,952—about a third more than for the intact family.[35] The loss of economies of scale would in itself cause the proportion of children below the poverty level in female-headed families to be approximately double that in male-headed families.[36]

But in fact the proportion is six times greater, a much larger difference than would be expected from economies of scale alone. What accounts for the rest? Part of the answer is that couples who divorce are likely to have had lower incomes to begin with.[37] A bigger problem, however, is that the family's income is not divided according to the relative needs of the two new families. If family income were divided between the two postdivorce families according to need, the mother and children would receive at least 60 percent of the income.[38] Mothers' earnings can, and do, provide a substantial chunk of this. The father, however, usually earns the bulk of the income for the family prior to the divorce, and both fathers and courts tend to see that income as his. Virtually nobody thinks that 60 percent should be taken away, even if the children are young and the mother unable to assume support responsibilities. Most child support awards are small, if they are made at all. Also, child support is hard to collect. After a few years it often dwindles to nothing. Consequently, the mother and children usually find themselves in much worse financial shape than the father.

One national survey followed the incomes of husbands and wives who separated in the period 1967 to 1973. The women who did not remarry had an average real income drop of 29.3 percent, while the income of the men who did not remarry dropped 19.2 percent. Since the women's incomes usually had to support more people than the men's, the differences in the ratio of income to needs were more dramatic. For the women, the ratio of income to needs dropped 6.7 percent after the separation, while that of the men *rose* 30 percent.[39]

In some cases, a father's ability to support his children is stretched to the limit by remarriage and his assumption of the financial burdens of a new family. In other cases, the husband's income is simply too low to share; nothing divided by two is still nothing. Even husbands who earn the average wage—in 1974, about $9,700 for adult men—do not seem well enough off to do without a large proportion of their income. Thus the economic difficulties of female-headed families cannot really be blamed on male wickedness, either among husbands or judges. When the husband earns the money, it seems only right that he be able to keep enough to live decently—and that certainly means more than the $2,396 low-income level.

Improvements in wages and work opportunities for women will ease the problem somewhat, but they will not solve it. Child care is, after all, a job that cannot be done simultaneously with another full-time job. So to hold a job a mother must pay someone else to provide child care while she works. A woman with average earning power then ends up with far less net income than most other workers. It would appear, in short, that single-parent families need more income than they are capable of earning. They need to be able to draw on their own savings, or on public savings put aside for the use of those in the difficult situation of raising children in a one-parent family.

In Great Britain, the Finer Committee, appointed by Parliament to investigate the situation of one-parent families, found widespread poverty among such families.[40] The committee found that maintenance (alimony and child support) payments were woefully inadequate as awarded and as actually paid. In most cases, no one was really to blame for the situation. No judge can award, and no husband can pay, more money than is left after providing for the husband's own basic needs.

To remedy the situation, the Finer Committee recommended that a guaranteed maintenance allowance be paid by the state to one-parent families. The allowance would be a flat social insurance benefit, paid to all one-parent families regardless of need. The benefit would be taxable, and thus the progressive British tax system would recover much of the benefit from better-off families. The government would attempt to recover additional money from the noncustody parents. Courts would determine the amount the noncustody parent should pay, as they do now, largely on the basis of available resources. These payments would be collected by the court, but the custody parent would receive guaranteed maintenance whether or not the other spouse actually paid. The difference between what the custody parent received and what the noncustody parent paid would be financed from general taxation, in the same manner as other social insurance benefits.

A similar scheme can be imagined for the United States. Single-parent families could receive a flat benefit high enough to bring them up to the poverty level. The benefit could be financed by an increase in the Social Security tax. If the benefit itself were taxable, it could be partly recovered from families with additional income. Courts would set the amount of the maintenance awards to be paid by noncustody parents on the basis of their ability to pay. The money would be collected by the court or another agency, perhaps the Internal Revenue Service, and turned over to the social insurance scheme up to the amount of the guarantee. Support payments above the level of the allowance would go directly to the family. Well-off fathers would thus support their children to the extent they do now.

A guaranteed maintenance allowance would have numerous benefits for single-parent families. It would also, of course, raise some problems. The biggest potential problem is cost. If the average allowance payment were equal to the poverty level, and if it were given to all one-parent families with children, the cost in 1973 would have been about $18.3 billion.[41] The cost would rise over the years, as the cost of living and the number of families continue to rise.

Much of the cost is theoretically recoverable from noncustody parents. If the distribution of earnings among noncustody parents were equal to that for adult men in general, and if the number of divorced and separated fathers equaled the number of mothers, setting support payments equal to 25 percent of earnings could potentially recover 40 percent of the cost of the program.[42] For various reasons, however, much of this money is not likely to be recoverable. Divorced and separated men, on the average, earn less than married men.[43] Moreover, the number of divorced and separated men is less than the number of women. Divorced men remarry faster than divorced women. And for some reason the number of women who report themselves as separated is nearly twice the number of men,[44] implying either substantial misreporting by single women with children or substantial bigamy among men. Whichever sex is lying, it is unlikely that the men can be easily found and collected from.

Perhaps as little as a half of the money potentially recoverable from noncustody parents could actually be collected. Some additional money would be recovered by taxing the benefits themselves, but the sum collected would be small since few single-parent families would be in the higher tax brackets. The likely cost of the benefit is, therefore, large enough to give Congress and taxpayers pause.

Other considerations will probably come into play in deciding whether or not the cost is justifiable. One is the effect of the benefit itself on divorce and remarriage. If the benefit induces couples to divorce or separate, the total cost of the program will increase. The benefit will be perceived as damaging families and the social insurance concept will be seriously compromised.

Remarriage is an even more complicated issue and raises all the "man-in-the-house" problems. A benefit to single-parent families should logically stop when the family stopped having only one parent. If it did not, the cost might be tripled. It would also be unfair, since families formed by a second marriage would receive a large benefit not available to a first marriage. It is not always clear, however, when a new family is formed. The Supreme Court has ruled that AFDC payments can be stopped only if the children are formally adopted by their mother's new husband.[45] This rule would presumably discourage adoption and require payments to be made to perhaps three times as many children as were actually living in single-parent families.[46]

Stopping payments with the remarriage of the mother would seem more realistic. But then one must deal with the problem of common law marriages and cohabitation. This is a highly emotional topic, but also one of some practical import. Studies of the relationships between AFDC levels and divorce and remarriage rates suggest that while AFDC may not motivate couples to divorce, it probably does motivate them to defer remarriage. Even if none of the women who put off remarriage were living with men, deferral of remarriage might be considered an unfortunate result—perhaps not morally, but certainly in terms of increasing the cost of the program.

The problem could be at least partially solved by a consistent rule on the responsibilities of the noncustody parent. Two approaches are possible. The first would hold natural parents responsible for support payments to their children, whether or not either parent remarried, and would continue benefits until the children reached maturity. Thus, if a noncustody father with children by a previous marriage married a woman with custody of her children, he would be responsible for his own children, but not for the children he was living with. This scheme should neutralize the incentives to cohabit or remarry—there would be no particular advantages to either. A second approach would stop the single-parent benefit to custody parents who remarried and also terminate the responsibilities of noncustody parents who remarried. This approach would provide an incentive for custody parents to cohabit rather than remarry, but an incentive for noncustody parents to remarry. The approach would also neutralize incentives as long as custody and noncustody parents usually married each other, and is more sensible in many ways. Adults would be responsible for contributing to the support of the families they live with, not the families in their past. Single-parent benefits would stop when families no longer had only one parent. The sums of money being moved around would be smaller, and the likelihood of collecting from fathers larger; thus the total costs should be considerably less. This would require an alteration in support laws, but assuming sensible laws were passed, the scheme should survive a constitutional test.

The real test for single-parent benefits will come, however, in people's perceptions of how fair the system is. The Finer Committee's recommendations for assisting single-parent families in Britain focused on a guaranteed maintenance allowance incorporated into the social insurance system. Social insurance is already a more broadly conceived notion in Britain than in the United States, however, and the single-parent benefit undoubtedly seems more acceptable in that country.[47] In this country, acceptance would probably only be possible if two conditions were met: that the risk of separation, and divorce, be distributed broadly and relatively randomly throughout the population; and that the decision to separate or divorce be made, and be perceived as made, independently of the existence of the benefit. In short, divorce and separation must be thought of as insurable risks.

Divorce and separation are well on their way to being widely distributed risks in the United States. The most recent projections estimate that 30–40 percent of the marriages now being contracted will end in divorce.[48] If divorces were randomly distributed the odds are that every American would have a close family member or a close friend who was or had been divorced. Such wide incidence should sensitize people to the risk of divorce and to the attendant problems, and the problems of single-parent families should become extremely visible.

The risk of divorce and separation is not, however, distributed randomly. Low-income people are somewhat more likely to divorce and separate than better-off people. Blacks are somewhat more likely to divorce than whites, although the differences in rates seem to be accounted for by differences in income.[49] Nothing is known about separation rates, but at any given time a much larger proportion of blacks than whites report themselves as separated.[50] Moreover, the proportion of black children living in single-parent families is much higher than the proportion of white children. In March 1974, for example, 35.5 percent of black children and 10.4 percent of white children lived in families headed by their mother without their father.[51] The black-white differential in the proportion of children living in female-headed families has narrowed somewhat in recent years,[52] but the change has been very small. These high black-white differentials may have contributed to a public perception that the single-parent family is a problem of "theirs"—the poor blacks in the central cities—and not of "ours."

The racial differentials in divorce and separation rates are not likely to change until the relative income position of black families changes. What is likely to happen quite quickly, however, is that divorce, separation, and single-parent rates among the well-off will rise to levels that, while still lower than rates among the poor, are so high that the problem cannot be ignored. If 20 percent of the children of the middle and well-off classes live in a single-parent family for a period of time during their childhood, which is entirely likely, the public may be goaded into action.

Neither a social insurance benefit for single-parent families nor a more generous AFDC benefit is likely to be enacted as long as the public believes that the benefit contributes to family breakup. The present structure of AFDC does appear to provide an incentive for men to desert their families, although little evidence shows that family breakups actually occur because of financial calculations.

There are only two ways of eliminating family-breakup incentives. One is a foolproof system for allocating support responsibilities between parents and collecting a level of payment from noncustody parents which is consistent with family needs. The other is a general program of transfers to children that would ensure a level of economic decency regardless of family type. Neither would be easy, and both would be costly. Even the first would require a substantial transfer of public funds to deal with the loss of economies of scale and the low incomes of some fathers. Both would work most sensibly in a society that ensured jobs at a decent minimum wage for all, so that working-age adults would indeed be able to support themselves, their retirement, and their children.

CONCLUSIONS

—

Persistent Commitments; Persistent Dilemmas

—

THE FACTS—as opposed to the myths—about marriage, child rearing, and family ties in the United States today provide convincing evidence that family commitments are likely to persist in our society. Family ties, it seems clear, are not archaic remnants of a disappearing traditionalism, but persisting manifestations of human needs for stability, continuity, and nonconditional affection. If, indeed, this view of the persisting centrality of family commitments is correct, then the makers of public policy cannot afford to ignore them.

Persistent family commitments generate persistent tensions between important public values. With Americans continuing to live in families and to value the responsibilities and satisfactions of family life, the polity is virtually required to respect family privacy and the family's role in raising children. But other social values—sexual equality, protection of children against abuse and neglect, provision of equal opportunities to children—seem in many situations to require governmental invasion of family privacy. These invasions are not easily justified nor easily implemented in a society with strong family loyalties.

The tensions between family privacy and other values are to some extent resolvable by a public stance that emphasizes the rights of individuals and leaves family roles to be worked out privately. For example, the most workable approach to sexual equality is probably to enforce the political and economic rights of women, and to rely on families to work through the power shifts and changing division of labor that political and economic equality imply. The protection of children, a more complicated task because of children's inherent dependency, may be partially dealt with by emphasizing the individual rights of children and designing mechanisms for articulating them. Yet another kind of tension, between family privacy and equal opportunities for children, may also be resolvable within an individualist framework. "Lifetime insurance"—which would make individuals responsible not only for their old age but also for their own childhood care—is a mechanism for equalizing opportunity with minimal intrusion on family privacy. An insurance scheme to provide benefits to single-parent families would also try to reconcile aid to children and noninterference in adult lives by emphasizing the notion of marital disruption as an insurable risk.

Other policy issues can perhaps also be dealt with by focusing on individual rights and inventing mechanisms that provide maximum freedom for individuals to shape their own family patterns. Such approaches are almost certainly more sensible than attempts to force conformity to traditional family patterns. History suggests that laws that, for example, require people to live in conventional families or forbid divorce are neither particularly effective nor particularly necessary. When left to their own devices, and even in the face of some severe discouragements, Americans continue to marry, have children, create homes, and maintain family ties.

There are, of course, some persistent tensions between family society and the polity that cannot be resolved, however much good sense and good will are available. Family life is incompatible with some aspects of equality among citizens. As long as children are raised even partially by families, their opportunities can never be equal; however much resources are equalized, affection, interest, and care remain idiosyncratically centered in families.

Equal treatment is, in a strict sense, also incompatible with family ties. Equal treatment implies an ethic wherein all men and women do unto others as others do unto them; strangers and brothers are treated similarly; and people are judged by what they do rather than what they are. Family loyalty follows quite different principles, treating people on the basis of special relationships, compatibility, and affection. Family members make no pretense of treating each other equally or of treating strangers the same as themselves. Family relationships are nonmeritocratic and based on characteristics over which people have no control. For these reasons some would have us believe that they are incompatible with modern life and represent an archaic holdover that need not be taken seriously.

Reality cannot, however, be discarded so simply. Family ties and family feelings are integral to the lives of most Americans. The ethic that governs relationships between people who love and care for each other inevitably intrudes into public life, coloring people's perceptions of what they and others ought to do. Policies that ignore this ethic—that imply that public facilities can replace parental care or that the public welfare system is responsible for supporting children—will almost surely be either widely resented or essentially disregarded. Even when family service programs respond to real needs, they are often perceived as undermining the fabric of society. Until such programs are designed to incorporate the very real and very strong values that underlie family life in America, and until they are perceived as doing so, they are doomed to failure.

Delay in designing constructive programs, consistent with family values, for promoting sexual equality and providing adequate resources to ensure some measure of equal opportunity to children serves no one. The historical trend has long been toward greater equality, and it is unlikely to come to a halt now. On the other hand, the strong commitment to family institutions and values, which is such a persistent theme in American society, is no more likely to go away. It is time to accept the persisting tension between family and public values and to design creative ways of living with both.

Appendix

Percentages Ever-married and Childless, and Mean Children per Mother,
Women Born 1846–1940, by Birth Cohort

Year of Birth of Women	Data Source Census Year	Age at Survey	Total Number of Women (thousands)	Percent Ever-Married	Percent Childless Among Ever-married	Average No. of Children per Woman with Children
1846–1855	1910	55–64	2,385	92.7	8.2	5.71
1856–1865	1910	45–54	3,868	91.3	9.2	5.33
1866–1875	1910	35–44	5,500	88.4	11.1	4.55
	1940	65–74	3,173	90.4	13.2	4.35
1876–1885	1940	55–64	5,122	91.0	15.2	4.02
1886–1890	1940	50–54	3,469	91.3	15.2	3.75
1891–1895	1940	45–49	3,987	91.4	15.4	3.62
1896–1900	1940	40–44	4,271	90.2	16.2	3.30
	1950	50–54	4,077	92.3	18.6	3.32
1901–1905	1950	45–49	4,480	92.0	20.4	3.13
1906–1910	1950	40–44	5,083	91.8	20.0	2.96
	1960	50–54	4,927	92.4	20.6	2.97
1911–1915	1960	45–49	5,560	93.5	18.2	2.94
1916–1920	1960	40–44	5,898	93.9	14.1	2.99
	1970	50–54	5,735	94.3	13.8	3.02
1921–1925	1970	45–49	6,250	94.7	10.6	3.20
1926–1930	1970	40–44	6,154	94.6	8.6	3.39
1931–1935	1970	35–39	5,711	94.1	7.3	3.42
1936–1940	1970	30–34	5,852	92.6	8.3	3.06

SOURCES: Calculated from 1940 Census, *Differential Fertility 1940 and 1910*, Tables 1–16; 1950 Census, *Fertility*, Tables 1, 2 and 16; 1960 Census, *Women by Number of Children Ever Born*, Tables 1, 2, 3, 16 and 17; and 1970 Census, *Women by Number of Children Ever Born*, Table 8.

TABLE A-2

Percentage Distribution of Mothers by Children Ever Born and of Children by Family Size, Selected Cohorts Born 1846–1949

Number of Children	Mothers by Children Ever Born — Women Born					Children by Family Size — Mothers Born				
	1846–55	1876–85	1906–10	1935–39	1945–49	1846–55	1876–85	1906–10	1935–39	1945–49
1	9.2	16.8	25.5	11.7	(10.0)	1.6	4.2	8.7	3.5	(4.1)
2	11.1	19.9	28.9	26.1	(54.2)	3.9	9.9	19.5	15.7	(43.9)
3	11.3	16.6	17.8	26.5	(23.4)	5.9	12.4	18.0	23.9	(28.4)
4	11.1	12.9	10.5	16.3	(8.4)	7.8	12.8	14.0	19.6	(13.6)
5–6	19.6	16.7	9.9	14.3	(3.5)	18.9	22.9	18.0	23.7	(7.8)
7–9	22.4	11.6	5.2	} 5.2	} (0.6)	31.4	23.1	} 13.6	} 13.5	} (2.1)
10+	15.2	5.5	2.1			30.6	14.8	} 8.4		
	100.0	100.0	100.0	100.0	100.0	100.0	100.0	100.0	100.0	100.0
Mean	5.71	4.02	2.97	3.32	(2.45)	7.65	5.83	4.58	4.34	(2.93)

SOURCES: For 1846–55 and 1876–85 cohorts, 1940 Census, *Differential Fertility 1910 and 1940*; for 1906–10 cohort, 1960 Census, *Women by Number of Children Ever Born*; for 1935–39 cohort, data on children ever born in CPR, P-20, No. 277, "Fertility Expectations, 1974"; for 1945–49 cohort, birth expectations data in CPR, P-20, No. 277, "Fertility Expectations, 1974." These last data are placed in parentheses to remind the reader that they are expected distributions, not real ones.

TABLE A–3

Distribution of Population by Type of Household and Relationship to Head, for Persons Aged 14 and Under

	Male				Female			
	1940	1950	1960	1970	1940	1950	1960	1970
Total population 14 years and under	16,726	20,690	28,494	29,553	16,247	19,961	27,407	28,461
Population in private households	99.4	99.0	99.1	99.5	99.5	99.1	99.6	99.7
Relationship to head:								
Head—of family	—	—	—	—	—	—	—	—
—primary individual [a]	N/A	N/A	—	—	N/A	N/A	—	—
Wife	—	—	—	—	—	—	—	—
Child	90.6	90.2	93.5	94.5	90.4	90.2	93.8	94.4
Grandchild	5.9	6.1	3.9	3.4	5.9	6.2	3.9	3.5
Parent	—	—	—	—	—	—	—	—
Other relative	1.8	1.8	1.3	1.0	2.0	1.9	1.4	1.2
Lodger	1.1	0.7	0.4	0.5	1.1	0.8	0.4	0.5
Servant or hired hand	—	—	—	—	—	—	—	—
Population outside private households	0.6	1.0	0.9	0.5 [b]	0.5	0.9	0.4	0.3 [b]

SOURCE: 1940 Census, *Characteristics by Age*, Tables 11 and 12; 1950 Census, *Characteristics of the Population*, Tables 107 and 108; 1960 Census, *Characteristics of the Population*, Tables 181 and 182; 1970 Census, *Detailed Characteristics*, Table 204. Calculations from census data made by Susan Bartlett.

TABLE A-4

Proportion of Children, Born 1901–70, Involved in Marital Disruption and Duration of Disruption

	Children Born						
	1901–10	1911–20	1921–30	1931–40	1941–50	1951–60 [d]	Around 1970 [e]
Percentages involved in disruption before age 18							
1. By death of father	11.9	11.7	9.2	8.5	6.4	(5.4)	(9)
2. By death of mother (estimate) [a]	10.7	10.5	7.4	6.0	3.8	(3.2)	
3. By divorce	5.2	4.9	7.0	9.8	9.2	(10.5)	(18–30)
4. By long-term separation (estimate) [b]	0.7	0.6	0.9	1.4	1.5	(1.7)	(3–5)
5. By "other reasons"	0.2	0.8	0.6	0.9	2.1	(2.4)	
6. Percentage whose mother never married	0.2	1.3	1.6	1.8	1.8	1.5	(2)
7. Total, all causes	28.9	29.8	26.7	28.4	24.8	(24.7)	(32–46)
Mean duration of disruption (years) [c]	6.35	5.49	6.23	5.57	5.15	(5.2)	
Number in sample	885	2,914	5,455	6,848	11,388	14,592	

SOURCE: Reproduced from Bane, 1976, with estimates added for 1970. The table was calculated using data from the Survey of Economic Opportunity, conducted in February and March 1967.

TABLE A-5

Distribution of Population by Type of Household and Relationship to Head, for Persons Aged 15 to 19

	Male				Female			
	1940	1950	1960	1970	1940	1950	1960	1970
Total population aged 15 to 19	6,180	5,323	7,076	9,714	6,153	5,322	6,589	9,479
Population in private households	97.7	91.3	85.4	90.8	98.3	94.5	94.3	93.3
Relationship to head								
Head—of family	1.0	1.9	2.1	2.9	0.2	0.5	0.3	0.5
—primary individual [a]	N/A	N/A	0.4	0.7	N/A	N/A	0.6	0.8
Wife	—	—	—	—	7.5	10.9	11.1	8.1
Child	87.0	80.3	76.0	81.9	78.7	72.1	74.0	77.5
Grandchild	2.6	2.6	2.2	1.8	2.3	2.3	1.9	1.6
Parent	—	—	—	—	—	—	—	—
Other relative	4.1	4.2	3.1	2.2	5.6	5.9	4.6	3.1
Lodger	2.2	2.0	1.4	1.4	2.4	2.5	1.6	1.6
Servant or hired hand	0.7	0.4	0.1	—	1.6	0.4	0.2	0.1
Population outside private households	2.3	8.7	14.6	9.2	1.7	5.5	5.7	6.7

SOURCES AND NOTES: Same as Table A-3.

TABLE A-6

Women by Marital Status, 1910, 1940, and 1970
(percentages)

| | | Age of Woman | | | | |
| | | 45–49 | | 50–54 | | 55–64 | |
	Census Year	Including "Unknown" *	Excluding "Unknown"	Including "Unknown"	Excluding "Unknown"	Including "Unknown"	Excluding "Unknown"
1. Married once, husband present	1910	68.1	70.2	62.9	64.7	53.8	55.0
	1940	63.6	68.6	59.6	64.0	51.5	54.9
	1970	—	69.9	—	65.7	—	56.6
2. Married more than once, husband present	1910	9.2	9.5	9.0	9.3	7.9	8.1
	1940	9.5	10.2	9.2	9.9	8.1	8.6
	1970	—	13.4	—	13.5	—	12.6
3. Widowed and divorced	1910	16.8	17.3	22.5	23.1	33.3	34.0
	1940	15.2	16.4	20.2	21.7	30.7	32.7
Widowed	1970	—	6.2	—	10.6	—	21.7
Divorced	1970	—	5.9	—	5.8	—	5.4
4. Ever widowed or divorced (Row 2 plus Row 3)	1910	—	26.8	—	32.4	—	42.1
	1940	—	26.6	—	31.6	—	41.3
	1970	—	25.5	—	29.9	—	39.7
5. Married, husband absent	1910	2.9	3.0	2.9	3.0	2.8	2.9
	1940	4.4	4.8	4.1	4.4	3.6	3.8
	1970	—	4.6	—	4.3	—	3.8
6. Married unknown times	1910	3.0	—	2.8	—	2.2	—
	1940	7.4	—	6.9	—	6.2	—

SOURCES: 1940 Census, *Differential Fertility 1940 and 1910*, Tables 13–16; and 1970 Census, *Marital Status*, Table 1.
* The 1970 census allocated "unknown" responses prior to publication.

TABLE A-7
Percentages Living with Parents or Other Relatives, 1960 and 1970

	1960		1970	
	Male	Female	Male	Female
Age 25–34: All	13.8	9.7	11.3	8.4
Single	57.7	60.3	50.9	49.6
Married, spouse present	2.7	1.9	1.5	1.0
Separated	44.7	30.8	36.0	19.8
Other spouse absent	27.0	44.9	17.9	40.1
Widowed	34.6	21.5	21.9	14.4
Divorced	43.3	29.8	34.2	19.6
Age 35–44: All	6.7	6.2	5.5	5.0
Single	47.3	52.6	43.3	47.3
Married, spouse present	1.1	1.0	0.5	0.4
Separated	30.1	19.7	23.8	12.4
Other spouse absent	21.4	30.7	13.0	32.9
Widowed	21.8	14.5	13.0	9.3
Divorced	31.6	19.6	24.3	11.8
Age 45–64: All	5.3	8.3	3.9	6.2
Single	33.0	39.8	31.7	36.3
Married, spouse present	0.9	1.0	0.5	0.6
Separated	20.5	21.7	16.9	16.7
Other spouse absent	19.2	26.7	10.8	33.1
Widowed	17.6	20.2	11.1	13.2
Divorced	21.3	20.2	17.0	13.8

SOURCES: 1960 and 1970 Census, *Persons by Family Characteristics*, Table 2.

TABLE A-8
Percentages of People Over 65 Living in Families, 1960 and 1970

	1960		1970	
	Male	Female	Male	Female
Age 65–74	82.8	70.2	82.2	63.9
Single	30.8	45.2	31.9	40.3
Married, spouse present	100.0	100.0	100.0	100.0
Separated	25.5	49.5	21.5	42.4
Other spouse absent	35.5	40.8	37.1	40.3
Widowed	44.4	48.7	30.1	34.6
Divorced	25.2	40.7	20.1	32.4
Age 75+	74.4	61.0	71.1	50.8
Single	28.4	40.6	32.5	37.9
Married, spouse present	100.0	100.0	100.0	100.0
Separated	30.6	53.1	23.2	42.0
Other spouse absent	34.9	36.2	26.4	31.1
Widowed	51.1	54.3	36.8	39.9
Divorced	29.8	43.2	21.0	35.9

SOURCES: Same as Table A-7.

TABLE A–9

Percentages of People Over 65 Living in Homes for the Aged and Other Institutions, 1960 and 1970

	1960		1970	
	Male	Female	Male	Female
Age 65–74	2.4	2.1	2.1	2.2
Single	12.3	6.6	10.7	6.4
Married, spouse present	—	—	—	—
Separated	6.4	4.7	7.2	4.2
Other spouse absent	25.5	25.8	20.6	23.4
Widowed	4.1	2.2	5.2	2.8
Divorced	8.2	3.7	7.1	3.2
Age 75+	5.8	8.0	6.7	10.9
Single	19.4	17.0	17.1	17.1
Married, spouse present	—	—	—	—
Separated	10.6	9.0	9.8	8.6
Other spouse absent	35.9	40.4	40.3	42.6
Widowed	8.9	8.1	12.3	12.4
Divorced	11.6	9.0	11.2	8.8

SOURCES: Same as Table A–7.

TABLE A–10

Distribution of Population by Type of Household and Relationship to Head, for Persons Aged 20 to 24

	Male				Female			
	1940	1950	1960	1970	1940	1950	1960	1970
Total population aged 20 to 24	5,692	5,559	5,559	7,754	5,896	5,878	5,520	8,351
Population in private households	95.4	86.7	80.0	84.5	97.3	94.5	95.0	94.4
Relationship to head:								
Head—of family	27.0	31.3	36.4	37.5	1.7	2.3	2.4	3.9
—Primary individual [a]	N/A	N/A	2.9	6.5	N/A	N/A	2.5	5.3
Wife	—	—	—	—	40.2	52.2	60.3	52.2
Child	58.3	41.4	30.7	31.6	39.7	27.7	21.2	24.3
Grandchild	1.1	1.0	0.9	0.9	0.7	0.7	0.5	0.7
Parent	—	—	—	—	—	—	—	—
Other relative	7.4	7.3	5.1	3.1	7.3	6.9	4.7	3.4
Lodger	6.2	5.2	3.8	4.9	5.4	4.2	3.1	4.2
Servant or hired hand	1.3	0.3	0.2	0.1	2.3	0.4	0.3	0.2
Population outside private households	4.6	13.3	20.0	15.5	2.7	5.5	5.0	5.6

SOURCES AND NOTES: Same as Table A–3.

TABLE A–11
Distribution of Population by Type of Household and Relationship to Head, For Persons Aged 25 to 34

	Male				Female			
	1940	1950	1960	1970	1940	1950	1960	1970
Total population aged 25 to 34	10,521	11,468	11,301	12,169	10,818	12,174	11,649	12,678
Population in private households	96.2	94.7	95.1	97.4	98.0	97.7	98.9	99.3
Relationship to head:								
Head—of family	62.2	71.0	75.8	77.7	4.4	4.4	4.8	8.0
—Primary individual [a]	N/A	N/A	3.6	6.4	N/A	N/A	2.1	3.5
Wife	—	—	—	—	67.3	74.6	80.9	77.8
Child	20.6	13.9	10.2	9.1	15.8	11.5	7.3	6.5
Grandchild	0.2	0.1	0.1	0.3	0.2	0.1	0.1	0.2
Parent	—	—	—	—	—	—	—	—
Other relative	6.6	5.9	3.2	1.8	4.8	4.1	2.3	1.6
Lodger	5.9	3.6	2.2	2.0	4.2	2.5	1.2	1.5
Servant or hired hand	0.7	0.2	0.1	—	1.3	0.3	0.2	0.1
Population outside private households	3.8	5.3	4.9	2.6	2.0	2.3	1.1	0.7

SOURCES AND NOTES: Same as Table A–3.

TABLE A–12
Distribution of Population by Type of Household and Relationship to Head, for Persons Aged 35 to 64

	Male				Female			
	1940	1950	1960	1970	1940	1950	1960	1970
Total population aged 35 to 64	22,535	25,427	29,887	31,266	21,881	26,159	30,962	33,688
Population in private households	96.0	95.4	96.1	98.3	97.8	97.3	98.6	99.0
Relationship to head:								
Head—of family	82.3	84.6	83.7	86.3	14.5	13.8	8.0	9.3
—Primary individual [a]	N/A	N/A	4.9	6.3	N/A	N/A	7.5	8.8
Wife	—	—	—	—	68.9	70.8	74.2	74.2
Child	3.6	3.1	2.7	2.6	4.1	3.7	3.0	2.5
Grandchild	—	—	—	—	—	—	—	—
Parent	0.7	0.7	0.4	0.3	2.6	2.6	1.8	1.3
Other relative	3.9	3.6	2.6	1.6	3.8	3.7	2.8	1.8
Lodger	4.9	3.2	1.7	1.2	2.5	2.0	1.0	0.9
Servant or hired hand	0.5	0.2	0.1	—	1.3	0.7	0.4	0.2
Population outside private households	4.0	4.6	3.9	1.7	2.2	2.7	1.4	1.0

SOURCES AND NOTES: Same as Table A–3.

TABLE A–13

Distribution of Population by Type of Household and Relationship to Head, for Persons Aged 65 and Over

	Male				Female			
	1940	1950	1960	1970	1940	1950	1960	1970
Total population aged 65 and over	4,406	5,736	7,766	8,437	4,616	6,523	8,898	11,664
Population in private households	95.4	93.8	90.0	95.7	96.3	94.7	94.9	93.7
Relationship to head:								
Head—of family	75.5	75.9	66.1	71.4	32.7	31.8	10.8	8.7
—Primary individual [a]	N/A	N/A	12.0	15.4	N/A	N/A	25.4	33.6
Wife	—	—	—	—	29.7	31.0	33.7	33.1
Child	—	—	0.1	0.6	—	0.2	0.2	0.5
Grandchild	—	—	—	—	—	—	—	—
Parent	10.4	9.4	6.2	4.2	22.2	20.7	16.0	11.9
Other relative	3.9	3.9	3.1	2.3	6.9	6.9	6.2	4.2
Lodger	5.3	4.3	2.4	1.7	3.9	3.4	1.9	1.3
Servant or hired hand	0.3	0.2	0.1	0.1	0.9	0.7	0.5	0.3
Population outside private households	4.6	6.2	10.0	4.3	3.7	5.3	5.1	6.3

SOURCES AND NOTES: Same as Table A–3.

TABLE A–14

Percentage Distribution of Workers by Type of Work and Size of Firm, 1956

Employed in agriculture	8.2	
Self-employed	9.2	
Employed in nonagricultural, private firms	71.2	
Size of firm:		
0–3 employees		4.9
4–7 employees		4.7
8–19 employees		8.0
20–49 employees		8.3
50–99 employees		6.4
100–499 employees		13.6
500+ employees		17.9
not known		7.4
Government employees	11.4	

SOURCES: Ray, 1975; and *County Business Patterns, 1956*, Table IC.

TABLE A–15

Social Participation, 1959–1974: Percentages of Respondents
Who Get Together with Relatives, Neighbors, and Friends

	National Sample 1974	Detroit Area 1959	Detroit Area 1971
Relatives:			
Almost every day	9	7	6
At least once or twice a week	38	42	37
At least several times a month	57	63	57
Neighbors:			
Almost every day	7	13	12
At least once or twice a week	31	32	29
At least once a month	61	55	49
Friends who live outside neighborhood:			
Almost every day	2		
Once or twice a week	22		
At least once a month	62		
Work colleagues:			
At least once or twice a week		15	14
At least once a month		37	38
Friends who are neither neighbors nor fellow workers:			
At least once or twice a week		25	29
At least once a month		62	65
Social evening at bar or tavern:			
Almost every day	2		
At least once or twice a week	12		
At least once a month	27		

SOURCES: National survey data from NORC General *Social Survey* 1974; Question 57. Detroit area data from Duncan, et al., 1973, Table 16.

TABLE A–16

Organizational Membership, 1959–1974: Percentages of Respondents Reporting Membership in Groups

	National Sample		Detroit Area	
	1967	1974	1959	1971
Fraternal groups	15	14	14	12
Service clubs	6	9		
Veterans groups	7	9	6	5
Political clubs	8	5	3	2
Labor unions	17	16	28	27
Youth groups	7	10		
School service groups	17	18	19	20
Hobby or garden clubs	5	10		
School fraternities or sororities	3	5		
Nationality groups	2	4	6	4
Farm organizations	4	4		
Literary, art, discussion, or study groups	4	9		
Professional academic societies	7	13	7	8
Church-affiliated groups	6	42	36	18
Business or civic groups			5	7
Neighborhood clubs or community centers			8	10
Neighborhood improvement associations			12	8
Sports teams (clubs)	12	18	11	15
Card clubs, women's or men's social clubs			12	13
Charitable and welfare organizations			9	7
Other groups	7	10		

SOURCES: The 1967 national survey comes from Verba and Nie, 1972, Table 2–2, and the 1974 national survey from NORC. General Social Survey 1974, Question 99. Detroit area data from Duncan, et al., 1973, Table 17.

Notes to Appendix Tables

Table A-1

When to look at completed fertility for a cohort is difficult to establish precisely. Ideally, one wants to look at a cohort after its members have completed childbearing, but before too many have died. For the older cohorts, this is very hard to do. However, for the older cohorts the question is answered by the data; it is only available for 1910 and 1940. The 1866–75 cohort illustrates the differences that are found when the cohort is looked at thirty years apart. For the younger cohorts, the problem is not so serious, since some of them can be looked at between ages 45 and 49, probably the ideal time, and others can be compared over two censuses.

Cohorts born after 1925 were still in their reproductive years at the time of the 1970 census. However, women now normally complete their childbearing before age 40. By the time women are aged 30–34, they have had 93 percent of all the children they expect to have; and by 35–39, they have had 99 percent (CPR, P-20, No. 277, "Fertility Expectations, 1974," Table 1). Thus, even the figures for the latter two cohorts can be considered fairly accurate.

The accuracy of the figures for women above age 45 at the time of the census is affected more by mortality rates. Cohort mortality rates illustrate that the problem is not terribly serious even for women in their 50s. The following figures show the percentages of white females alive at age 20 who survived to ages 45, 50, 55, 60, and 65 (among women born 1899–1903 and 1908–1912):

Alive at:	Born 1899–1903	Born 1908–1912
45	91.2	93.9
50	89.1	92.2
55	86.3	89.7
60	82.7	86.0
65	77.6	—

(From U.S. National Center for Health Statistics, *Cohort Mortality and Survivorship*, 1972. The 1908–12 cohort had not yet reached age 65 when the tables were calculated.) These are cohort mortality figures, based on actual mortality experience, rather than the more common period mortality figures. The cohort figures are more accurate and considerably higher than period figures.

Mortality is a problem in these figures because women with more children may die earlier. Kitagawa and Hauser, 1973, report that mortality rates for women aged 45 and over are higher than normal for those with no children (1.01 times the average rates), lower for those with one (.95 of normal), two (.98), and three (.95) children, and higher for those with four (1.01), five or six (1.00), and seven or more (1.12) children. These mortality differences are not great, luckily.

Table A-2

In calculating the percentages for the 1846–55 and 1876–85 cohorts, the average number of children in the 5–6 interval was assumed to be 5.5 and in the 7–9 interval, 8. The average number in the 10+ interval was calculated as the number needed to make the mean number of children equal that in Table A–1, which was calculated by dividing total children by total mothers. For the 1846–55 cohort that number is 11.5; for 1876–85 it is 10.8. For women born 1906–10 the 1960 census gave the distribution by single numbers up to 11. The average for 12+ was calculated to be 12.7. For women born 1935–39 and 1945–49 the 5–6 interval was assumed to have a mean of 5.5. The mean for the 7+ interval was assumed to be equal to that in the data for women born 1906–10, i.e., 8.8.

Table A-3

Total population in thousands. All other data in percentages. Percentage not shown if less than 0.1; a dash in the table indicates either a percentage too small to report or an inappropriate category, e.g., "wife" for men or "parents" for children.

a A primary individual is either an individual living alone or with persons not related to him. In 1940 and 1950 the distinction between the head of a family and a primary individual was not made; all heads were heads of families. NA indicates that the breakdown was not available.

b Data was given for age categories under 5 years, 5–13 years, and 14–15 years. The figures for 14–15 years was divided by two.

Table A-4

The Survey of Economic Opportunity, conducted in February and March 1967, surveyed a representative national sample of households. The calculations reported in this table are based on 20,989 women who had borne children. Since the mothers reported dates of divorces, death of husbands and birth of children, it was possible to calculate from their reports the number of children who experienced disruptions. The age of the mother at the time of the survey must be kept in mind in interpreting the data. The 1901–10 cohort is distorted in a number of ways, deriving from the fact that children born 1901–10 were aged 57 to 66 themselves in 1967 and their mothers must have been at least 75 at the time of the survey. The estimates from this cohort are included mostly for comparative purposes.

a Since the data in the survey were collected on living women, children whose mothers had died were not represented in the sample. The estimate of the number of children affected by death of a mother was made by adjusting Row 1, death of father, for the ratio of female to male death rates for adults aged 25–64 in 1915, 1925, 1935, 1945, 1955, and 1965 (calculated from Grave and Hertzel, 1968, Table 56).

b The number of children affected by long-term separations not ending in divorce was estimated by applying to Row 3 the ratio of the proportion of women affected by long-term separation to the proportion of women affected by divorce, by birth cohort.

c Based only on data for divorce and death of father.

ᵈ All estimates for the 1951–60 cohorts are extrapolations from the data, since not all children born 1951–60 had reached age 18 by the time of the survey in 1967. I estimated the proportion of children involved in divorce by age 6 and 12 for all cohorts. Since children's age at death and divorce were roughly similar for all cohorts, I used the proportions of children involved in divorce and death by age 12 in the 1931–50 cohorts to extrapolate from available data to overall estimates for the 1951–60 cohort.

ᵉ Estimates for children born around 1970 were obtained as follows. Death rate of parents were assumed to be the same as those for children born 1951–60. Separation and annulment rates were also assumed to remain about constant, although both may possibly fall if divorce rates rise. Illegitimacy was assumed to rise slightly.

Two estimates of divorce were made. The low estimate begins with projected divorce rates for women born 1940–44 and multiplies by the average number of children per divorce. The high estimate multiplies the proportion of children affected by divorce in 1973 by 18, assuming that rates remain constant at the 1973 rate and that divorces affect children of various ages evenly. The high estimate is probably closer to being correct. Even it may be low, however, since it assumes constant rates. Divorce rates and children per divorce from U.S. National Center for Health Statistics, *Divorces*, 1973.

Table A–15

The wording of the Detroit area question was the same in both years. The national survey asked how often the respondent "spent a social evening" with relatives, neighbors, and other friends, while the Detroit area survey asked how often "do you usually get together with" relatives, neighbors, and friends. The latter wording would be expected to result in larger proportions.

Table A–16

The two national surveys used exactly the same question wording. The responses to "church-affiliated groups" suggest, however, that interviewers in the 1967 survey explained the question differently from the others. The Detroit area surveys both used the same wording, which differed from the two national surveys.

Notes

Introduction

1. Russell, 1929, p. 173.

2. This statement began an *Ithaca Journal* article (June 19, 1975) entitled "Statistics Show the U.S. Family is Falling Apart," reporting on Urie Bronfenbrenner's testimony before the U.S. Senate Subcommittee on Children and Youth during hearings on a proposed Child and Family Services Act in 1975.

3. For example, Toffler 1970; and Packard, 1972.

4. For example, Gilder, 1973 from the male supremacist position; and Oakley, 1974, from the radical feminist.

5. See, for example, Laslett, 1965; Laslett and Wall, 1972.

6. See Ariès, 1962, and Shorter, 1975, for rich and interesting descriptions of the making of the modern family. Hunt, 1970, is another classic book on French families. Lloyd de Mause, 1974, presents material challenging the notion that life was better in the old days; his interpretation may be overdone, but the data are formidable. See also Laslett, 1965, for a fascinating description of English family history, which is quite different from the history of the Continent.

Chapter One (pages 3–20)

1. Coale, 1974; McKeown and Brown, 1965; McKeown, Brown, and Record, 1972; and Rozzell, 1974.

2. Greven, 1970, found extremely low mortality rates at all ages in seventeenth-century Andover, Mass. If these rates were typical of the colonies, white Americans may never have experienced the high death rates characteristic of seventeenth-century Europe.

3. See Coale, 1974, for a summary of general demographic history.

4. As long as the number of women of reproductive age grows, reflecting birth rates before 1970 that were above replacement level, the population will continue to grow, even though each woman of reproductive age reproduces only at the replacement level. CPR, P-25 #480 "Illustrative Population Projections, 1972." (CPR references appear throughout the book. CPR refers to the Current Population Reports published by the U.S. Bureau of the Census. Several surveys are conducted each year, and the results published in a series of reports. Only the publication number [P-20, No. 277] and short title will be given in notes. Complete references are given in the Bibliography under U.S. Bureau of the Census, Current Population Reports. In the Bibliography, series [P-20, P-23, P-60] are arranged in numerical order, and publication numbers [e.g., No. 277] are arranged numerically within series.)

5. Grabill, Kiser, and Whelpton, 1973, citing Samual Blodget's table in *Economica, A Statistical Manual for the United States of America*, 1806, gives the growth rate for 1800. Other growth rates are calculated from population figures in the *Statistical Abstract*.

6. Ryder, 1975. Model age distributions for populations with different birth and death rates can be found in Coale and Demeny, 1966.

7. Keyfitz and Flieger, 1971.

8. U.S. Bureau of the Census, *Historical Statistics*, and 1970 Census, *Detailed Characteristics*. Ryder calculated that adults aged 15–64 make up 63 percent of a stable population with high death rates, 65 percent of a population with low death rates, and 51–54 percent of a population growing at 3 percent per year. The 1940 population was the oldest recorded in any census year, because of the very low birthrates of the 1930s. Later years suffer from the postwar baby boom.

9. Ariès, 1962, seems to imply this. Arthur Clarke in *Childhood's End* makes the same point in a more entertaining format.

10. The reader may wish to speculate on some data from the last forty years. Although the general trend in U.S. history has been toward a steady aging of the population, two recent fluctuations have disturbed the pattern. During the 1930s, birthrates dropped precipitously in response to the Great Depression. During the 1950s, in contrast, birthrates were unusually high. These fluctuations resulted in changing proportions of children and teenagers in the population, as follows:

Census Year	Proportion of Population Aged 0–9	Proportion of Population Aged 10–19
1930	19.6	19.2
1940	16.1	18.3
1950	19.5	14.4
1960	21.7	16.8
1970	18.3	19.7

SOURCES: For 1930–50, U.S. Bureau of the Census, *Historical Statistics*, Series A-71-85; and for 1960–70, 1970 Census, *Detailed Characteristics*, Table 189.

11. Women born 1846–55 were aged 55–64 in 1910. Data were gathered on older women as well, but older cohorts would have been subject to high mortality, perhaps differentially by class or childbearing history. See Table A–1 in the Appendix.

12. The data on which this and the following discussions are based are presented in the Appendix, Table A–1. The numbers in Table A–1 come from the decennial census. Projections recently published in the Current Population Reports (P-25, No. 613, "Illustrative Projections of First Births"), however, show somewhat lower rates of childlessness for women born around the turn of the century.

13. Infant mortality rates remained stable during the nineteenth century. Improvements in medicine seem to have been balanced by the degeneration of the environment, especially in cities. See Shorter, 1975.

14. 1970 Census, *Children Ever Born*, Table 16. Twenty-five percent of ever-married black women were childless compared to 16.7 percent of ever-married white women. (Throughout the book, citations are given of publications of the U.S. Bureau of the Census covering the 1970 Census of Population and Housing. The complete references appear in the Bibliography under U.S. Bureau of the Census, Census of Population: 1970. In the notes, references are given as 1970 Census, followed by a short title.)

15. 1970 Census, *Children Ever Born*, Table 16. Among white women 17.7 per-

cent of those born in the Northeast were childless compared to 16.7 percent in the nation.

16. 1970 Census, *Children Ever Born*. Data on age from Table 24, and on urban-rural from Table 35.

17. 1970 Census, *Women by Number of Children Ever Born*, Table 46.

18. In 1974, 8.2 percent of the married women born 1935–39, 10.0 percent of those born 1940–44, and 19.6 percent of those born 1945–49 were actually childless. Data in notes 18 to 21 come from CPR, P-20, No. 277, "Fertility Expectations 1974," and CPR, P-20, No. 288, "Fertility History 1975."

19. When 25- to 29-year-olds were surveyed in 1967, only 2.2 percent of them expected to have no children. In 1975 about 5 percent of these same women and about 5 percent of the contemporary 25- to 29-year-olds expected to remain childless.

20. Among 25- to 29-year-olds in 1975, 6.7 percent of those who attended college expected to have no children, compared with 3.9 percent of high-school graduates. In the same year, 3.6 percent of 18- to 39-year-old black wives expected to be childless, compared with 4.8 percent of white women.

21. The census surveys wives over 18; those 18 in 1974 were born in 1956. Many of these young women are not yet married and responses of the sample under 25 are probably not worth much. For the record, though, in 1974 the proportion expecting to have no children was 5.4 percent among 22- to 24-year olds, 4.8 percent among 20- and 21-year-olds, and 4.1 percent among 18- and 19-year-olds.

22. Sklar and Berkov, 1975.

23. Hastings and Robinson, 1974.

24. CPR, P-25, No. 613, "Illustrative Projections of First Births."

25. Greven, 1970; and Demos, 1970 give estimates from the colonies. Other figures are from Table A–1 in the Appendix.

26. In 1975, 18- to 24-year-old black wives expected an average of 2.5 children, down from 2.8 in 1967. White wives in that age bracket expected 2.1 children, down from 2.9 in 1967. Wives 18 to 24 who were less than high school graduates expected an average of 2.3 children, compared with 2.1 for women who had attended college. CPR, P-20, No. 288, "Fertility History 1975."

27. See Appendix, Table A–2.

28. Calculated from the distributions of children ever born to women born 1846–55, 1876–85, 1906–10, and projected 1945–49. See Appendix, Table A–2. Expected birth data is, of course, not as reliable as real data. The real data suggest that children born to women born between 1935–39 will have an average of 3.3 brothers and sisters. But many of these would have been baby-boom babies—a quite peculiar circumstance.

29. Duncan, Featherman, and Duncan, 1972; and Jencks, forthcoming.

30. Lindert, 1974.

31. Lindert used Kathryn Walker's Cornell time study data on 1,296 Syracuse families, collected in 1967–68.

32. For this part of the study Lindert used a 1963 sample of 1,087 siblings. Leibowitz, 1974, using a rather odd sample of 1,464 high-I.Q. individuals, also found significant relationships between the amount of time parents spent with children and achievement.

33. Studies on family size are reviewed in Terhune, 1974, and Clausen and Clausen, 1973. The cross-cultural material is from Whiting and Whiting, 1975, Ch. 5.

34. See Appendix, Table A–3.

35. These numbers were calculated from data on the 1967 Survey of Economic Opportunity and from divorce and death rates. See Appendix, Table A–4; and Bane, 1976.

36. Cutright, 1974.
37. CPR, P-20, No. 287, "Marital Status 1975," Table 4.
38. See Appendix, Table A–4; and Bane, 1976.
39. Studies summarized in Howrigan, 1975.
40. Mnookin, 1973, summarizes some of these studies.
41. The historical trend points in this direction, as does cross-sectional data. See Chapter Three.
42. R. Weiss, 1975.
43. Rubenstein, et al., 1972.
44. 6 hours/day times 164 days (see note 46 below) divided by 52 weeks.
45. *Statistical Abstract*, Table 183. (Another U.S. Bureau of the Census publication, listed under that auspice in the Bibliography.)
46. Ferriss, 1969.
47. Hayghe, 1975 and 1976.
48. Data cited in Emlen and Perry, 1975, from a 1970 Office of Economic Opportunity survey.
49. Survey Research Center, 1966.
50. Walker and Woods, 1976.
51. The correlation between the amount of time wives spent on family care activities and age of the youngest child was 0.6 in the Syracuse study; between time spent and number of children, 0.28. For physical care, the correlation with age of youngest child was 0.70; for non-physical care, 0.18. See Walker and Woods, 1976.
52. White and Watts, 1973.
53. The correlation of wives employment and non-physical care by all family members was −0.05 when age of youngest child was held constant. The correlation with wives' time in non-physical care was −0.21. See Walker and Woods, 1976.
54. Evidence summarized in Hoffman and Nye, 1974.
55. Glueck and Glueck, 1962.
56. Howrigan, 1973; Hoffman and Nye, 1974.
57. Mead, 1928.
58. Katz, 1976; and Modell and Hareven, 1973.
59. Katz, 1976.
60. Colonial life is well described in Greven, 1970. The historical phenomenon of boarding is discussed in Modell and Hareven, 1973. See also Glasco, 1975.
61. See Appendix, Table A–5.
62. Lazerson, 1971.
63. CPR, P-20, No. 271, "Marital Status, 1974," Table 2. I counted those who were heads of subfamilies as living with their parents and those women who were heads of families as living on their own. Primary and secondary individuals were also considered to be living on their own.

Chapter Two (pages 21–36)

1. President's Research Committee on Social Trends, 1933.
2. Sorenson, 1973; and Yankelovich, 1974.
3. Greven, 1970, p. 121; and Wells, 1972, for colonial data. For more recent data see Appendix, Table A–1. Almost 95 percent of the women born between 1921 and 1925, for example, had married by the age of 50, and the proportion is probably just as high for women born during the 1930s. Women born after 1925 had not yet reached age 50 (by 1970) and thus are not quite comparable with the cohort born 1921–25. The proportions married by age 35 or 40, however, are sufficiently high to suggest that by age 50 they will have caught up.

4. Data from CPR, P-20, No. 271, "Marital Status, 1974."

5. Demos, 1970, p. 193; Greven, 1970, pp. 206–9; Seward, 1973; and Wells, 1972.

6. Ages at first marriage from U.S. Bureau of the Census, *Historical Statistics* and *Statistical Abstract.* Proportions married from CPR, P-20, No. 271, "Marital Status, 1974."

7. See section on The Correlates of Divorce, pages 31–33.

8. Norton, 1973. The experience of the 1930–39 cohort was projected by using childbearing experience of the cohort to date and age at completion of childbearing for the older cohorts.

9. See Chapter Three for data on how long children live at home.

10. The 1971 Census Bureau survey found that the average woman had her first child 1.5 years after her marriage and her later children 2.5 years apart. Spacing patterns varied little with age. They also varied little with number of births. I have therefore assumed that these intervals were the same in the past and will persist into the future. This assumption is shaky but may not be too far wrong. Age at first marriage for the women is assumed to equal that for women in 1890 for the older cohort and that in 1970 for the younger. Age at first marriage of children is equal to the mean for men and women. For women born 1846–55 death of spouse is predicted on the basis of life expectancy at age twenty, in 1871 in England and Wales. American life table values are not available for this period, but later values are very similar to those of England and Wales. For women born 1946–55 the figure is based on expectancy of life at age 20 in 1960. Death of spouse is calculated from male life expectancy minus difference between male and female age at first marriage. Own death is calculated from female life expectancy.

11. In fact, the expectation of the life of a marriage in 1960, considering both first and later marriages, was 30.8 years. (Schoen and Nelson, 1974). Marriages that did not end in divorce (some second and third marriages) were expected to last 38.2 years. If second and third marriages lasted on the average half as long as first, then stable first marriages, according to these calculators, would be expected to last 43.9 years.

12. U.S. National Center for Health Statistics, *Divorces*, 1973.

13. Data for 1971 is from the "Quality of American Life" survey, reported in Campbell, Converse and Rodgers, 1976. I calculated 1974 figures from the National Opinion Research Council (NORC) General Social Survey tape. I defined eight life-cycle stages and cross-tabulated them by answers to the question: "Taking things all together, how would you describe your marriage? Would you say that your marriage is very happy, pretty happy, or not too happy?" The eight-cycle stages, the number of respondents in each stage, and the percentages or respondents who answered that their marriages were "very happy" are as follows:

Childless couples, no children expected	(32)	46.9
Childless couples, children expected	(68)	83.8
Small families with young children	(232)	64.7
Large families with young children	(52)	65.4
Small families with school age children	(105)	68.6
Large families with school age children	(103)	57.3
Families with teenage children	(99)	72.7
Families with all children grown	(81)	80.2

I also calculated the proportions of respondents who answered that they were "very happy" in response to the question: "Taken all together, how would you say things are these days—would you say that you are very happy, pretty happy, or not too happy?"

The proportion of married men who answered that they were very happy varied by the number of children in the household as follows: no children, 36.7 percent; one child, 34.2 percent; two children, 30.7 percent; three children, 35.6 percent. For married women, the proportions "very happy" were, with no children, 44.7 percent; one child, 34.1 percent; two children, 48.0 percent; three children, 40.8 percent. Too few respondents had more than three children living at home to warrant calculations on happiness.

14. They note, however, that this evidence, although consistent with the findings of other researchers, is not necessarily conclusive. Age effects and historical circumstances influence the results in ways that cannot be separated out without longitudinal data. Spanier, Lewis, and Cole, 1975.

15. Glenn, 1975b.

16. See Ryan, 1975, Feldberg, 1975; and Hartman, 1975. On women in Europe, see Scott and Tilly, 1975.

17. For data, see Sweet, 1973; and Hayghe, 1975.

18. Studies summarized in Hoffman and Nye, 1974. Figures given in the text were calculated from the 1973 NORC General Social Survey tape. Campbell, Converse and Rodgers, 1976, report data on a wide variety of satisfaction measures. They find very few differences between housewives and employed married women.

19. Studies summarized in Hoffman and Nye, 1974. On marital stability, see also Bane, 1975; Ross and Sawhill, 1975; and Hoffman and Holmes, 1976. Marital dissatisfaction may reflect the fact that husbands are not always crazy about their wives' working. In the 1973 General Social Survey, the proportion of husbands who responded that they were "very happy" to the general happiness question varied with the employment status of their wives, as follows: husbands of full-time working wives, 38.6 percent "very happy"; husbands of part-time working wives, 44.9 percent "very happy"; husbands of housewives, 50.0 percent "very happy."

20. H. Weiss, 1975; Jackson, 1974; and Sweet, 1973. On the use of time, see Robinson and Converse, 1972. See also Lein, et al., 1974. Walker and Woods, 1976, found the average workday of women employed full time to be 10.1 hours, compared with 9.2 hours for men.

21. Wives, whether working or not, perform the vast majority of household tasks. Walker and Woods, 1976, found that husbands of non-employed women spent an average of 1.6 hours per day on household work. The husbands of employed women also spent 1.6 hours. See also Robinson and Converse, 1972; and the review of studies in Bahr, 1974.

22. Glick and Norton, 1974; and Norton and Glick, 1976.

23. Data for 1910 and 1940 are for native-born whites and Negroes only; data for 1970 are for all races. Also, in 1910 and 1940, up to 7 percent of the women were reported as "married unknown times," a category eliminated in 1970 by allocating nonrespondents. I eliminated the "married unknown times" in calculating the percentages for 1910 and 1940. The adjustments are shown in the Appendix, Table A-6.

24. Thirty-five percent will have been divorced. Another 8–10 percent will have been widowed, assuming that death rates for midle-aged men fall little from their levels in 1970. A large proportion of both these groups will show up in the 1990 census as "married more than once." Another 4–5 percent will be separated.

25. Bane, 1975; and Stetson and Wright, 1975.

26. Rheinstein, 1972.

27. Schoen, Greenblatt, and Mielke, 1975.

28. The proportion of young marriages is the best demographic predictor of state to state differences in divorce rates. Weed, 1974. Age at first marriage is also the best predictor of the probability of an individual's divorcing, although with regard to individuals the predictive power is very low. Ross and Sawhill, 1975; and Bane, 1975.

29. Cutright, 1973, looked at the effect of timing of first birth on the probability

of becoming a female head of household, using the 1967 Survey of Economic Opportunity. He found that the risk of female headship was not very different for mothers who conceived before marriage than for mothers who conceived after marriage.

30. Effect of family income was first noticed by Goode, 1956, who expected it to have the opposite effect. Cutright, 1971, identified income, rather than socio-economic status in general, as the important variable. See also Carter and Glick, 1970; Ross and Sawhill, 1975; Bane, 1975; and Hoffman and Holmes, 1976.

31. Sawhill et. al., 1975.

32. Ross and Sawhill, 1975.

33. Honig, 1974; and Hoffman and Holmes, 1976.

34. Ross and Sawhill, 1975; Sawhill et. al., 1975; Bane, 1975; and Moles, 1976.

35. Bernstein and Meezan, 1975.

36. CPR, P-20, No. 223, "Social and Economic Variations, 1967."

37. Norton and Glick, 1976.

38. Ross and Sawhill, 1975; and Bane, 1975.

39. Bane, 1975.

40. Ross and Sawhill, 1975.

41. Bane, 1975.

42. Ross and Sawhill, 1975; and Bane, 1975. Duncan, 1976, found a less strong effect of welfare on remarriage.

43. Calculated from NORC General Social Survey, 1972 and 1973. Each sample contained about 1,500 individuals over 18. Level of well-being was established by answers to the question, "Taken all together, how would you say things are these days— would you say that you are very happy, pretty happy, or not too happy?" In 1972, 32.4 percent of the married men and 37.5 percent of the married women said they were "very happy," compared to 11.2 percent of the single men and 25.9 percent of the single women. In 1973, 30.9 percent of the married men and 45 percent of the married women said they were "very happy," compared to 16.5 percent of the single men and 25.0 percent of the single women. Glenn (1975b) reports a similar analysis, with similar results. See also Campbell, Converse, and Rodgers, 1976.

44. Bernard, 1972.

45. Kitagawa and Hauser, 1973.

46. R. Weiss, 1975, gives excellent clinical descriptions of the difficulties involved in marital separation. See also Epstein, 1974, for a personal description.

47. Le Masters, 1975, describes the marital conflicts that occur among a group of skilled workers.

Chapter Three (pages 37–49)

1. See, for example, the testimony in U.S. Senate Subcommittee on Children and Youth, 1974 and 1975.

2. Laslett and Wall, 1972. Laslett's conclusions have been challenged with regard to non-English societies, and some of his interpretations have also been challenged. See Berkner, 1975; and Shorter, 1975.

3. Laslett, 1972. About 29 percent included lodgers, and perhaps 15 percent included servants (p. 134).

4. Thomas Burch, who calculated what household sizes would be if a stem or extended family existed whenever demography permitted, observed that "populations with high fertility, relatively low mortality and moderate household size (e.g., 5 or under) are operating under an actual family system that involves considerable departure from an extended family idea." Burch, 1972, p. 96.

5. Wells, 1974.

6. Calculated by dividing the population by the number of households; data in 1970 Census, *Number of Inhabitants*.

7. Demos, 1972.

8. Blumin, 1975.

9. Pryor, 1972.

10. See also Anderson, 1972, for a fascinating discussion of the impact of industrialization on household composition in England.

11. 1970 Census, *Family Composition*.

12. Modell and Hareven, 1973; and Katz, 1976.

13. Income data from 1970 Census, *Persons by Family Characteristics*, Tables 10 and 12.

14. Morgan, 1974. See also Hill and Hill, 1976, for an analysis of the older children's decisions to leave home for all family income levels.

15. 1970 Census, *Persons by Family Characteristics*, Table 12.

16. Baerwaldt and Morgan, 1973.

17. The average divorced woman under 25 remarries after about two years. CPR, P-20, #223, "Social and Economic Variations, 1967." Therefore, half of the under-25 divorced women at a given time are in the first year of divorce. If they lived with their parents only for the first year, forty-three out of fifty or 86 percent of young divorced women would live with their parents for a period after divorce. There is no data on how long people actually live with their parents.

18. Calculated from 1970 Census, *Persons by Family Characteristics*, Table 2. The Census Bureau does not publish data on living arrangements by presence of children. I arrived at the above estimates by computing the proportion of heads of families—who almost always have children—who were heads of subfamilies.

19. CPR, P-20, No. 223, "Social and Economic Variations, 1967."

20. Life expectancies at age 65 from *Statistical Abstract*, Table 81. These are computed from period rather than cohort data and may be somewhat low. They seem high because life expectancy is usually reported as life expectancy at birth.

21. A national health survey in 1971 found that 56.3 percent of those over 65 experienced no chronic limitation of activity. The figures were not broken down into over and under 75. Sixty-five percent of those over 65 in 1970 were also over 75, so the figures are compatible with quite good health for those 65–75, and even with good health for a substantial minority of those over 75. U.S. National Center for Health Statistics, *Current Estimates*, 1973.

22. Reports on people's relationships to the heads of households do not give a completely accurate picture of actual relationships. For example, when a mother lives with an unmarried child, the family decides who to call the head. If the child is designated the head of household, then the mother becomes the parent of the head and shows up in the figures. But if the mother is designated the head, census figures conceal the fact that she is living with her child. A second example comes from two sisters living together. When this happens, one is called the head by the census and the other is called the sister of the head. Because of these reporting confusions, a better picture of the living arrangements of unmarried old people is given by looking at the proportions living in families.

23. Data from 1970 Census, *Persons by Family Characteristics*. Interestingly, forty over-75 widows are listed by the census as living in military barracks. One hopes this is a coding error.

24. Data for 1960 and 1970 are given in the Appendix, Tables A–7 to A–9. See also Bernard, 1975, on changes between 1970 and 1974.

25. The data are given in the Appendix, Tables A–10 to A–13. The tables show relationship to head of household by sex and age. The data are not broken down by

marital status and thus allow for only educated guesses about single, widowed, and divorced persons.

26. Data for women are considerably more useful in examining changes than those for men, because before 1960 primary individuals were not separated out from heads of households. Thus, for men, it is impossible to tell whether changes in the proportion that are heads of households result from more marriages or more men living on their own. Women heads of households, in contrast, are by definition not living with their husbands. The data on 20- to 24-year-olds are given for both sexes in the Appendix, Table A–10.

27. Data for both sexes in the Appendix, Table A–11.

28. See Appendix, Table A–12.

29. Percentages of over-65s calculated from the Appendix, Table A–13, by adding the proportion "parent" and the proportion "other relative" and dividing by the total number minus the number of wives. Over-75s calculated in the same way from 1940 Census, *Characteristics by Age*, and 1970 Census, *Detailed Characteristics*.

30. Anderson, 1972, on rural nineteenth-century England; Katz, 1976, on Hamilton, and Glasco, 1975, on Buffalo.

31. See figures on childlessness in the Appendix, Table A–1.

Chapter Four (pages 50–66)

1. See R. Weiss, 1973, on loneliness; also Bradburn, 1969, and Bradburn and Caplovitz, 1965.

2. See articles on Women in Politics and Domestic Groups in Rosaldo and Lamphere, 1974; also articles in Reiter, 1975.

3. Whiting and Whiting, 1975.

4. The potential has been shown by the Citizen's Action Program (CAP) in Chicago and Arkansas Community Organizations for Reform Now (ACORN) in Arkansas. See Dorfman, 1975; and Kopkind, 1975.

5. See, for example, Nisbet, 1953. For discussions of isolation and community as they affect the family, see testimony in U.S. Senate Subcommittee on Children and Youth, 1974. For a fascinating discussion of the relationship of family and community in premodern Europe, see Shorter, 1975.

6. Adams, 1968; Klatzky, 1972; and Reiss, 1962.

7. As will be shown in a later section, about 50 percent of all adult Americans seem to live in the state of their birth at any given time. The probability of two siblings living in the state of their birth is, therefore, $(0.5)(0.5) = 0.25$. Some moves away from the state of birth will have occurred while the siblings were living at home. Since most moves are short distance, there is a positive probability that adult siblings will move to the same, probably contiguous state. Also, siblings may move to be near each other.

8. Campbell, Converse, and Rodgers, 1976. Size of place correlated .24 with community satisfaction; a positive relationship held after other factors were held constant. This study also looked at the relationships between satisfaction with neighbors and neighborhoods and various objective characteristics. They found that respondents in larger cities, in racially mixed neighborhoods, and in less well kept up neighborhoods tended to be less satisfied, but that the three attributes taken together explained only 14 percent of the variance in satisfaction. Size of community explained 5 percent.

9. In 1880, 72 percent of the population lived in rural areas, according to the census definition. But only 44 percent of the employed labor force were farmers or employed on farms. Since farm families tended to be larger than urban families, the

farm population was probably proportionally larger than the farm labor force. Source: 1880 Census, Volume 1, *Population*. 1930 and 1970 data from 1970 Census, *Detailed Characteristics*, Table 189.

10. Data on mobility of sons of farmers from Blau and Duncan, 1967, p. 278.

11. 1970 Census, *Number of Inhabitants*, Table 7.

12. CPR, P-20, No. 273, "Mobility 1970–1974."

13. Verba and Nie, 1972, pp. 239–241. For an elegant analysis of the relationship between size and democracy, see Dahl and Tufte, 1973.

14. U.S. Bureau of the Census, *Census of Manufactures: 1967*.

15. Averages calculated from 1880 Census, Vol. II, *Manufactures*, and *Census of Manufactures: 1972*. Average firm size was larger in 1967 than in 1972. Compare 1967 and 1972 *Census of Manufactures*.

16. A table comparable to Table 4–2 for 1956 is found in the Appendix as Table A–14.

17. Quinn and Shepard, 1974.

18. Hill, 1974.

19. Guest, 1975.

20. The data for all SMSAs with population over 100,000 show that only about 16 percent of the work force are commuters in the standard sense of people who live in the suburbs and come into the central city to work. The rest either work outside the central city, or both live and work in the central city. In the Los Angeles/Long Beach metropolitan area, for example, 27 percent both live and work in the city of Los Angeles and 15 percent commute into Los Angeles. Of the workers who live in the smaller cities in the Los Angeles/Long Beach area, about a third work in the same city in which they live. The rest work in a city other than Los Angeles, but not the same city they live in. In the Boston area, 16 percent of the metropolitan work force both live and work in Boston. In the seven other area cities for which the Census Bureau publishes data, a quarter of the workers commute into central cities while 40 percent live and work in the same city. All data from 1970 Census, *Journey to Work*.

21. Campbell, Converse, and Rodgers, 1976. Kasarda and Janowitz, 1974, came to the opposite conclusion in a study of community feeling in Great Britain.

22. Katz, 1976.

23. Thernstrom, 1973.

24. All data from CPR, P-20, No. 273, "Mobility 1970–1974."

25. Morgan, et al, 1974.

26. 1960 and 1970 Census, *Lifetime and Recent Migration*, Table 1.

27. Katz, 1976, on Hamilton; Morgan, et al., 1974, on household heads; Parnes, et al., 1972, on older men.

28. See Appendix, Table A–15.

29. See the Appendix, Table A–16, for details.

30. *Statistical Abstract*, Table 589.

31. Some trends in organizational membership are presented in the Appendix, Table A–16.

32. Ferriss, 1971, p. 172.

33. *Statistical Abstract*, Table 781.

34. *Statistical Abstract*, Table 1009. In 1970, there were more farm coop members than farmers, which makes numbers somewhat hard to interpret.

35. Verba and Nie, 1972, p. 42, found 37 percent active among union members.

36. Verba and Nie, 1972, p. 42.

37. Ferriss, 1971, Series I-029.

38. Duncan, et al, 1972, p. 48.

39. Verba and Nie, 1972, p. 31.

40. McWilliams, 1973, provides an interesting perspective on these groups.
41. Kanter, 1972.
42. Gans, 1967; and Stack, 1974.
43. Garson, 1975; and Terkel, 1972.

Chapter Five (pages 69–74)

1. Statement of Dr. Edward Zigler before the Senate Subcommittee on Children and Youth, September 24, 1973. For other examples of testimony, see U.S. Senate Subcommittee on Children and Youth, 1974 and 1975.
2. E. Morgan, 1944, p. 133, quoting Thomas Cobbitt, *A Fruitfull and Usefull Discourse Touching the Honour due from Children to Parents and the Duty of Parents towards their Children* (London, 1656.)
3. E. Morgan, 1944, p. 145, quoting *Massachusetts Records*, I, 186, Dec. 13, 1636.
4. Farber, 1972.
5. See Foote, Levy, and Sander, 1966, ch. 2C.
6. See Foote, Levy, and Sander, 1966, ch. 7.
7. *Griswold* v. *Connecticut*, 381 U.S. 479 (1965). Justice Douglas wrote the opinion for the majority. He articulated the notion that "specific guarantees in the Bill of Rights have penumbras, formed by emanations from those guarantees that help give them life and substance." He then noted the right of association in the First Amendment, the Third Amendment's prohibition against quartering of soldiers, the Fourth Amendment's protection against search and seizure, the Fifth Amendment's self-incrimination clause, and the Ninth Amendment's vesting of rights in the people as constitutional guarantees whose "penumbras" define a zone of privacy. Several justices apparently disagreed with the "penumbra" argument, since three wrote concurring opinions articulating less esoteric arguments. Goldberg cited the Ninth Amendment, and Harlan and White the Fifth and Fourteenth Amendments' due process guarantees. The Griswold case dealt with reproduction within marriage. The court extended its protection of privacy with regard to reproduction to unmarried people in *Eisenstadt* v. *Baird*, 405 U.S. 438 (1972).
8. *Roe* v. *Wade*, 410 U.S. 113 (1973). Roe was an unmarried woman, so the case affirmed the rights of both unmarried and married women to abortion. Arguments for and against legalized abortion are, I believe, quite complicated, and I do not wish to join them here. The point is only that a right of privacy has been affirmed in the courts.
9. In *Cleveland Board of Education* v. *La Fleur*, 414 U.S. 632 (1974), the court said that having children was "one of the basic civil rights of man [sic]." On sterilization, see discussion in Davidson, Ginsburg, and Kay, 1974, pp. 381–90.
10. *Baker* v. *Nelson*, 291 Minnesota 310 (1971).
11. *Reynolds* v. *U.S.*, 98 U.S. 145 (1878).
12. *Village of Belle Terre* v. *Boraas*, 416 U.S. 1 (1974).

Chapter Six (pages 75–97)

1. The *Worcester Spy*, 1855, reprinted in Davidson, Ginsburg, and Kay, 1974, p. 174.
2. Blackstone, *Commentaries on the Laws of England*, 1765, quoted in Davidson, Ginsburg, and Kay, 1974, p. 117.
3. See discussion in Davidson, Ginsburg, and Kay, 1974, pp. 124–130.

4. For example, Paul Freund began his testimony opposing the Equal Rights Amendment with the statement: "I am in wholehearted sympathy with the efforts to remove from the statute books those vestigial laws that work an injustice to women, that are exploitative or oppressive discriminations on account of sex." Quoted in Kanowitz, 1973, p. 533.

5. See Rosaldo, "Women Culture and Society: A Theoretical Overview," in Rosaldo and Lamphere, 1974.

6. See articles in Rosaldo and Lamphere, 1974; and in Reiter, 1975, especially Draper.

7. See references in Note 16, Chapter Two.

8. Kanowitz, 1969, p. 40.

9. Eight states now have such laws. See discussion in Davidson, Ginsburg, and Kay, 1974, p. 157.

10. Davidson, Ginsburg, and Kay, 1974, pp. 158–71.

11. *Statistical Abstract*, Table 552. On women's labor force participation over the lifetime, see the article by Polachek in Lloyd, 1975; and Jaffe and Ridley, 1976.

12. Title VII of the 1964 Civil Rights Act as amended by the Equal Employment Opportunity Act of 1972.

13. The landmark case in this regard is *Griggs v. Duke Power Co.*, 401 U.S. 424 (1971). For a discussion of the current law on burden of proof in employment discrimination cases, see chs. IV and V of Cooper, Rabb, and Rubin, 1975.

14. *Weeks v. Southern Bell Telephone and Telegraph*, 408 F2d 228 (1969).

15. There are obviously a variety of complex issues involved in implementing Title VII that are not discussed here and that may make my optimism premature. But while litigation will be required for a long time, I believe the trend is clear. See ch. II of Davidson, Ginsburg, and Kay, 1974; and Cooper, Rabb, and Rubin, 1975, for excellent discussions of the issues.

16. Equal Pay Act of 1963. The Equal Employment Opportunity Act also forbids discrimination in compensation, as well as hiring and promotions.

17. *Shultz v. Wheaton Glass Co.*, 421 F2d 259 (1970); certiorare denied, 398 U.S. 905.

18. *Hodgson v. Miller Brewing Co.*, 457 F2d 221 (1972).

19. Hoffman and Nye, 1974. See also Walker and Woods, 1976.

20. Walker and Woods, 1976.

21. In 1973, for example, the wife earned about as much as or more than the husband in only 12 percent of American families. Calculated from CPR, P-60, No. 97, "Money Income in 1973," Table 39.

22. Ross and Sawhill, 1975. See discussion in Chapter Two.

23. Preston and Richards, 1975.

24. Day care is currently available disproportionally to the rich and the poor; to the rich because they can afford to pay for it and to the poor because their day care is subsidized under Title IV of the Social Security Act. Thus current day care usage is not a good basis for predicting future usage. The argument here is based only on intuitions about work incentives.

25. These ratios are written into the Federal InterAgency guidelines for child care programs.

26. The evidence is reviewed in S. White, et al., 1973.

27. The cost of day care at $2,500/year per child times an average of 1.35 children. For cost figures see Rowe and Husby, 1973. For more on day care see Roby, 1973; Center for the Study of Public Policy, 1971; and Bane, 1974. The best arguments for providing some way for mothers to get out of the house are made by Beatrice Whiting. See, for example, Whiting, 1972.

28. Suter and Miller, 1973; and Mincer and Polacheck, 1974.

29. *Phillips* v. *Martin Marietta Corp.*, 400 U.S. 542 (1971).

30. Women are generally in worse jobs than men, and both men and women in low-status, low-pay jobs quit and are absent more than men and women in better jobs. Thus, overall rates for women are higher.

31. John R. Brown dissenting in *Phillips* v. *Martin Marietta Corp.*, 411 F2d 1 (1969).

32. Equal Employment Opportunity Commission, 1972, quoted in Davidson, Ginsburg, and Kay, 1974, p. 497.

33. See discussion in Davidson, Ginsburg, and Kay, 1974, pp. 495–510.

34. See *Cleveland Board of Education* v. *La Fleur*, 414 U.S. 632 (1974).

35. *Dessenberg* v. *American Metal Forming Co.*, 6EPD P 8813, N.D. Ohio (1973).

36. The Supreme Court case was *Geduldig* v. *Aiello*, 417 U.S. 484 (1975). It was brought on Fourteenth Amendment grounds. In contrast, *Turner* v. *Department of Employment Security*, 44 Law Week 3298 (1975), was brought on due process grounds and the decision went in favor of the plaintiff. Cases may also be brought under Title VII of the 1964 Civil Rights Act. Two such cases are before the courts at the time of writing.

37. *Danielson* v. *Board of Higher Education*, 358 F Supp 22 (1972).

38. A bibliography on part-time work and flexible scheduling has been assembled by Margaret Wilkinson of the Center for the Continuing Education of Women, University of California, Berkeley.

39. *Graham* v. *Graham*, 33 F Supp 936 (1940).

40. *Murphy* v. *Murphy*, 232 Ga. 352 (1974); certiorare denied April 1975.

41. *McGuire* v. *McGuire*, 157 Neb. 226 (1953).

42. *Sillery* v. *Fagan & Fagan*, 120 N.J. Super 416 (1972).

43. See, for example, *Lefler* v. *Lefler*, 264 So 2d 112 (1972).

44. Hoffman and Holmes, 1976.

45. Brown, Emerson, Falk, and Freedman, 1971, p. 946.

46. I am parodying here the famous Shulman (1970) marriage contract, which is, I believe, rightfully derided.

47. Contracts in lieu of marriage are the subject of Weitzman, 1974. The discussion is equally applicable to marriage contracts. See also Krauskopf and Thomas, 1974.

Chapter Seven (pages 98–113)

1. Turnbull, 1972.

2. Ariès, 1962.

3. Ariès, 1962, p. 413.

4. de Mause, 1974, p. 250.

5. de Mause, 1974; and Stone, 1975.

6. Hunt, 1970.

7. See de Mause, 1974; Shorter, 1975; Stone, 1975; and Ariès, 1962.

8. Shorter, 1975.

9. Shorter, 1975.

10. Ariès, 1962; and Shorter, 1975.

11. Demos, 1970, p. 66.

12. U.S. National Center for Health Statistics, 1972. See Shorter, 1975, for European estimates.

13. E. Morgan, 1944.

14. N.Y. Statutes, Sec. 712; Quoted in Foote, Levy, and Sander, 1966, p. 421.

15. See Rothman, 1971; Platt, 1969; and the articles in Faust and Brantingham, 1974. For the third point on parental abrogation of responsibility, I am indebted to Barbara Brenzel.

16. Statute cited in a case before the Missouri Court of Appeals, *In the Interest of S.K.L.* v. *Smith*, 480 S.W. 2d 119 (1972).

17. See discussion of neglect in Paulson, 1973.

18. See Platt, 1969; Rendleman, 1971; and in general, Faust and Brantingham, 1974. For court statements, see *Commonwealth* v. *Fisher*, 213 P 48 (1905); and *People ex rel O'Connell* v. *Turner*, 55 Ill. 280 (1870).

19. See the court's statement in *In re Clark*, 210 F2nd 86 (1962); and, in general, Part III of Goldstein and Katz, 1965.

20. An excellent discussion can be found in Baskin, 1974.

21. See Ohlin, Coates, and Miller, 1974, and references cited therein. See also the opinion of the U.S. Supreme Court in *In re Gault*, 387 U.S. 1 (1967), which also cites studies of recidivism.

22. Studies described and cited in Mnookin, 1973, especially footnotes 83–90.

23. Phillips, et al., 1971.

24. *Stanley* v. *Illinois*, 405 U.S. 645 (1972). This is a case establishing the rights of unwed fathers in dependency cases, but takes notice of the procedural protection due in custody cases of other sorts.

25. Mnookin, 1973; Baskin, 1974; also Faust and Brantingham, 1974, chs. IV and V. Baskin argues that when a child is to be taken from parents on the grounds of "state interest," the judicial standards of strict scrutiny ought to apply. When the child's own welfare is to be served, Baskin argues that the state ought to be required to prove that leaving the child at home would cause "severe and irreversible damage to well being."

26. *Valent* v. *New Jersey State Board of Education*, 114 N.J. Super 63 (1971).

27. *Medeiros* v. *Kyosadi*, 52 Hawaii 436 (1970).

28. For example, *Parducci* v. *Rutland* 316 F Supp 352 (1970).

29. See, for example, *Maillous* v. *Kiley*, 323 F Supp 1387 (1971).

30. *Wisconsin* v. *Yoder*, 406 U.S. 205 (1972).

31. *Pierce* v. *Society of Sisters*, 268 U.S. 510 (1925).

32. See Chapter Two and Bane, 1975.

33. See discussion in Davidson, Ginsburg, and Kay, 1974, pp. 271–77.

34. Nine states have now established marital breakdown as the major basis for divorce, and three other states have added it to their list of grounds. Many other states interpret their divorce laws so as to have "no fault" in fact. See Davidson, Ginsburg, and Kay, 1974, pp. 222–25. As of September 1975, Massachusetts, one of the last holdouts, was about to pass a no-fault divorce law.

35. Uniform Marriage and Divorce Act, 1970. Copies are distributed by the National Conference of Commissioners on Uniform State Laws, Chicago, Illinois.

36. *Moezie* v. *Moezie*, Supreme Court of the District of Columbia, Family Division #D-3535-71 (1973).

37. Ohio and Utah.

38. See Sloan, 1974, for a compact summary of the various definitions of youth.

39. Such a petition was made in 1953 by a 14-year-old California boy who wanted to live with his grandmother instead of his mother and stepfather. The court refused his petition. (*In re Guardianship of Kenters*, 41 Cal. 2d 639 (1953).)

40. Jean Piaget is primarily responsible for formulating stages of cognitive development. A good bibliography and discussion is found in Flavell, 1963.

41. Ariès, 1962.

Chapter Eight (pages 114–137)

1. CPR, P-60, No. 102, "Characteristics of the Population Below the Poverty Level: 1974," p. 143.

2. Ibid., Appendix A. This appendix gives a detailed explanation of the poverty standard, and also gives a table of needs standards by family size and composition.

3. Margaret Wynn uses this notion, which she calls "prosperity numbers," in her book on family policy, 1972.

4. CPR, P-60, No. 98, "Characteristics of the Low-Income Population: 1973," Table 26. The proportions in poverty are as follows: all families, 8.8 percent; families with head under age 65 and no children, 4.8 percent; families with head under 45 and all children under 6, 11.0 percent; families with head under age 45, some children under 6, and some 6–17, 14.7 percent; families with head under age 45 and all children over 6, 9.6 percent; families with head aged 45–65 and children under 18 (mostly older children), 8.4 percent.

5. *Statistical Abstract*, 1975, Table 471 and 443.

6. Calculated from *Statistical Abstract*, Tables 443 and 471; Consumer Price Index from Table 666.

7. Wilson, 1975.

8. 43 Eliz., c 2 (1601) quoted in Cooper and Dodyk, 1973, p. 8.

9. 43 Eliz., c 2 S 7 (1601), quoted in Cooper and Dodyk, 1973, p. 8.

10. Rothman, 1971, p. 6. This book provides a good overview of the history of poor relief up to the nineteenth century. Piven and Cloward, 1972, provide a good general history.

11. Rothman, 1971, ch. 2.

12. See Chapter Seven.

13. Cooper and Dodyk, 1973, pp. 13–14.

14. 394 U.S. 618 (1969).

15. *U.S. v. Guest*, 383 U.S. 745 (1966).

16. 60 Cal. 2d 716 (1964).

17. *County of San Mateo v. Boss*, 3 Cal. 3d 962 (1971).

18. Subchapter XVI of the Social Security Act enacted in October 1972 to take effect January 1, 1974.

19. *King v. Smith*, 392 U.S. 309 (1968).

20. *Lewis v. Martin*, 397 U.S. 552 (1970).

21. *Dandridge v. Williams*, 397 U.S. 471 (1970). The case challenged a Maryland regulation that set an upper limit on the benefits that a family could receive. Maryland's welfare benefits were based on a standard of need that increased with family size. The maximum benefit provision, however, meant that large families received considerably less than they "needed" according to the official standard. The case was brought on the grounds that the regulation discriminated against large families, in violation of the equal protection clause of the Fourteenth Amendment. The court decided, however, that the Maryland regulation was a rational and reasonable way of keeping costs down and of keeping welfare levels below wage levels.

22. The change would not, however, necessarily improve the situation of large numbers of welfare recipients, as the debates over Nixon's proposed Family Assistance Plan illustrate. See Moynihan, 1973; and Jencks, 1974.

23. A good history of American education, properly cynical about the motives and results of education, is Tyack, 1974.

24. Coleman, et al., 1966; Jencks, et al., 1972; Averch, et al., 1972.

25. White, et al., 1973.

26. Coleman, et al., 1966; Plowden, 1967; Blau and Duncan, 1967; Jencks, et al., 1972; Jencks, forthcoming.

27. Bronfenbrenner, 1973.

28. Schiltz, 1970.

29. Another aspect of the basic regressivity of Social Security taxes. The rich, on the average, live longer than the poor.

30. The tax credit is the most straightforward form of income maintenance. The basic advantages of tax credits are their simplicity, their redistributive potential, and their fairness. Rainwater, 1973. A children's allowance tax credit would work as follows. Suppose the allowance were set at $1,000 for each child under 18, financed by a flat tax of 7 percent on all personal income. Families without children would pay 7 percent of their income in taxes for transfers to children, in addition to what they pay for other government programs. Families with children would be entitled to a credit. Suppose, for example, that a family with two children had an income of $12,000. Their federal income taxes might be 7 percent for transfer, plus perhaps 10 percent for other federal spending, for a total $2,040. Since their two children would entitle them to a credit of $2,000 they would pay only $40 in taxes. Families with three children would pay no taxes unless their income was above $17,700.

31. Sheila Tobias brought up this idea in conversation, and I am grateful to her for focusing my attention on it.

32. College education is probably most fairly paid for by loans to students, which are paid back as a percentage of adult earnings.

33. See Bell, 1975.

34. There were about 67 million children in 1973. The total cost of a $1,000 children's allowance would thus be about $67 billion. Total personal income was about $1,000 billion.

35. Numbers from Appendix A of CPR, P-60, No. 98, "Characteristics of the Low-Income Population: 1973."

36. In 1973 the ratio of the low-income level for broken families to intact families ranged from 1.5 for families with one child to 1.12 for families with five children. At a maximum, then, the proportion of children below the poverty level in female-headed families should equal the proportion below 150 percent of the poverty level in husband-wife families. In 1973, that number was 18 percent, compared with 8 percent below the poverty level itself. CPR, P-60, No. 98, "Characteristics of the Low-Income Population: 1973."

37. See Chapter Two.

38. For a family of four: $3,556 (low-income level for mother plus two children) ÷ 3,556 + 2,396 (low-income level for single man) = 0.6.

39. Hoffman and Holmes, 1976.

40. Finer, 1974.

41. Cost calculated by multiplying the low-income level for each family size by the number of female-headed families with children of that size. The number of male-headed one-parent families is small and would increase the cost only a little.

42. Calculations using the distribution of income for men over 14 from CPR, P-60, No. 97, "Money Income, 1973," Table 51. I assumed that men with earnings under $3,000 would be assessed nothing, and that the rest were assessed 25 percent of earnings. For men with incomes over $15,960, only $3,990 of their assessment would go toward recovery of the benefit cost; the rest would go to their families. I further assumed that the number of fathers involved was equal to 72 percent of the number of female-headed families with children to allow for widows. Using these assumptions, the total recoverable is $7.3 billion.

43. In 1969 mean incomes for married men living with spouses were $9,073; for

divorced men, $6,500; and for separated men, $5,724. 1970 Census, *Marital Status*, Table 7.

44. In 1974, for example, 1.8 million men and 3.0 million women reported themselves as separated. CPS, P-20, No. 271, "Marital Status 1974," Table 1.

45. *King* v. *Smith*, see note 19 above.

46. About 15 percent of children live in single-parent families at any given time. Between 35 and 50 percent are predicted to live in single-parent families at some point during their childhood. See Bane, 1976.

47. As of January 1976, Great Britain gave single parent families a flat benefit of £1.50 per week under an Interim Child Benefit for one-parent families. The government proposes to incorporate this benefit into a Comprehensive Child Benefit at some later time.

48. Ross and Sawhill, 1975; and Bane, 1975.

49. CPR, P-20, No. 271, "Marital Status, 1974," Table 1. The problem is complicated because the number at any given time reflects both rates and duration.

50. CPR, P-20, No. 271, "Marital Status, 1974," Table 4.

51. In 1967 the white rate equaled 27.9 percent of the black rate; in 1974 the white rate equaled 29.3 percent of the black rate.

Bibliography

Adams, Bert N. *Kinship in an Urban Setting.* Chicago: Markham Publishing Co., 1968.

Anderson, Michael. "Household Structure and the Industrial Revolution; Mid-Nineteenth Century Preston in Comparative Perspective." In *Household and Family in Past Time,* edited by Peter Laslett and Richard Wall, pp. 215–36. Cambridge: Cambridge University Press, 1972.

Ariès, Philippe. *Centuries of Childhood: A Social History of Family Life.* Translated by Robert Baldick. New York: Vintage Books, 1962.

Averch, Harvey A., et al. *How Effective is Schooling? A Critical Review of Research.* Santa Monica: The Rand Corporation, 1972.

Baerwaldt, Nancy A., and Morgan, James N. "Trends in Inter-Family Transfers." In *Surveys of Consumers, 1971–72.* Edited by Lewis Mandell. Ann Arbor: Institute for Social Research, University of Michigan, 1973.

Bahr, Stephen J. "Effects on Power and Division of Labor in the Family." In *Working Mothers,* edited by Lois Hoffman and F. Ivan Nye, pp. 167–85. San Francisco: Jossey-Bass, 1974.

Bane, Mary Jo. "Who Cares About Child Care?" *Working Papers* 2 (1974):33–40.

―――. "Economic Influence on Divorce and Remarriage." Mimeographed. Cambridge, Mass.: Center for the Study of Public Policy, 1975.

―――. "Marital Disruption and the Lives of Children." *Journal of Social Issues* 32 (1976): 103–17.

Baskin, Stuart J. "State Intervention into Family Affairs: Justification and Limitations." *Stanford Law Review* 26 (1974):1383–1409.

Bell, Carolyn Shaw. "Should Every Job Support A Family." *Public Interest* 40 (1975): 109–18.

Berkner, Lutz K. "The Use and Misuse of Census Data for the Historical Analysis of Family Structure." *Journal of Inter-disciplinary History* 5 (1975):721–38.

Bernard, Jessie. *The Future of Marriage.* New York: Bantam Books, 1972.

―――. "Notes on Changing Life Styles 1970–1974." *Journal of Marriage and the Family* 37 (1975):582–93.

Bernstein, Blanche, and Meezan, William. "The Impact of Welfare on Family Affairs." New York: Center for New York City Affairs, New School for Social Research, 1975.

Blau, Peter, and Duncan, Otis Dudley. *The American Occupational Structure.* New York: John Wiley & Sons, 1967.

Blumin, Stuart M. "Rip Van Winkle's Grandchildren: Family and Household in the Hudson Valley, 1800–1860." *Journal of Urban History* 1 (1975):293–315.

Bott, Elizabeth. *Family and Social Network.* New York: Free Press, 1971.

Bradburn, Norman M. *The Structure of Psychological Well-Being.* Chicago: Aldine Publishing Co., 1969.

Bradburn, Norman M., and Caplovitz, David. *Reports on Happiness.* Chicago: Aldine Publishing Co., 1965.

Bronfenbrenner, Urie. "Is Early Intervention Effective?" Mimeographed. Ithaca: Cornell University, 1973.

Brown, Barbara A.; Emerson, Thomas; Falk, Gail; and Freedman, Ann E. "The Equal

Rights Amendment: A Constitutional Basis for Equal Rights for Women." *Yale Law Journal* 80 (1971):871.

Burch, Thomas K. "Some Demographic Determinants of Average Household Size: An Analytic Approach." In *Household and Family in Past Time*, edited by Peter Laslett and Richard Wall, pp. 91–102. Cambridge: Cambridge University Press, 1972.

Campbell, Angus; Converse, Philip E.; and Rodgers, Willard L. *The Quality of American Life*. New York: Russell Sage Foundation, 1976.

Carter, Hugh, and Glick, Paul C. *Marriage and Divorce: A Social and Economic Study*. Cambridge, Mass.: Harvard University Press, 1970.

Center for the Study of Public Policy. *An Impact Study of Day Care*. Report to U.S. Office of Economic Opportunity. Cambridge, Mass.: Center for the Study of Public Policy, 1971.

Clausen, John A., and Clausen, Suzanne R. "The Effects of Family Size on Parents and Children." In *Psychological Perspectives on Population*, edited by James T. Fawcett. New York: Basic Books, 1973.

Coale, Ansley J. "The History of the Human Population." *Scientific American*, 231 (September 1974):30–39.

Coale, Ansley J., and Demeny, Paul. *Regional Model Life Tables and Stable Populations*. Princeton, N.J.: Princeton University Press, 1966.

Coleman, James S., et al. *Equality of Educational Opportunity*. Washington D.C.: U.S. Government Printing Office, 1966.

Coleman, James S. *Power and the Structure of Society*. New York: W. W. Norton Co., 1974.

Cooper, George, and Dodyk, Paul M. *Cases and Materials on Income Maintenance*. St. Paul, Minn.: West Publishing Co., 1973.

Cooper, George; Rabb, Harriet; and Rubin, Howard J. *Fair Employment Litigation*. St. Paul, Minn.: West Publishing Co., 1975.

Cutright, Phillips. "Income and Family Events: Marital Stability." *Journal of Marriage and the Family* 33 (1971):291–306.

———. "Timing the First Birth: Does It Matter?" *Journal of Marriage and the Family* 35 (1973):585–96.

———. "Components of Change in the Number of Female Family Heads Aged 15–44: United States 1940–1970." *Journal of Marriage and the Family* 36 (1974): 714–21.

Dahl, Robert A. and Tufte, Edward R. *Size and Democracy*. Stanford, Calif.: Stanford University Press, 1973.

Davidson, Kenneth M.; Ginsburg, Ruth B.; and Kay, Herma H. *Sex Based Discrimination: Text, Cases and Materials*. St. Paul, Minn.: West Publishing Co., 1974.

de Mause, Lloyd, ed. *The History of Childhood*. New York: The Psychohistory Press, 1974.

Demos, John. *A Little Commonwealth: Family Life in Plymouth Colony*. New York: Oxford University Press, 1970.

———. "Demography and Psychology in the Historical Study of Family-Life: A Personal Report." In *Household and Family in Past Time*, edited by Peter Laslett and Richard Wall, pp. 561–570. Cambridge: Cambridge University Press, 1972.

Dorfman, Ron. "Greenlining Chicago: The Citizen's Action Program." *Working Papers* 3 (1975):32.

Draper, Patricia. "Kung Women: Contrasts in Sexual Egalitarianism in Foraging and Sedentary Contexts." In *Toward an Anthropology of Women*, edited by Rayna R. Reiter. New York: Monthly Review Press, 1975.

Duncan, Greg J. "Unmarried Heads of Households and Marriage." In *Five Thousand*

American Families, vol. 4, edited by Greg J. Duncan and James N. Morgan, pp. 77–116. Ann Arbor: Institute for Social Research, University of Michigan, 1976.

Duncan, Greg J., and Morgan, James N. *Five Thousand American Families—Patterns of Economic Progress*, vol. 3. Ann Arbor: Institute for Social Research, University of Michigan, 1975.

Duncan, Otis Dudley; Featherman, David; and Duncan, Beverly. *Socio-economic Background and Achievement*. New York: Seminar Press, 1972.

Duncan, Otis Dudley; Schuman, Howard; and Duncan, Beverly. *Social Change in a Metropolitan Community*. New York: Russell Sage Foundation, 1973.

Durbin, Elizabeth. "Work and Welfare: The Case of Aid to Families with Dependent Children." *Journal of Human Resources* 8, Supplement (1973):103–25.

Emlen, Arthur C., and Perry, Joseph B. "Child-Care Arrangements." In *Working Mothers*, edited by Lois Hoffman and F. Ivan Nye, pp. 101–25. San Francisco: Jossey-Bass, 1975.

Epstein, Joseph. *Divorced in America*. New York: E. P. Dutton & Co., 1974.

Farber, Bernard. *Guardians of Virtue*. New York: Basic Books, 1972.

Faust, Frederic L., and Brantingham, Paul J. *Juvenile Justice Philosophy: Readings, Cases and Comments*. St. Paul, Minn.: West Publishing Co., 1974.

Feldberg, Roslyn. "Women's Work: Changing Patterns of Women's Activity in Paid and Unpaid Work." Paper prepared for Center on Research on Women in Higher Education and the Professions, Wellesley College, 1975.

Ferriss, Abbott L. *Indicators of Trends in American Education*. New York: Russell Sage Foundation, 1969.

———. *Indicators of Trends in the Status of American Women*. New York: Russell Sage Foundation, 1971.

Finer, Sir Morris, chairman. *Report of the Committee on One-Parent Families*. London: Her Majesty's Stationary Office, 1974.

Flavell, John H. *The Developmental Psychology of Jean Piaget*. New York: Van Nostrand Reinhold Co., 1963.

Foote, Caleb; Levy, Robert J.; and Sander, Frank E. A. *Cases and Materials on Family Law*. Boston: Little Brown & Co., 1966.

Gans, Herbert. *The Levittowners*. New York: Pantheon Books, 1967.

Garson, Barbara. *All the Livelong Day*. New York: Doubleday & Co., 1975

Gilder, George F. *Sexual Suicide*. New York: Quadrangle Books, 1973.

Glasco, Laurence A. "The Life Cycles and Household Structure of American Ethnic Groups: Irish, Germans and Native-born Whites in Buffalo, New York, 1855." *Journal of Urban History* 1 (1975):339–64.

Glenn, Norval D. "The Contribution of Marriage to the Psychological Well-Being of Males and Females." *Journal of Marriage and the Family* 37 (1975):594–99.

———. "Psychological Well-Being in the Postparental Stage: Some Evidence from National Surveys." *Journal of Marriage and the Family* 37 (1975): 105–12.

Glick, Paul C., and Norton, Arthur J. "Perspectives on the Recent Upturn in Divorce and Remarriage." *Demography* 10 (1974):301–14.

Glueck, Sheldon, and Glueck, Eleanor. *Family Environment and Delinquency*. Boston: Houghton Mifflin Co., 1962.

Goldstein, Joseph, and Katz, Jay. *The Family and the Law*. New York: Free Press, 1965.

Goode, William J. *Women in Divorce*. New York: Free Press, 1956.

Grabill, Wilson H.; Kiser, Clyde V.; and Whelpton, Pascal K. "A Long View." In *The American Family in Social Historical Perspective*, edited by Michael Gordon. New York: St. Martin's Press, 1973.

Grave, Robert D., and Hetzel, Alice M. *Vital Statistics Rates in the United States*

1940–1960. U.S. Department of Health, Education and Welfare, Public Health Service, National Center for Health Statistics, 1968.

Greven, Philip J., Jr. *Four Generations: Population, Land and Family in Colonial Andover, Massachusetts.* Ithaca: Cornell University Press, 1970.

Guest, Avery M. "Journey to Work 1960–70." *Social Forces* 54 (1975):220–25.

Hartmann, Heidi. "Historical Perspectives on Job Segregation by Sex or the Fruits of Patriarchy." Paper prepared for Conference on Occupational Segregation, Wellesley College, May 1975.

Hastings, Donald W., and Robinson, J. Gregory. "Incidence of Childlessness for United States Women Cohorts Born 1891–1945." *Social Biology* 21 (1974): 178–84.

Hayghe, Howard. "Marital and Family Characteristics of Workers, March, 1974." *Monthly Labor Review* 98 (1975):60–64.

———. "Families and the Rise of Working Wives—an Overview." *Monthly Labor Review* 99 (1976):12–19.

Hill, Daniel, and Hill, Martha. "Older Children and Splitting Off." In *Five Thousand American Families,* vol. 4, edited by Greg J. Duncan and James N. Morgan, pp. 117–154. Ann Arbor: Institute for Social Research, University of Michigan, 1976.

Hill, Martha. "Modes of Travel to Work." In *Five Thousand American Families,* vol. 2, edited by James Morgan, et al., pp. 107–20. Ann Arbor: Survey Research Center, University of Michigan, 1974.

Hoffman, Lois Wladis, and Nye, F. Ivan. *Working Mothers.* San Francisco: Jossey-Bass, 1974.

Hoffman, Saul, and Holmes, John. "Husbands, Wives and Divorce." In *Five Thousand American Families,* vol. 4, edited by Greg J. Duncan and James N. Morgan, pp. 23–76. Ann Arbor: Institute for Social Research, University of Michigan, 1976.

Honig, Marjorie. "AFDC Income, Recipient Rates and Family Dissolution." *Journal of Human Resources* 9 (1974):303–22.

Howrigan, Gail. "The Effects of Working Mothers on Children." Reprint. Cambridge, Mass.: Center for the Study of Public Policy, 1973.

———. "The Effects of Divorce and Separation on Children." Reprint. Cambridge, Mass.: Center for the Study of Public Policy, 1975.

Hunt, David. *Parents and Children in History.* New York: Basic Books, 1970.

Jackson, Gregory. "Models of Mothers' Labor Force Participation: Consideration of 1970 Data." Special Qualifying Paper, Harvard Graduate School of Education, 1974.

Jaffe, A. J., and Ridley, Jeanne Clare. "The Extent of Lifetime Employment of Women in the United States." *Industrial Gerontology* Winter (1976):25–36.

Jencks, Christopher, et al. *Inequality: A Reassessment of the Effect of Family and Schooling in America.* New York: Basic Books, 1972.

Jencks, Christopher. "The Poverty of Welfare." *Working Papers* 4 (1975):5.

———, ed. *Who Gets Ahead?* New York: Basic Books, forthcoming.

Kanowitz, Leo. *Women and the Law.* Albuquerque: University of New Mexico Press, 1969.

———. *Sex Roles in Law and Society.* Albuquerque: University of New Mexico Press, 1973.

Kanter, Rosabeth. *Commitment and Community.* Cambridge, Mass.: Harvard University Press, 1972.

Kasarda, John D., and Janowitz, Morris. "Community Attachment in Mass Society." *American Sociological Review* 39 (1974):328–39.

Katz, Michael J. *The People of Hamilton, Canada West.* Cambridge, Mass.: Harvard University Press, 1976.

Keeley, Michael C. "A Comment on 'An Interpretation of the Economic Theory of Fertility.'" *Journal of Economic Literature* 13 (1975):461–86.
Keyfitz, Nathan, and Flieger, Wilhelm. *Population: Facts and Methods of Demography.* San Francisco: W. H. Freeman, 1971.
Kitagawa, Evelyn M., and Hauser, Philip M. *Differential Mortality in the United States.* Cambridge, Mass.: Harvard University Press, 1973.
Klatzky, Sheila R. *Patterns of Contact with Relatives.* Washington, D.C.: American Sociological Association, 1972.
Komarovsky, Mirra. *Blue-Collar Marriage.* New York: Random House, 1962.
Kopkind, Andrew. "ACORN Calling: Door to Door Organizing in Arkansas." *Working Papers* 3 (1975):13.
Krauskopf, Joan M., and Thomas, Rhonda C. "Partnership Marriage: The Solution to an Ineffective and Inequitable Law of Support." *Ohio State Law Journal* 35 (1974):558.
Laslett, Peter. *The World We Have Lost.* New York: Charles Scribner's Sons, 1965.
———. "Mean Household Size Since the Sixteenth Century." In *Household and Family in Past Time,* edited by Peter Laslett and Richard Wall, pp. 125–58. Cambridge: Cambridge University Press, 1972.
Laslett, Peter, and Wall, Richard. *Household and Family in Past Time.* Cambridge: Cambridge University Press, 1972.
Lazerson, Marvin. *Origins of the Urban School: Public Education in Massachusetts, 1870–1915.* Cambridge, Mass.: Harvard University Press, 1971.
Leibenstein, Harvey. "An Interpretation of the Economic Theory of Fertility: Promising Path or Blind Alley?" *Journal of Economic Literature* 12 (1974):457–79.
Leibowitz, Arleen. "Home Investments in Children." *Journal of Political Economy* 82 (1974):S111–31.
Lein, Laura, et al. "Work and Family Life." Final report to the National Institute of Education, Project No. 3–3094, 1974.
Le Masters, E. E. *Blue-Collar Aristocrats.* Madison: University of Wisconsin Press, 1975.
Lindert, Peter A. "Family Inputs and Inequality Among Children." Discussion paper. Madison: Institute for Research on Poverty, University of Wisconsin, 1974.
Lloyd, Cynthia B., ed. *Sex, Discrimination and the Division of Labor.* New York: Columbia University Press, 1975.
McKeown, Thomas, and Brown, R. G. "Medical Evidence Related to English Population Changes in the Eighteenth Century." In *Population in History,* edited by D. V. Glass and D. E. C. Eversley. Chicago: Aldine Publishing Co., 1965.
McKeown. T.; Brown, R. G.; and Record, R. C. "An Interpretation of the Modern Rise of Population in Europe." *Population Studies* 26 (1972):345.
McWilliams, Wilson Carey. *The Idea of Fraternity in America.* Berkeley: University of California Press, 1973.
Mead, Margaret. *Coming of Age in Samoa.* New York: William Morrow & Co., 1928.
Mincer, Jacob, and Polachek, Solomon. "Family Investments in Human Capital: Earnings of Women." *Journal of Political Economy* 82 (1974):S76–108.
Mnookin, Robert H. "Foster Care—In Whose Best Interest?" *Harvard Educational Review* 43 (1973):599–638.
Modell, John, and Hareven, Tamara K. "Urbanization and the Malleable Household: An Examination of Boarding and Lodging in American Families." *Journal of Marriage and the Family* 35 (1973):467–79.
Moles, Oliver C. "Marital Dissolution and Public Assistance: Variations Among American States." *Journal of Social Issues* 32 (1976): 87–101.
Mondale, Walter. "Anticipating the Needs of Families and Children." *Journal of Current Social Issues* 12 (1975):20–23.

Morgan, Edmund S. *The Puritan Family.* New York: Harper and Row, 1944.

Morgan, James N. "Family Composition." In *Five Thousand American Families,* vol. 1, edited by James N. Morgan, et al. Ann Arbor: Institute for Social Research, University of Michigan, 1974.

Morgan, James N., et al. *Five Thousand American Families—Patterns of Economic Progress,* vols. 1 and 2. Ann Arbor: Institute for Social Research, University of Michigan, 1974.

Moynihan, Daniel P. *The Politics of a Guaranteed Income.* New York: Random House, 1973.

Nisbet, Robert A. *The Quest for Community.* New York: Oxford University Press, 1953.

Norton, Arthur J. "The Family Life Cycle Updated: Components and Uses." Paper presented at the annual meeting of the Population Association of America, New Orleans, La., 1973.

Norton, Arthur J., and Glick, Paul C. "Marital Instability: Past, Present and Future." *Journal of Social Issues* 32 (1976): 5–20.

Oakley, Ann. *Women's-Work.* New York: Pantheon Books, 1974.

Ohlin, Lloyd E.; Coates, Robert B.; and Miller, Alden D. "Radical Correctional Reform." *Harvard Educational Review* 44 (1974):74–111.

Packard, Vance. *A Nation of Strangers.* New York: David McKay Co., 1972.

Parnes, Herbert S.; Nestil, Gilbert; and Andrisiani, Paul. *The Pre-retirement Years: A Longitudinal Study of the Labor Market Experience of Men,* Vol. III. Columbus, Ohio: Center for Human Resource Research, Ohio State University, 1972.

Paulsen, Monrad G. *Cases and Selected Problems in Family Law and Poverty.* St. Paul. West Publishing Co., 1973.

Phillips, Michael H., et al. *Factors Associated with Placement Decisions in Child Welfare.* New York: Child Welfare League of America, 1971.

Piven, Frances Fox, and Cloward, Richard. *Regulating the Poor.* New York: Vintage Books, 1972.

Platt, Anthony M. *The Child Savers.* Chicago: University of Chicago Press, 1969.

Plowden, Lady Bridget, et al. *Children and Their Primary Schools.* London: Central Advisory Council for Education, Her Majesty's Stationary Office, 1967.

President's Research Committee on Social Trends. *Recent Social Trends in the United States.* New York: McGraw-Hill Book Co., 1933.

Preston, Samuel H.; Keyfitz, Nathan; and Schoen, Robert. *Causes of Death: Life Tables for National Populations.* New York: Seminar Press, 1972.

Preston, Samuel H., and Richards, Alan Thomas. "The Influence of Women's Work Opportunities on Marriage Rates." *Demography* 12 (1975):209 22.

Pryor, Edward T., Jr. "Rhode Island Family Structure: 1875 and 1960." In *Household and Family in Past Time,* edited by Peter Laslett and Richard Wall, pp. 571–89. Cambridge: Cambridge University Press, 1972.

Quinn, Robert P., and Shepard, Linda J. *The 1972–73 Quality of Employment Survey.* Ann Arbor: Institute for Social Research, University of Michigan, 1974.

Rainwater, Lee. "Economic Inequality and the Credit Income Tax." *Working Papers* 1 (1973):50.

Ray, Robert N. "A Report on Self-employed Americans in 1973." *Monthly Labor Review* 98 (1975):49–54.

Reiss, Paul J. "The Extended Kinship System: Correlates of and Attitudes on Frequency of Interaction." *Marriage and Family Living* 24 (November 1962):332–39.

Reiter, Rayna R. *Toward an Anthropology of Women.* New York: Monthly Review Press, 1975.

Rendleman, Douglas R. "Parens Patriae: From Chancery to the Juvenile Court." *South Carolina Law Review* 23 (1971):205. Reprinted in Faust and Brantingham.

Rheinstein, Max. *Marriage Stability, Divorce and the Law*. Chicago: University of Chicago Press, 1972.

Robinson, John P., and Converse, Philip E. "Social Change Reflected in the Use of Time." In *The Human Meaning of Social Change*, edited by Angus Campbell and Philip E. Converse. New York: Russell Sage Foundation, 1972.

Roby, Pamela, ed. *Child Care—Who Cares?* New York: Basic Books, 1973.

Rosaldo, Michelle Zimbalist, and Lamphere, Louise, eds. *Woman, Culture and Society*. Stanford, Calif.: Stanford University Press, 1974.

Ross, Heather L., and Sawhill, Isabel V. *Time of Transition: The Growth of Families Headed by Women*. Washington, D.C.: The Urban Institute, 1975.

Rothman, David J. *The Discovery of the Asylum*. Boston: Little Brown & Co., 1971.

Rowe, Mary Potter, and Husby, Ralph D. "Economics of Child Care: Costs, Needs and Issues." In *Child Care—Who Cares?*, edited by Pamela Roby. New York: Basic Books, 1973.

Rozzell, P. E. "An Interpretation of the Modern Rise of Population in Europe—A Critique." *Population Studies* 26 (1974):5–18.

Rubinstein, Eli A.; Comstock, George A.; and Murray, John P., eds. *Television and Social Behavior*. Report to the Surgeon General's Scientific Advisory Committee on Television and Social Behavior, U.S. Department of Health, Education and Welfare, 1972.

Russell, Bertrand. *Marriage and Morals*. New York: Horace Liveright Co., 1929.

Ryan, Mary P. *Womanhood in America*. New York: New Viewpoints, 1975.

Ryder, Norman B. "Notes on Stationary Populations." *Population Index* 41 (1975): 3–28.

Sawhill, Isabel V.; Peabody, Gerald E.; Jones, Carol A.; and Caldwell, Steven B. *Income Transfers and Family Structure*. Washington: The Urban Institute, 1975.

Schiltz, Michael E. *Public Attitudes Toward Social Security 1935–1965*. U.S. Department of Health, Education and Welfare, Social Security Administration, Research Report No. 33, 1970.

Schoen, Robert; Greenblatt, Harry N.; and Mielke, Robert B. "California's Experience with Non-Adversary Divorce." *Demography* 12 (1975):223–44.

Schoen, Robert, and Nelson, Verne E. "Marriage, Divorce and Mortality: A Life Table Analysis." *Demography* 11 (1974):267–90.

Schultz, Theodore W., ed. *Economics of the Family: Marriage, Children and Human Capital*. Chicago: University of Chicago Press, 1975.

Scott, Joan, and Tilly, Louise. "Women's Work and the Family in Nineteenth Century Europe." In *The Family in History*, edited by Charles E. Rosenberg. Philadelphia: University of Pennsylvania Press, 1975.

Seward, Rudy Roy. "The Colonial Family in America: Toward a Socio-Historical Restoration of Its Structure." *Journal of Marriage and the Family* 35 (1973): 58–70.

Shorter, Edward. *The Making of the Modern Family*. New York: Basic Books, 1975.

Shulman, Alix. "A Marriage Agreement." *Up from Under* 1 (1970):5–8.

Sklar, Jane, and Berkow, Beth. "The American Birth Rate: Evidences of a Coming Rise." *Science* 189 (1975):693–700.

Sloan, Irving J. *Youth and the Law: Rights, Privileges and Obligations*. 2d ed. Dobbs Ferry, N.Y.: Oceana Publications, 1974.

Sorenson, Robert. *Adolescent Sexuality in Contemporary America*. New York: World Publishing Co., 1973.

Spanier, Graham B.; Lewis, Robert A.; and Cole, Charles L. "Marital Adjustment Over the Family Life Cycle: The Issue of Curvilinearity." *Journal of Marriage and the Family* 37 (1975):263–76.

Stack, Carol. *All Our Kin*. New York: Harper and Row, 1974.

Stetson, Dorothy M., and Wright, Gerald C. "The Effects of Laws on Divorce in American States." *Journal of Marriage and the Family* 37 (1975):537–47.

Stone, Lawrence. "The Rise of the Nuclear Family in Early Modern Europe." In *The Family in History*, edited by Charles E. Rosenberg. Philadelphia: University of Pennsylvania Press, 1975.

Survey Research Center. "Summary of United States Time Use Summary." Mimeographed. Ann Arbor: Survey Research Center, University of Michigan, 1966.

Suter, Larry E., and Miller, Herman P. "Income Differences Between Men and Career Women." In *Changing Woman in a Changing Society* edited by Joan Huber, pp. 200–212. Chicago: University of Chicago Press, 1973.

Sweet, James A. *Women in the Labor Force*. New York: Seminar Press, 1973.

Terhune, Kenneth H. *A Review of the Actual and Expected Consequences of Family Size*. U.S. Department of Health, Education and Welfare, National Institutes of Health, Publication No. (NIH) 75–779. Washington, D.C.: U.S. Government Printing Office, 1974.

Terkel, Studs. *Working*. New York: Pantheon Books, 1972.

Thernstrom, Stephan. *The Other Bostonians*. Cambridge, Mass.: Harvard University Press, 1973.

Toffler, Alvin. *Future Shock*. New York: Random House, 1970.

Turnbull, Colin M. *The Mountain People*. New York: Simon & Schuster, 1972.

Tyack, David. *The One Best System*. Cambridge, Mass.: Harvard University Press, 1974.

U.S. Bureau of the Census. *Census of Manufactures: 1967*. Vol. II, Industry Statistics. Washington, D.C.: U.S. Government Printing Office, 1971.

U.S. Bureau of the Census. *Census of Manufactures: 1972*. Washington, D.C.: U.S. Government Printing Office, 1975.

U.S. Bureau of the Census. *Census of Population: 1880*, Vol. I, *Population*. Washington, D.C.: U.S. Government Printing Office, 1883.

U.S. Bureau of the Census. *Census of Population: 1880*, Vol. II, *Manufactures*. Washington, D.C.: U.S. Government Printing Office, 1883.

U.S. Bureau of the Census. *Census of Population: 1940, Characteristics by Age*, Vol. IV, Part 1, U.S. Summary. Washington, D.C.: U.S. Government Printing Office, 1943.

U.S. Bureau of the Census. *Census of Population: 1940, Differential Fertility 1940 and 1910: Women by Number of Children Ever Born*. Washington, D.C.: U.S. Government Printing Office, 1945.

U.S. Bureau of the Census. *Census of Population: 1950, Characteristics of the Population*, Vol. II, Part 1, U.S. Summary. Washington, D.C.: U.S. Government Printing Office, 1953.

U.S. Bureau of the Census. *Census of Population: 1950, Fertility*, Final Report P-E, No. 5C. Washington, D.C.: U.S. Government Printing Office, 1955.

U.S. Bureau of the Census. *Census of Population: 1960, Characteristics of the Population*, Vol. II, Part 1, U.S. Summary. Washington, D.C.: U.S. Government Printing Office, 1964.

U.S. Bureau of the Census. *Census of Population: 1960, Lifetime and Recent Migration*, Final Report PC(2)-2D. Washington, D.C.: U.S. Government Printing Office, 1963.

U.S. Bureau of the Census. *Census of Population: 1960, Persons by Family Characteristics*, Final Report PC(2)-4B. Washington, D.C.: U.S. Government Printing Office, 1963.

U.S. Bureau of the Census. *Census of Population: 1960, Women by Number of*

Children Ever Born, Final Report PC(2)-3A. Washington, D.C.: U.S. Government Printing Office, 1963.

U.S. Bureau of the Census. *Census of Population: 1970, Detailed Characteristics*, Final Report PC(1)-D1, U.S. Summary. Washington, D.C.: U.S. Government Printing Office, 1973.

U.S. Bureau of the Census. *Census of Population: 1970, Family Composition*, Final Report PC(2)-4A. Washington, D.C.: U.S. Government Printing Office, 1973.

U.S. Bureau of the Census. *Census of Population: 1970, Journey to Work*, Final Report PC(2)-6D. Washington, D.C.: U.S. Government Printing Office, 1973.

U.S. Bureau of the Census. *Census of Population: 1970, Lifetime and Recent Migration*, Final Report PC(2)-2D. Washington, D.C.: U.S. Government Printing Office, 1973.

U.S. Bureau of the Census. *Census of Population: 1970, Marital Status*, Final Report PC(2)-4C. Washington, D.C.: U.S. Government Printing Office, 1972.

U.S. Bureau of the Census. *Census of Population: 1970, Number of Inhabitants*, Final Report PC(1)-A1, U.S. Summary. Washington, D.C.: U.S. Government Printing Office, 1971.

U.S. Bureau of the Census. *Census of Population: 1970, Persons by Family Characteristics*, Final Report PC(2)-4B. Washington, D.C.: U.S. Government Printing Office, 1973.

U.S. Bureau of the Census. *Census of Population: 1970, Sources and Structure of Family Income*, Final Report PC(2)-8A. Washington, D.C.: U.S. Government Printing Office, 1973.

U.S. Bureau of the Census. *Census of Population: 1970, Women by Number of Children Ever Born*, Final Report PC(2)-3A. Washington, D.C.: U.S. Government Printing Office, 1973.

U.S. Bureau of the Census. *County Business Patterns 1956, U.S. Summary*. Washington, D.C.: U.S. Government Printing Office, 1957.

U.S. Bureau of the Census. *County Business Patterns 1972, U.S. Summary*. Washington, D.C.: U.S. Government Printing Office, 1973.

U.S. Bureau of the Census. "Social and Economic Variations in Marriage, Divorce and Remarriage: 1967." *Current Population Reports*, Series P-20, No. 223. Washington, D.C.: U.S. Government Printing Office, 1971.

U.S. Bureau of the Census. "Social and Economic Characteristics of Students: October 1971." *Current Population Reports*, Series P-20, No. 241. Washington, D.C.: U.S. Government Printing Office, 1972.

U.S. Bureau of the Census. "Living Arrangements of College Students: October 1971." *Current Population Reports*, Series P-20, No. 245. Washington, D.C.: U.S. Government Printing Office, 1973.

U.S. Bureau of the Census. "Fertility Histories and Birth Expectations of American Women: June 1971." *Current Population Reports*, Series P-20, No. 263. Washington, D.C.: U.S. Government Printing Office, 1974.

U.S. Bureau of the Census. "Marital Status and Living Arrangements: March 1974." *Current Population Reports*, Series P-20, No. 271. Washington, D.C.: U.S. Government Printing Office, 1974.

U.S. Bureau of the Census. "Mobility of the Population of the United States: March 1970 to March 1974." *Current Population Reports*, Series P-20, No. 273. Washington, D.C.: U.S. Government Printing Office, 1974.

U.S. Bureau of the Census. "Fertility Expectations of American Women: June 1974." *Current Population Reports*, Series P-20, No. 277. Washington, D.C.: U.S. Government Printing Office, 1975.

U.S. Bureau of the Census. "Marital Status and Living Arrangements: March 1975."

Current Population Reports, Series P-20, No. 287. Washington, D.C.: U.S. Government Printing Office, 1975.

U.S. Bureau of the Census. "Fertility History and Prospects of American Women: June 1975." *Current Population Reports*, Series P-20, No. 288. Washington, D.C.: U.S. Government Printing Office, 1976.

U.S. Bureau of the Census. "Illustrative Population Projections for the United States: The Demographic Effects of Alternate Paths to Zero Growth." *Current Population Reports*, Series P-25, No. 480. Washington, D.C.: U.S. Government Printing Office, 1972.

U.S. Bureau of the Census. "Illustrative Projections of First Births for the United States: 1975–2000." *Current Population Reports*, Series P-25, No. 613. Washington, D.C.: U.S. Government Printing Office, 1975.

U.S. Bureau of the Census. "Money Income in 1973 of Families and Persons in the United States." *Current Population Reports*, Series P-60, No. 97. Washington, D.C.: U.S. Government Printing Office, 1975.

U.S. Bureau of the Census. "Characteristics of the Low-Income Population: 1973." *Current Population Reports*, Series P-60, No. 98. Washington, D.C.: U.S. Government Printing Office, 1975.

U.S. Bureau of the Census. "Money Income and Poverty Status of Families and Persons in the United States: 1974." *Current Population Reports*, Series P-60, No. 99. Washington, D.C.: U.S. Government Printing Office, 1975.

U.S. Bureau of the Census. "Characteristics of the Population Below the Poverty Level: 1974." *Current Population Reports*, Series P-60, No. 102. Washington, D.C.: U.S. Government Printing Office, 1976.

U.S. Bureau of the Census. *Historical Statistics of the United States: Colonial Times to 1957*. Washington, D.C.: U.S. Government Printing Office, 1960.

U.S. Bureau of the Census. *Statistical Abstract of the United States*, 95th ed. Washington, D.C.: U.S. Government Printing Office, 1974. Also published as *The U.S. Fact Book*. New York: Grosset and Dunlap, 1975.

U.S. National Center for Health Statistics. *Cohort Mortality and Survivorship: United States Death Registration, States 1900–1968*. Vital and Health Statistics, Series 3, No. 16. Washington, D.C.: U.S. Government Printing Office, 1972.

U.S. National Center for Health Statistics. *Current Estimates from the Health Interview Survey*. Vital and Health Statistics, Series 10, No. 79. Washington, D.C.: U.S. Government Printing Office, 1973.

U.S. National Center for Health Statistics. *Divorces: Analysis of Charges, United States 1969*. Vital and Health Statistics, Series 21, No. 22. Washington, D.C.: U.S. Government Printing Office, 1973.

U.S. Senate Subcommittee on Children and Youth of the Committee on Labor and Public Welfare. *American Families: Trends and Pressures 1973*. Washington, D.C.: U.S. Government Printing Office, 1974.

U.S. Senate Subcommittee on Children and Youth of the Committee on Labor and Public Welfare. *Child and Family Service Act, 1974*. Washington, D.C.: U.S. Government Printing Office, 1975.

Verba, Sidney, and Nie, Norman H. *Participation in America*. New York: Harper and Row, 1972.

Walker, Kathryn E., and Woods, Margaret E. *Time Use: A Measure of Household Production of Family Goods and Services*. Washington, D.C.: American Home Economics Association, 1976.

Weed, James A. "Age at Marriage as a Factor in State Divorce Rate Differentials." *Demography* 2 (1974):361–76.

Weiss, Heather M. B. "A Review of the Literature on the Determinants of Married

Women's Labor Force Participation." Special Qualifying Paper, Harvard Graduate School of Education, 1975.

Weiss, Robert S. *Loneliness: The Experience of Emotional and Social Isolation.* Cambridge, Mass.: MIT Press, 1973.

————. *Marital Separation.* New York: Basic Books, 1975.

Weitzman, Lenore J. "Legal Regulation of Marriage: Tradition and Change." *California Law Review*, 62 (1974):1169–1288.

Wells, Robert V. "Quaker Marriage Patterns in Colonial Perspective." *William and Mary Quarterly* 29 (1972):413–42.

————. "Household Size and Composition in the British Colonies in America 1675–1775." *Journal of Interdisciplinary History* 4 (1974):543–70.

White, Burton L., and Watts, Jean Carew. *Experience and Environment.* Englewood Cliffs, N.J.: Prentice Hall, 1973.

White, Sheldon H., et al. *Federal Programs for Young Children.* Washington, D.C.: U.S. Government Printing Office, 1973.

Whiting, Beatrice. "Work and the Family: Cross-Cultural Perspectives." Paper presented to conference on "Women: Resource for a Changing World," 17–18 April 1972 at Radcliffe Institute, Cambridge, Mass.

Whiting, Beatrice B., and Whiting, John W. M. *Children of Six Cultures.* Cambridge, Mass.: Harvard University Press, 1975.

Wilson, E. O. *Sociobiology.* Cambridge, Mass.: Harvard University Press, 1975.

Wynn, Margaret. *Family Policy.* Harmondsworth, England: Penguin Books, 1972.

Yankelovich, Daniel. *The New Morality.* New York: McGraw Hill Book Co., 1974.

Young, Michael, and Willmott, Peter. *The Symmetrical Family.* New York: Pantheon Books, 1973.

Index